The Development of Milton's Thought

Medieval & Renaissance Literary Studies

General Editor:
Albert C. Labriola

Advisory Editor:
Foster Provost

Editorial Board:
Judith H. Anderson
Diana Treviño Benet
Donald Cheney
Ann Baynes Coiro
Mary T. Crane
Patrick Cullen
A. C. Hamilton
A. Kent Hieatt
Margaret P. Hannay
Michael Lieb
Thomas P. Roche Jr.
Mary Beth Rose
John T. Shawcross
John M. Steadman
Humphrey Tonkin
Susanne Woods

The Development of Milton's Thought

Law, Government, and Religion

John T. Shawcross

DUQUESNE UNIVERSITY PRESS
PITTSBURGH, PENNSYLVANIA

Copyright © 2008 Duquesne University Press
All rights reserved

Published in the United States of America by
DUQUESNE UNIVERSITY PRESS
600 Forbes Avenue
Pittsburgh, Pennsylvania 15282

No part of this book may be used or reproduced,
in any manner or form whatsoever,
without written permission from the publisher,
except in the case of short quotations
in critical articles or reviews.

Library of Congress Cataloging-in-Publication Data

Shawcross, John T.
 The development of Milton's thought : law, government, and religion / John T. Shawcross.
  p. cm. — (Medieval & Renaissance literary studies)
 Includes bibliographical references and index.
 ISBN 978-0-8207-0411-1 (cloth : acid-free paper)
 1. Milton, John, 1608–1674—Criticism and interpretation. 2. Milton, John, 1608–1674—Knowledge and learning. 3. Milton, John, 1608–1674—Religion. I. Title.
 PR3588.S465 2008
 821'.4—dc22
                                            2008030619

∞Printed on acid-free paper.

Contents

	Preface	vii
One	Milton and Constancy of Thought	1
Two	Milton and Legal Matters	25
Three	Milton the Republican	49
Four	Milton, the Church, and Theology	63
Five	Theological Concerns, Especially the Trinity	82
Six	Theological Concerns, the Son, and the Divine Presence	111
Seven	Conceptual Reflections in Milton's Poetry and Prose	135
Eight	The Three Major Poems	159
Nine	Unchanging Belief and the Changed Mind	171
	Notes	197
	Works Cited	256
	Index	275

Preface

Criticism has frequently viewed John Milton as having a mind that never changed, not over time, not according to any subject, not for any reason. Unrealistic as that view is, it quite often underlies the reading of both his poetry and his prose, as well as whatever biographical correlation might arise. In this study I look at the pertinence of that idea in personal matters, political ideas, religious and theological worlds and beliefs. While some change occurs, a more accurate term for the differences that Milton's mind entertains over time is "development," in this case "conceptual development." I do not find an unchanged mind except and only in his always-present, never-rejected faith in God. There may be some questioning of why life turns as it does, why failures happen and unjustified oppositions succeed, but all things continue for Milton "as ever in [his] great task-maisters eye." God has so provided for humankind—rescuing the faithful even in the height of greatest cataclysm—that all God's ways can be justified. Providence lies in the Son, in the Christ, whose whole being is charity, love, *agape*. This belief emerges in Milton's earliest days and never subsides; it may, with reflection, with adverse experience, with the rise of unrighteousness in the world, be challenged, but it endures and through such crises becomes stronger, indeed thus "develops." In other venues the development is such that thought and attitudes and externals are changed, yielding different life experiences, other and more definitely defined political thought, attitudes toward the visible church and its administrators, and even basic beliefs in a theology that drives his unchanging faith.

This study follows upon three previous volumes: *John Milton: The Self and the World* (1993), *"The Arms of the Family": The Significance of John Milton's Relatives and Associates* (2004), and *Rethinking Milton Studies: Time Present and Time Past* (2005), as well as three books devoted individually to the three major poems. I try to present Milton and his thought and attitudes: I do not present my own. I fully recognize that Milton's prose is usually polemic (even his *De doctrina Christiana*, which should be devoid of real argumentation as an investigation into Christian doctrine drawn from Scripture alone is not entirely without such disputation), and that his poetry, especially *Paradise Lost,* is fiction. Unfortunately, much criticism of his prose seems to ignore audience and occasion in its argumentation, thus deriving most explicitly what is alleged as Milton's belief. His depiction of God the Father, particularly within the dramatic plot of the epic, seems to represent Milton's theological belief without the least hint of the fictionality of the character, who becomes a kind of allegoric figure. Sin and Death, too, are allegories, and obviously then Satan, as part of his daughter and son's allegory, must also be allegoric. Milton appears to believe in the existence of Satan, adversary to God, but the figure and his actions in the poem are made up, drawn from references in the Bible but still in fictionalized narrative and psychology to explain what human beings experience in life and the world, and why. The Milton that emerges may not always be the model, complete thinker, totally admirable person that centuries of readers have deemed him to be. But I must risk the hostility of my reader and present the less-than-perfect person—rather, the *human* person—whom I find.

Sadly, it is evident that some readers need to be reminded that translations of the Bible are *not* always the words and therefore *not* the meanings of the Bible that they believe were communicated by God. The Hebraic, Aramaic, and such language forms that are the Old Testament and the Greek that is the New Testament do not always appear in the translations—and these erroneous forms often appear in a number of significant places. The same problem occurs with translations of Milton's Latin (and some Greek and Hebrew) in *De doctrina Christiana;* translations even alter his quotations of the Bible, although such quotations are themselves Latin translations of the original texts. The translations are *not* what Milton wrote. In addition, we must remember that the Bible had many transcribers, underwent recessions at different historical times (for example, Isaiah), and at times had words supplied by later writers where disjunctions (omissions, παραλειπψες) exist in the original received texts (for example, in Luke 10:21, 23:17; John 7:54–8:11).

Milton's theological position in both *De doctrina* and *Paradise Lost* is unorthodox; it has some likenesses to various sectarian beliefs, but it is not the same as these beliefs on significant points. It is only logical and accurate, therefore, *not* to assign Milton a label that is inaccurate for his thinking (for example, Arminian, Arian, Socinian, and even Calvinist). Examined objectively, his theological position can be classified only as individual—though reflecting some Calvinistic, Arminian, Socinian, and what is inaccurately called Arian ideas—and at the same time *confused*. Is God only God the Father? Does Godhead include the Son? While an orthodox Trinity is denied, does the Holy Spirit enjoy a triunal relationship with the Father and the Son? And if so, what is the full understanding of the Godhead for him? Topics taken up in this study interface frequently, creating, therefore, repetitions of citation and statement. This arises in fitting, as briefly as possible,

Milton's work and concepts into those advanced by others during, prior to, and after his own human existence. Again, I am trying to present Milton's beliefs—which show confusion at times—not my own and not any specific theism or deistic principle.

The research and analyses of many critics, of the past and of the present, many of whom I know (or knew) and count as my friends, have contributed overwhelmingly to this study: their work is reflected everywhere in the text. My sincere and unqualified thanks for and appreciation of their outstanding investigations can be read in what I write. There will be some disagreements, but anything that appears questionable has been evoked by those valuable readings, those important analyses. Two people are, and must be, especially acknowledged for their help through discussion and suggestion: Michael Lieb and Edward Jones. *Ewig! Ewig! meine Freunde!*

A few paragraphs in chapter 2 and in chapter 7 appear in *John Milton: Reasoning Words*, edited by Kristin A. Pruitt and Charles W. Durham (Selinsgrove, Pa.: Susquehanna University Press, 2008), in my essay "Milton's Loaded Language: 'Convey' and Other Examples," 50–59. I wish to thank and acknowledge the Press for permission to reprint these paragraphs in this book.

ONE

Milton and Constancy of Thought

Critical attitudes have long held that John Milton was unwaveringly aware of his thinking about his career and vocation, social life, government and politics, and religion in both doctrine and discipline. It has been alleged that his thinking was always constant, unchanged by time or event—somewhat like Satan's boast. In *Paradise Lost* 1.252–53, Satan calls himself "One who brings / A mind not to be chang'd by Place or Time."[1] The concept becomes more horrendous as we think about it and about all the circumstances of changed venue (or context) and progression of time that might alter any thought the mind might engage—ever. What Milton the literary artist is doing in this line, of course, is depicting the psychology of this antihero who attempts to justify his unjustifiable actions *to himself,* not a hero who knows that his course of action is valid. Milton is certainly not praising the "unchanged mind." The Satan who continues in the poem repeatedly changes his mind about many things, even to admitting that "Pride and worse Ambition threw me down / Warring in Heav'n against Heav'ns *matchless* King" (4.40–41; my emphasis). Certainly if God is "matchless," revolt against him is irrational, and if this is to be construed only as a post hoc realization, then it shows a "mind" that *has* been changed by time *and* event. The inadequate reading of the self-deceptive Satan since John Dryden until today need not be reprised here.

One example of this claim of constancy is Edward Le Comte's publication of three essays under the title of *Milton's Unchanging Mind*.[2] The first, "Milton *versus* Time," relates time and Milton's career; the second, "*Areopagitica* as a Scenario for *Paradise Lost*," studies the relationship between remarks in *Areopagitica* involving the Adam and Eve story and the Fall and in *Paradise Lost* as well as the aborted Arthuriad. The third reprints "Milton as Satirist and Wit." The first is a clear example of William Riley Parker's comment about the "legend" of Milton's career, quoted below. For Le Comte, repetition and echo of language or image verifies an "unchanging mind."[3] In the first essay, recurrent attitudes toward unrelenting time define Milton's "consistency." The second essay indicates Milton's epic ambitions expressed in 1638–39 concerning an Arthuriad that gave way (was "changed," that is) to contemplation of a telling of the familiar and frequent biblical story in 1640–42 (and pursued intermittently thereafter until about 1665), and the evidential use of that story in 1644. The third offers satiric and witty examples of Milton's writing over a number of years, with nothing indicating a lack of change. The first set of language examples does not support the idea of an ambitious/career/conceptual constancy. The second is an important contribution to understanding what Milton was thinking about in 1644 when he wrote *Areopagitica* and employed the story of the Fall to argue humankind's need to undergo "triall" to achieve true virtue, while Milton was *at the same time* writing a dramatic version of the loss of Paradise as told in Genesis.[4] That need offers a theological and moral concept that pervades Milton's thinking. Le Comte's third essay is simply not relevant to the subject at hand.

In his foreword to *Milton's Unchanging Mind*, Douglas Bush relates the echoes of that book to Milton's adaptation of Horace's "Epistles," 1.11.27, in Count Camillo Cerdogni's album when Milton was in Geneva on June 10, 1639: "Cœlum non animu[m] muto du[m] trans mare curro" (I change the sky but not my mind when I cross the sea). The point in adding this line to the last two of *Comus* ("—if Vertue feeble were / Heaven it selfe would stoope to her") *when he was in Geneva*, the seat of Protestant theology, is to confirm Milton's concordant belief in a benevolent God who looks out for the faithful, and notably in reference to the potential harm that his sea voyage and unfamiliar surroundings might have brought up. We can imagine Milton feeling that this "Calvinist" position sustained him during his experiences, social and religious, when in Roman Catholic Italy. The lines from *Comus* and Horace iterate his Protestant beliefs: they have not changed despite the change in venue. This constancy of belief in God's omnipresence and omnipotence is basic for Milton.

1

Milton's thinking has been cast as consistent, his attitudes almost unchanging, the man himself always having a purpose intact, making his life thus different from that of most (if not all) human beings. The rest of us wake up to the world around us and its benightedness as we add years, questioning and often rejecting the beliefs and "wisdom" of our elders, or what we once were firmly convinced were our own principles and knowledge of life, finally understanding that the meaningfulness of an action—perhaps all actions—may be a chimera. For many, personal, social, political, and religious concepts change, some almost completely, some only partially though the challenge has undoubtedly had effect. For some religion may remain most unchanged, a perpetual though questionably factitious conviction. Upon analysis, some of this continued belief and action is hypocritical, unacknowledged, revealed in thoughts and actions that contradict other sincere thoughts and actions. On the surface, at least, such thought *seems* to be persistent and unchanged. Still, one may frequently come to the conclusion later on that an earlier conclusion is just plain wrong. Perhaps this happens most often with external matters, like career or evaluations of people, but at a point in time when the earlier conclusion was made, the thought was believed and trusted and could not be denied as operative and of importance *at that point in time*.

Further, part of one's social life relates to (or is governed by) legalities, and perspectives can be substantially altered by one's experiences with law. Some of the legal constructions that we must abide by may remain, be altered, or be rejected altogether. The same may be said of social, political, and religious constructions, and yet some basic attitudes do not really change. That John Milton experienced these human questionings and such revisions, rejections, and even persistence in some matters like anyone else is the burden of this study of some human concepts that have too often been appropriated for Milton by commentators writing about him and his works. At least today no one accepts as truly accurate William Wordsworth's delusive hope that Milton could be a star that dwelt apart.

Readers will have heard repeatedly that Milton was a Puritan, a republican, and a misogynist; that he was mean to his daughters, particularly in forcing them to be his amanuenses, and that he was not truly compatible with his first wife Mary née Powell; that he was an Arminian and an Arian and an anti-Trinitarian.[5] Regardless of the position for which a commentator argues, three problems seem to emerge in many treatments of Milton: first, what Milton wrote is not objectively read and not all of what he wrote has been read, although broad, all-inclusive statements, implying many works, are made; second, some language is employed without knowing or without abiding by its meaning, thus becoming a stereotypical categorization like a racial, ethnic, religious, or gendered epithet that is rightly the bane of current discourse ("political correctness"); and third, others' studies of a topic under discussion have been disregarded (as comments on the Internet also may demonstrate), thus either repeating some seemingly "dead horse" or misinterpreting through inadequate attention and knowledge.[6] Too often critics espouse their own thinking as Milton's position or find Milton's thinking so opposed to theirs that Milton therefore is wrong. A kind of idolatrous or adversarial role prompted by one's own concerns is played out, not allowing for differences of thought even when no fact is available to determine the validity of either or any other contention. Further, the context and audience for Milton's writing are often ignored, making what is published absolute, an exact and exacting statement of his beliefs and attitudes well beyond its context and its then current intent and audience. (I am not alleging that he did not believe everything that he published, and certainly am not suggesting downright fabrications, whether by commission or by omission of pertinent matter. But different interpretations of material may exist that are valid as well as potentially negative, or there may be oppositional information that critics have avoided.) Perhaps one way of stating the critical impasse is this: Milton is always right, and he always knows what he wants to say, and he says it. Or, only some of his position is correct, with countervailing rebuttals that he has erred or has inadequately thought out an issue. The latter appraisals are often accompanied by opprobrious evaluations of him as thinker, poet, and person. It becomes not simply a difference of opinion.

Indeed, we have not dispelled the religious antagonism of a Charles Leslie, the political antagonism of a Samuel Johnson, the literary antagonism of an F. R. Leavis or a T. S. Eliot.[7] Strong questions have been raised about Milton's toleration, his thinking involving monarchy, his attitude toward "the people," and even his seemingly learned use of allusion.[8] We are discovering a Milton who is still an important writer, presenting positions that should be positively considered, even embraced, yet one who is not in all respects the paragon of objectivity some have made him, the unswerving savant and mentor. These questions join the uncertainties that the past has sometimes advanced about gender attitudes, religious beliefs, and sociopolitical positions.

William R. Parker summarizes the critical attitudes of those who see only a steadfast Milton when it comes to his career: "Milton's life was preternaturally consistent: that he knew early what he intended to do, set about it simply and directly, never swerved from his determined course, and died with every item on his mental list neatly ticked off as completed.... But, unfortunately," he continues, "lives are not lived that way, even if a Milton is doing the living."[9] As I read and hear discussions about Milton's republicanism, his heterodoxy—his Arianism, anti-Trinitarianism, Arminianism—his concepts of women, marriage, and divorce, and his poetry, this legend of his constancy frequently underlies the argument or interpretation—almost 70 years after Parker pointed out its potential error. While Parker was speaking largely about matters biographical (and thus more prominently external), the comment does relate to thought, internal matters, and an absolute view of Milton's unchanging mind.

An important, brief article challenging the consistency attitude is Robert Ellrodt's "Milton's Unchanging Mind and the Early Poems," in which he refutes Cleanth Brooks's and John Edward Hardy's claim that the 1645 *Poems* "testifies to the clear consistency of Milton's whole career, anticipating in many ways...the major works to come," as well as Le Comte's "fixity of idea and emotional and verbal pattern." Noting that "thematic and verbal recurrence...does not preclude change" and that "Milton repeatedly modified his views on political and religious problems," Ellrodt proceeds to argue for "changelessness in the structures, not the content, of the mind" where left "unchanged" are "some distinctive modes of consciousness." My emphasis on Milton's faith fits neatly into Ellrodt's term, "consciousness."[10]

Commentators do not recognize that myth of consistency (often a traditional view simply taken over and repeated) operating behind their analyses. It takes many forms, influences in varied ways, and underlies an idolatry that will not allow Milton to be wrong, unsure, or not so thorough in his thought as we might wish. Yet for Milton there may be a commonplace lack of total follow-through in thinking about issues; there may be a reluctance to accept where his mind is leading him at a specific point in time; there may be a rejection of what he does not approve of in the realms of politics and religion and their spillover into social and domestic life.

The specter of uncertainty—just as we do not know how many universes are out there in space or how they got there, thus provoking metaphysical answers supplied for the answerless question—is relentlessly rejected for Milton, and with it the sufficiency that faith can provide for many a questioning individual. These matters do beset human beings, and I argue, Milton. Ultimately he may have recognized these failings in the human psyche—in his psyche—and both unswerving and complete constancy and a sense of accomplishment thus may have fallen away. Yet the sense of truth to his self and to his God remains. Culture is what remains after we have forgotten all we set out to know, Ezra Pound perceived: for Milton, his meritorious performance is what remains after the desiderata of "the visible Diurnal Sphear" have evansced into time. "Unchanging" and "constant" may rear up as valid adjectives to apply to Milton's mind, but such a focus generates from faith in his God and God's ways. "Yet once more" thought has been shaken and what cannot be shaken remains.

2

An important warning sounded against the frequent peremptory and absolute reading of a composition by Milton is Jonathan Goldberg's punningly titled essay "Dating Milton." Examining *Sonnet XIX* ("When I consider how my light is spent"), he posits: "In place of a narrative which imagines a Milton who was always the same, always himself (and in which the dating of the poem is part of that self-unfolding), I would offer a different account, and that refuses self sameness either to 'Milton' or to the supposed regularities of a temporal progression."[11] The argument raises questions about, or indeed denies, first, the "growth" of Milton's mind,[12] where a sense of the end-product is a complete and final culmination always aimed at and always advanced toward. Second, questions arise concerning the historicist attempt to pinpoint a "moment" that has effected Milton's writing, that is, the point of view of the author at that writing without regard to the possible layers of experience and background that may have accrued and be fundamental to the artifact that is the composition. "The poet is imagined as always 'growing' into himself, never changed, or split, by historical experience," Goldberg notes; rather, revision over time "would imbed the lyric in a history that refuses the teleological imperative of historicism."[13]

I wish to offer a kind of inclusive, "both" rather than "this" or "that," understanding of Milton. While he has hopes and expectations, like all of us, about his life and what will or will not happen, it is not always consistent or persistent: his mind changes. And the externals of life change (not just career), and so many of those changes are a result of the changes of mind and the accrual of life experiences upon that mind. The concept of the "growth" of the mind implies a teleological development and culmination, which, like Goldberg, I consider unrealistic despite the possibility of a close relationship with early ambition at some later plateau. But it is not only the larger career-related concept that may alter: attitudes and beliefs change; what was accepted at one time may be rejected at another and supplanted. An author is affected by many historical moments, and those moments accumulate and may emerge influentially in his or her thinking and actions. Yet any expression that encompasses them may be provoked by a specific moment: that moment in time is important but is not necessarily the all-encompassing and final and only important moment in time, either before or after that moment in time. We should not, *we cannot validly* ignore the historical build-up, the psychological effect that recognition of existence and significance of anything at certain specific times may create. We may find the catalyst for the writing down of *Sonnet XIX* to be the creation of the Major-Generals' controls over areas of England, as I have suggested elsewhere,[14] but many of the concepts displayed within it harken back (at the very least psychologically) to the contemplation of blindness and its advent and to whatever hopes Milton bore of being a factor in establishment of a "just and pious Nation."

Realization to the conscious mind may occur or be forced upon one after some alteration to one's life has occurred. At times we need an event, a personal happening, a historical moment to make us aware that we have changed in our thinking about ourselves, about life, about what we would have cast as truth at some prior time. Such a moment may bring forth a specific statement—public or private—that a later moment may alter. For the author, and that definitely means for Milton, a thought, attitude, "conclusion" expressed in writing, published or unpublished, may be revised and its alteration evidenced by revision in writing, published or unpublished. Milton's personal reaction to *Sonnet XIX* a year or so after it had been written, we might imagine, would have rejected that possible catalyst or, indeed, any further governmental maneuver of the various leaders or hope for the creation of a "just and pious Nation." Nonetheless, at the same time we might expect him to iterate its well-known last line (as perhaps we all iterate—in possibly unrealistic hope—to ourselves now and then): "They also serve who only stand and wait." The line, despite its possible validity, may be a psychological crutch.

"Development," which I employ in my title, implies change: it can be interpreted to mean a movement from the kernel of being or thought to something fuller, more explicit; and it may as often mean the rejection or total forgetting of whatever that kernel of thought was at some other point in time. It does imply a seed that existed and was altered, or rejected, or out of which something evidential came into existence (for the writer, something concrete), even when disguised so as to be difficult to recognize.[15] But it does not demand a teleological end or demand that it involve positive change. Implied as well is a realization that at any moment the author's work may be only a stage in further development, and thus that when we talk of development we are speaking of a specific point in time to which concepts have moved. Perhaps in ensuing points in time those concepts will have moved again. Why a concept, especially the concretized evidence of that concept (as in a piece of writing), may have moved can include many dissimilar reasons, but this points to development and is constituted by influences. Development does not present us with a constant, unchanging Milton ("the same Milton"), nor with "some temporal progression" as if it were steady. It does not mean progress in some positive sense, nor a Milton "growing into himself" and reaching toward some teleological imperative. It is the simple fact of experience that human beings—including Milton—do change, do move from this to that ("develop"), even if "that" is reactionary to "this." Change is always a moment on a path that has been preceded by other moments and which may alter as and if that path continues in time.

I am in strong agreement with John P. Rumrich's important (and, it seems, inadequately known) study of *Milton Unbound: Controversy and Reinterpretation*. He writes, "Milton was a poet of indeterminacy who found ways to incorporate the uncertain and the evolving into his most highly realized works of literary art: a poetics of *becoming*." Based on a theory of communication that "presents all communication, including literary art, as a means of actively and intentionally coping with what is not already known, with what is developing, with change," Rumrich's revision of repeated criticism placing Milton in "a tradition of Christian orthodoxy" and certain aspects of "material culture" is clearly pertinent to my view of Milton's changing and unchanging mind.[16]

3

An important study of Milton and his works that counters the assumption of an "unchanged" mind that has arisen so often—explicitly and tacitly—is Peter Herman's *Destabilizing Milton*.[17] He is concerned primarily with the three major poems and the ambiguities, doubt, incertitude, and unreliability of meaning in Milton's language, images, apparent "statements" in the poetry (as both "author" as in the proem to book 7 of *Paradise Lost* and as a "narrative voice"), and the way in which such readings have led to epitomes of Milton the person in political, social, and religious matters. A development of Milton's conceptual thinking lies behind the discussion, although Herman is concerned most with refutations of critical statements that seem to assign absolute meanings to Milton's works and language. He recognizes that even the "author" may (almost surely does) present language that destabilizes whatever the reader thinks he or she is reading, regardless, for example, of the factual blindness behind the proem to *Paradise Lost*, book 3, or the "evil dayes...evil tongues" alluded to in book 7. Herman does not examine Milton's unchanged or changed mind, but he does argue for a shift from certitude to incertitude over the years.[18]

A major concern in using this language to describe what Milton does or does not write is that "certitude" and "incertitude" imply something much more than "destabilization" and "ambiguity." On the one hand, the words imply uncertainty on Milton's part about content rather than the purposeful use of words and images, which brings into play multiple meanings, ideas, and attitudes (see chapter 7 for some examples). On the other hand, "certitude" or "incertitude" may arise from unthought-out or changed concepts. The difference is important.

Milton's "incertitude," as Herman uses that concept, existed well before 1660 in specific situations and for some specific topics (as I suggest below), although it may have expanded and intensified as time went on. There have been expressions that read as "certainty" (the Trinity, for example, in the Nativity ode of 1629), but there is also the "incertitude" that underlies (in 1637) "What boots it with incessant care / To tend the homely slighted shepherds trade / And strictly meditate the thankless muse?" (*Lycidas*, 65–67). The answer given to that question implicates a belief in God's omniscience and award to faithful servants. We have, thus, incertitude *and* certitude of faith in God. We should also, however, observe that while "all-judging *Jove*" and Phœbus (thus Father and Son) as well as "him that walkt the waves" (the Incarnated Son) are part of this poem, *there is no Spirit*. Omission may be as important as commission.[19] Has Milton been experiencing some uncertainty about a triunal being by 1637 that will emerge in *Paradise Lost* and *De doctrina Christiana*? Or perhaps it has not yet been fully altered as the quotation from *Of Reformation* (1641) suggests?[20]

The certitude and incertitude that emerge in these earlier poems (and perhaps the prose of 1641) will also be found in such prose as *Tetrachordon* (March 1645): In this tract Milton argues for divorce on grounds of what we would call incompatibility (desertion and adultery need not be pursued since they already existed as causes), and his audience is the *male* and "Christian" Parliament. He lines up for his Christian audience, among other corroborations, "Scripture," "testimony of ancient Fathers," "civill lawes in the Primitive Church," "famousest Reformed Divines," and the "Act of Parliament and Church of England in the last yeare of EDVVARD the sixth" (title page). And he remarks that the biblical "Created he him" means that "it must have bin male and female created he him," except for that male audience, for whom he resorts to quoting Saint Paul, who "ends the controversie by explaining that the woman is not primarily and immediatly the image of God, but in reference to the man" (3; YP 2:589).[21] While Milton may have accepted this rationalization because of his reliance on acceptance of the word of Scripture, and Paul is always of major significance for him, we modern readers should recognize the "incertitude" that that seemingly ubiquitous interpretation of Milton's attitude, critically delimited to the statement from Paul, has cast over it when Milton *immediately* notes, "Not but that particular exceptions may have place, if she exceed her husband in prudence and dexterity, and he contentedly yeeld, for then a superior and more naturall law comes in, that the wiser should govern the lesse wise, whether male or female" (589). That is hardly the positive, misogynist position that has been accorded Milton—this statement creeps in despite his male audience's probable disallowance of the possibility that a woman could meaningfully "govern" a man.[22] (We are well beyond the time that Elizabeth ruled; however, this is the period when Charles I's French queen Henrietta-Maria and her French courtiers were far from obscure and praiseworthy in governmental matters.) The modification of the Pauline statement is really a questioning of God's great prescience and creative ability for the masculine absolutist, and places a negative evaluation on Paul's "law" as *less* "superior" and *less* "naturall." Herman accepts the questionable critical extrapolation from the citation of Paul and ignores the further statement to argue a change in attitude later on in the characterization of Eve.

Herman cites only the "absolute rule" of Paul's New Testament bias in order to stress that revision of Milton's thinking in the latter part of *Paradise Lost*.[23] The matter is not that simple. The "revision" may be primarily the result of inadequate readers and what thus become misreadings of some of the literary texts and, in turn, the misassignment of alleged Miltonic "certitude." There *is* incertitude in what he wrote in *Tetrachordon*, but it is not until that incertitude develops into an apparently clear rejection of second-class status for woman that such incertitude has been more fully recognized and acknowledged. In turn, this leads to a conclusion about woman, particularly in relation to man, although any such apperception is potentially subject to further revision or even stronger acceptance. Perhaps Milton's concepts of gender were changing in 1645, or perhaps they had already changed but had to be mollified for his male audience. Lines 297–99 in book 4 of *Paradise Lost* introduce the two human characters of the myth of human creation seen through the narrator's words. The legend of the Fall, as Milton presents it, iterates on the one hand the weakness of the woman (a most commonplace, traditional, and biblical attitude), but on the other hand in book 9 Milton also assigns a lack of adequate "contemplation" and of true "valour" on the part of the man (not at all a usual or biblical reading).

The ensuing characterizations after book 4 refute the certitude about Milton's attitude toward the feminine that Herman also challenges and these characterizations lead to his view of the incertitude established by later lines since later passages change the alleged import that people have derived from the earlier ones. Herman does not, however, recognize that same incertitude in *Tetrachordon,* and I am unsure whether he recognizes its hovering in those lines in book 4: "Milton in *Paradise Lost* does not always confirm his earlier positions, but puts them into question, and the same applies to his views on gender and marriage" (137). Are we talking about *Milton*'s "earlier positions" or readers' perceptions of what those positions were? Are we presented in both *Tetrachordon* and *Paradise Lost* with a certitude on Milton's part that says that Paul's dictum is to be assented to, or are we to recognize at the same time in both works that such a biased absolute dictum should be modified and thus, as stated, rejected? It is not a closed issue. Rather than a simple reading that in book 4 Eve is inferior to Adam's superiority but that by the end of the poem woman has been asserted as equal (even the superior to man if he is represented by the Adam figured in books 10–12), we should recognize the range of gender attitude that Milton presents. The contrast between books 4 and 9 and books 10 and 12 where the presentations of Eve alter so meaningfully within the same poem demonstrates Herman's argument for Milton's changed attitude but in a much more complicated way than Herman seems to realize. I do not see the poem as of one piece and altered only from what has been purported for Milton in the divorce tracts. Rather, we have instead a poem that builds and develops within its own being. The poem recapitulates the sociofamilial Hebraic world of the Bible as well as Paul's narrow and prejudiced pronouncement, which has been emended by the end of the poem. There is development of thought—demonstrated even within the poem—that may reject part or parts of past beliefs. Milton may have been influenced by his mid-1640s real life experiences of marriages and family, and an awareness of biblical (both Old and New) untrustworthiness in many things. But we are looking at a changed mind, a development in the terms that Herman argues for, a nonconstancy roaming around in at least one sphere of what man alleges is God's creation.

In the epic, Milton the literary artist is contrasting the commonplace male attitude about gender with a gendered alteration that will appear in books 10–12. Milton the literary artist plants ideas, situations, and characterizations that may play out in the full work or that may be altered and thus raise new insights for the reader about the people, events, and "message" inhering in the literary work. The conclusion that a reader may reach in either prose or poem is neither easy nor one that is unchallengeable. As I read *Paradise Lost* (in agreement with what is really the important point that Herman is making), Milton overthrows Paul's—and the still commonplace, both male and very often female—genderization as we proceed to a fuller appreciation of love, *agape*. Perhaps Milton is still "masculinist" when he completes his epic—man and woman may not be truly or totally "equal," but the incertitude that has arisen in the divorce tracts has developed into a strong position depicting woman's status in the world of humankind. The mind has changed.

The comments in *Tetrachordon* involving gender attitudes do show incertitude on Milton's part because of Saint Paul's dictum, pointing to an underlying question about such issues: at any one historical moment (like the seeming acceptance of Paul's misogyny), Milton may express certitude even though further thought and future time will lead to modifications or rejections. What certitude one can extract from the epic lies in the unabating evil of Satan and in what is provided by "Love / By name to come call'd Charitie, the soul / Of all the rest" (*PL* 12.583–85). Faith in God and God's Providence subtends such *agape*.

4

In this book I will look at some concepts—legal and social, governmental, political, religious—that do not persist unchanged through time. Yet with Milton, as with us all, there are elemental beliefs that will persist despite questioning, uncertainty, contrariness of evidence, incomplete examination—and those persistent beliefs revolve around the religious (and moral). Of course, there may be denial to the self, or submerging of fact or analysis, a resorting to a comfortable acceptance that things are as one wishes and as they have always been. To reach those denials one closes off a part of the mind, hides one's head in the sand. By "development," I mean change with certain concepts changing, triggering different attitudes, different expressions of those concepts, and differences that are not final and are not necessarily corroborative of concepts that one's past had maintained. I reject the connotation that development means an end, a desired end, a constant moving toward some conceived conviction. One may proceed with one's life toward some conceived end, perhaps reaching it, perhaps not. But reaching it will stop that development only if one stops (or seems to stop) at that point; other concerns or life activities may discontinue that line of development, dropping any inkling of continued interest in such an end. The end is reached and accepted or then ignored as different concerns take over. Development—of the mind, of one's activities—has shifted.

Two obvious and contrasting examples of changed thought (yet the circumstances pointing to such change are generally ignored) are Milton's reference to "Trinal Unity" (11) in *Ode on the Morning of Christs Nativity*, which seems so often forgotten when remarks of uncertainty about the Trinity and especially about the exact nature of the Holy Spirit are raised in *De doctrina Christiana*, and the frequent readings of *A Mask* (*Comus*) as if the received text of 1637 (1638?) were the text presented three years earlier at Ludlow Castle, with interpretations of the theme of virginity and chastity and with analyses of the Lady and feasible length of her speeches being based on the revised text. The early acceptance of the Trinity should alter a critic's interpretation of the treatise on this point: the concept has developed from acceptance of Trinity to an uncertainty. It is plausible that the concept of Trinity in 1629 may be only that which was unthinkingly iterated because it was a concept repeatedly heard from parents and early religious upbringing.[24] Realizing that, the critic should weigh the reason for the questioning that Milton admits in the treatise. Milton's skepticism on the issue is taken up in chapter 5.

The other example of changed thought, which does not deny literary echo, transumption, or expansion at a later time, raises warnings of treating only a "final" text rather than one developed over time as the same in substance *at all times without change*. Such a reading of a literary work collapses time and denies an awareness on the author's part of altered thought, thesis, or clarification, even to himself or herself, of what his or her thought and thesis have been.[25] Many critics' employment of their interpretation of the received 1637 text to analyze the circumstances of the 1634 performance at Ludlow Castle offers a clear example of the inept reading of *Sonnet XIX* that Goldberg points out. The number of lines that the Lady speaks is much less in 1634 than the text of 1637 presents. And recognition of the revision of just the epilogue to the masque in 1637[26] forces the reconsideration of "virginity" as presented in 1634, of Milton's thesis intentions when he seems to feel compelled in 1637 to add line 997, "(List mortals, if your ears be true)," and of the "unspotted" "bride"—later to be praised in terms of "wedded Love" and opposed to "Harlots" and "Casual fruition" (*PL* 4.750, 766–67). In this latter echo of moral belief consistency does reside, but it tells us more about Milton's psyche than about a perceptive interrogation of sexual matters and marriage.

But Milton's career must enter our discussion as well: the intended clerical career gives way to a poetic one and that to an adversarial one in prose—or rather, according to Milton himself, the poetic career is interrupted in 1641–42 when prose became the "manner of writing wherin knowing my self inferior to my self, led by the genial power of nature to another task, I have the use, as I may account it, but of my left hand" (*Reason of Church-Government*, YP 1:808). The reason for both career moves is very similar: both concerned the way in which he saw himself fitting into the demands of the church and the state of the church with its political involvements. A few years later, religiosocial antagonism aided a reversion to his poetic career, although in the years from 1639 through around 1648 and from time to time incidentally thereafter activity of a kind of "career" emerged in his teaching a few students in his home—a necessary move at first to educate his perhaps orphaned nephews Edward and John Phillips, which then expanded slightly over the years.[27] That reversion to poetry and more personal writing like *The Art of Logic* from late 1645 through 1649 and spasmodically thereafter until 1660 and the Restoration returned him to "the inspired guift of God" to be employed

> to imbreed and cherish in a great people the seeds of vertu, and publick civility, to allay the perturbations of the mind, and set the affections in right tune, to celebrate in glorious and lofty Hymns the throne and equipage of Gods Almightinesse, and what he works, and what he suffers to be wrought with high providence in his Church, to sing the victorious agonies of Martyrs and Saints, the deeds and triumphs of just and pious Nations doing valiantly through faith against the enemies of Christ, to deplore the general relapses of Kingdoms and States from justice and Gods true worship. (YP 1:816–17)

It is wiser to refer here to "vocation" as John Spencer Hill discusses it rather than "career."[28] This divine vocation persists despite alterations in the external activities Milton pursued in prose writings, governmental employment, educational work, and even in his poetic "career," which identifies the medium that divine vocation will follow. Jameela Lares views "preaching" as almost tantamount to "the ministry,"[29] and thus with recognition of his inadequacy as a preacher he turned from the ministry as vocation. Yet ministerial (not clerical) endeavors and actions—"divine vocation"—is something more than just preaching, which is but one activity of the minister, important and dominating though it may be. Such divine vocation persists, and the communicative approach that "sermo" provides will emerge as passages in *Paradise Lost*.[30] His ambition and its execution can be seen in his poetry as well as his prose (once one downplays refutation of an opponent as his intention), but important through all his work is the emphasis upon the religious environment of these aspirations.

A second interruption in Milton's poetic career occurs with the advent of a new government in 1649 and lasts through 1660 when that government ceased to exist. All of these changes in activity and work force a kind of changing of the mind, of his uppermost concerns, and of Milton's development of other arenas of thought; and yet, Milton's mind, in another sense, is not necessarily changed but may persist in his religious beliefs and their interrelationship with sociological and political worlds. Such beliefs, however, also show a development, a clarification, an alteration at various points, even though the basic beliefs (of faith, of God and his ways, of his Providence) remain. The effect of such a change coupled with persistence is reflected in Milton's poetic career. Peter Herman argues in a different book, "Despite Milton's reputation among the majority of his critics for absolute certainty over his calling, several of the earlier poems suggest that Milton, like Spenser and Sidney, had his own questions about the efficacy of poetry and the difficulty of distinguishing licit from illicit uses of the imagination."[31] Is Milton's prior ambition carried out in the poetry that is wrought, in the prose that results from his entanglements in civic questions and activities? Does its achievement in either or in both forms question the efficacy of poetry and, indeed, the efficacy of any public writing or teaching or attempt to create a world of truth? Are the questions of the efficacy of any action ever resolved?

The underlying affirmation of "All is.../ As ever in my great task-maisters eye" (*Sonnet VII*, 13–14) predicates a belief that is certainly constant in Milton's work: the value in life and the prescience and omnipotence of God and his mercy for humankind.[32] The sonnet, written during his last year as a graduate student at Christ's College, Cambridge, as well as the letter to an unknown friend in the Trinity Manuscript into which he copied it, both attest to his recognition of inadequacy as a practicing cleric, although this has been ostensibly his educational and career goal. It does not reject ministerial and religious thought or writing, but it does present outward change and some kind of mindful development—a kind of "waking up," an apparently realistic assessment of self, an admission that father does not necessarily know best. The great taskmaster has led him through philosophic and religious study with purpose, but a purpose that, now that the cleric's life appears no longer viable for him, he cannot identify. The unchanging mind has changed while it also has remained consistent in its orientation of belief. Despite the time spent in "studious retirement" in Hammersmith and Horton, as well as Milton's move out of his father's home in 1637 after his mother died[33] and his travel to France, Italy, and Geneva in 1638, the sonnet in 1631 or 1632 and the letter in 1633–37 counter that myth of a determined course for his life, although study and religious belief in his God do not alter.

Milton records in *Pro populo anglicano defensio secunda* (1654) that his continental sojourn was to see "foreign parts and especially Italy" ("regiones exteras, & Italiam potissimùm" [83]) and "for the cultivation of [his] mind" ("me animi causâ" [85]). In those places, he attests, he frequently discussed religion (that is, his Protestant religion) with those of Roman Catholic faith, returning safely "by the will of God" ("Deóque sic volente" [86]) from Rome to Florence, despite warnings of possible harm because of theological animosity. He also notes that during his travels amid so many sinful enticements that were rife everywhere he traveled, in repudiation of accusations of licentiousness made by "Alexander More" (that is, Peter Du Moulin), he knew that he could not hide from the eyes of God ("si hominum latere oculos possem, Dei certè non posse" [87]).[34] His belief in God, in God's omniscience and omnipresence, does not waver, nor does his belief in God's omnipotence and mercy, which are constant for the true, obedient servant as Milton always cast himself.

The belief dominates Milton's first full poem, his translation of Psalm 114, written in 1624 at age 15. I will discuss this kind of constancy—one different in nature from external, public, communal constancy—in chapter 9. This belief answers the questions that rear up with shifts in public postures and political milieus, but it also verifies the efficacy of poetry for Milton in the domain most important to him, the purview of his God. While trust in the efficacy of his writing for humankind may decline and even disappear with time (the "fit audience" indeed has always been "few"), it is always a reality that may bring "praise" and "Fame," which does not grow on "mortal soil,...But lives and spreds aloft by those pure eyes / And perfet witness of all-judging *Jove*" (*Lycidas*, 76–83). A different efficacy, to be sure, but there is the hope (if we take him at his word) that at least there are a few who will understand and heed the exhortations and dissection of the anatomy of evil and *amend their lives*.

This development of Milton's attitudes and thoughts, changes of an external nature that may occur as a result, as well as his persistence of belief and its possible inculcation in others are consonant with John N. King's position about Milton and church discipline and career (vocation) and with Christopher R. Hair's analysis of the depth of meaning abiding in the "Paradise within...happier farr" (*PL* 12.587).[35] King demonstrates that, beginning in such a poem as *In Quintum Novembris* (1626), Milton's vision of clerical probity steadily disintegrated in stages until 1637 when *Lycidas* and its so-called digression on the corrupt clergy (emphasized in the later headnote to the poem) make clear his being "Church-outed" (*Reason*, YP 1:823). Milton is explicit in his 1641/42 tract that he could not join such clerics who had commandeered the church and still assert his conscience: one would have to "perjure, or split his faith." Milton's mind has changed, and the factors within church administration that had in the past been credited to true faith and godly work are now seen as not *his* faith or godly work. It is an awakening over time, a development of attitude and recognition. A moment in time may have made him realize what had been happening to "his" church and thus to him. That moment may have been the imprisonment and mutilation meted out to John Bastwick, William Prynne, and Henry Burton in the summer of 1637, but the substance of the realization had been there for some time—from at least 1626, according to King, and surely more aggressively from around 1632 (when, we recall, he was graduated with a master's degree from Cambridge University and began his "studious retirement") and 1633 when the policies of the new Archbishop of Canterbury, William Laud, spawned reactions that could not be ignored. (Chapter 4 will go into this matter in greater detail.) Yet most strongly implied in this rejection of what the "discipline" of the church had become is the belief in "the holy reformed Church, and the elect people of God" (YP 1:861; these are the last words of *The Reason of Church-Government*). Milton will "not cease to hope through the mercy and grace of Christ, the head and husband of his Church," and the belief that "God...ordain'd his Gospell to be the revelation of his power and wisdome in Christ Jesus" (YP 1:749, 750). His mind has not changed.

This belief and trust are internal; the rejection of matters concerned with the church deals with externalities, which to Milton oppose and thus negate the internalities of his faith. In his examination of the "paradise within" in various authors including Milton, Christopher Hair concludes:

24 The Development of Milton's Thought

> Milton contemplates inwardness with a surprising regularity throughout his works, but, as one might expect, what 'inwardness' means to Milton shifts and changes over the course of his life.... Surely there is a growing association of inward with spiritual power as Milton matures, and this spiritual power comes to be presented as a real force at work in the world.
>
> In the image of the paradise within, Milton's principal subject throughout his canon becomes manifest, taking on a substantial and theological dimension beyond simply inner knowledge, light, or righteousness.[36]

Again we are confronted with a "changed" mind *and* an "unchanged" mind: a persistence of that which remains after all that is shaken has been removed (as Saint Paul asserts). His faith cannot be shaken; those things that are shaken are "things that are made"—human structures, human actions, human conceptions.

Two

Milton and Legal Matters

For the most part any legalities in reference to Milton's biography have been relegated to chancery concerns involving loans, transference of property, and default by some of those failing to comply with required actions. Another aspect of legality for Milton lies in its metaphoric possibilities for textual readings in his literary works, a topic little touched upon by Milton criticism. The import of such legalistic language joins the substantive connotations of other words that flair up to lead us to deeper meanings in what he presents for government, religion, and the social world in which he engages. We can infer some change in legal attitude and in usage of symbolic or metaphoric language, and yet there is a continuance of what most people would classify as a hypocritical attitude, highlighting what nearly all would call a fraudulent deception in which Milton allowed himself to indulge.

1

A significant word that has not, to my knowledge, been discussed in connection with Milton is "convey" and its substantive form, "conveyance." In a most provocative study of Sidney, Spenser, and Shakespeare, Charles Ross examines the legal significance of these words, particularly "fraudulent conveyance." He argues the underlying illegality to which these writers refer in employing allusions to the way people—one might say now as well as then—avoided taxation on inheritances and thwarted assessments on legal transference of property. Fraudulent transference of property (no matter what its nature) allowed the "former" owner to retain ownership although it would appear in legal terms as a bona fide transfer from one person to another. It was a means of reducing what were alleged as the full assets of someone who perhaps was being sued or who was in a position to lose control over that property, allowing them not to have to pay a higher assessment should the case be lost or thereby not running afoul of some law dealing with ownership. "Fraudulent conveyances operate in a shifting moral sphere, where power blurs the line between right and wrong," Ross states. At issue is the question: "to what extent frauds, deceptions, concealments, and conveyances would be legal to protect property from creditors, including the state."[1] A "creditor" is "one that gives Credit, one that lends or trusts another with Money or Goods."[2] The creditor might be an heir or a relative, of course, and the transaction often required secrecy of one's assets even from that person. Notably, fraudulent conveyance was most employed in landownership and transfer in the period of social upheaval during the sixteenth and seventeenth centuries when "prosperity and social status of the lesser landowners," which led to founding of families, increased. According to A. B. Simpson, conveyances were employed to "ensure that the family estate should not be alienated out of the family in the future."[3] These uses of "convey" all deal with transference of property in some form, *not* with the simple denotation of "communicate," such as an idea or information. This latter usage appears, for example, in *Of Education:* "language is but the instrument convaying to us things usefull to be known" (YP 2:369).

Milton, of course, was the son of a scrivener who had much to do with drawing up deeds, bonds, bills, leases, releases, and the like, and the brother and brother-in-law of lawyers. Aside from his governmental salary and whatever monies his publications and limited teaching brought, Milton's financial status and landowning were inherited and dependent upon loans and rentals, and upon any additional ownership and investments he made. What must have been a substantial accumulated income from such sources has been generally ignored. Milton's financial condition has been referred to from time to time, but usually without realistic inferences that the few known facts suggest. These facts of loans and other financial transactions by his father and by him are detailed elsewhere,[4] but possible inferences are only seldom hinted at in scholarship on Milton. Significantly, Stephen Fallon comments on "The scrivener's son, whose leisure was purchased by the interest earned from his father's loans (and who met his first wife while collecting on one of those loans)"; and David Hawkes remarks that the "father's fortune, on which the poet lived for long periods, was made largely by moneylending." Importantly, Nicholas von Maltzahn writes, "For money-lending was not just part of Milton's youth, some immediate legacy of his father's business, but rather his own lifelong means of making a living, a source of income more lasting than the salaries he drew as a teacher and then state servant."[5]

In proceeding to examine Milton's attitude toward church matters, such as hirelings (reflected both in *Sonnet XVI* [1652] and *Considerations Touching the Likeliest Means to Remove Hirelings Out of the Church. Wherein is also discourc'd Of Tithes, Church-fees, Church-revenues; And whether any maintenance of ministers can be settl'd by law* [1659]),⁶ Hawkes adds, "Although he sometimes repeats commonplace criticism of covetousness, Milton never condemns exchange for profit as such, as many of his contemporaries do," which is a major point of my present discussion. Yet he disputes Blair Hoxby's position in *Mammon's Music* on Milton's purported positive acceptance of a system of commerce and exchange, for "Greek philosophy and Judeo-Christian religion indict large-scale exchange for profit as unethical." Hawkes then contends that "laudable *spiritual* effects," being absent in the marketplace, oppose Milton's being a proponent of commerce in all the ways it might invade the church. The division of these worlds of the church and mundane life, while recognized and thereby surely evoking modified or opposed conceptions of financial matters in each, is insufficiently acknowledged here by Hawkes to allow him to entertain Milton's hypocritical position and his incomplete and biased view when the full subject is addressed. What Hawkes says about the relationship with the church holds up, but the world outside the church is decidedly different. To me, both Hoxby and Hawkes are correct, but that is because each is talking about different, and for Milton conflictive, worlds.⁷

Most importantly, Hawkes in his recent edition of *Paradise Lost* pays direct attention to this "very controversial" and "disreputable" profession of moneylending. Although "Milton senior seems to have avoided criminal prosecution," others did not. "Many people felt that taking interest on a loan ipso facto constituted the sin, and the crime, of usury, which was regarded as an unnatural vice akin to sodomy and as an antisocial practice demonstrating a rapacious avarice utterly at odds with Christian charity." He also—I think with good reason—remarks upon the circumstances of Milton's marriage to Mary Powell in conjunction with this financial world, and suggests that perhaps both "were aware that she was in some sense an interest payment on a loan."⁸

Nicholas von Maltzahn builds on French's presentation in *Milton in Chancery* and the evidence of Milton's continued moneylending in 1666, stating that, "whatever his losses at the Restoration, he presumably did not lose his business acumen, even as he lost his other means of making a living," recalls Milton's losses of £2000 when the Excise Office failed. I suggest that it was not poor financial judgment on Milton's part (as had often been advanced as cause) but faulty allegiance to and foundationless hope in a government doomed to failure and on the edge of replacement.[9] To be acknowledged is Milton's experience in this world of commerce, of financial arrangements, of potential fraud, and his acceptance of what appears to many people as hypocrisy and equivocation when activities were to his advantage, particularly financial advantage.

"Milton's usury" has been noted (although in connection with the stereotype of the Jew as usurer).[10] Milton was *not* just "one of the people," as some recent critics have tried to make him: he was not a kind of Leveller (a concept not even fully understood by John Lilburne), a believer in absolute equity for all people (certainly not in financial matters and, omission from any consideration shows, not for both sexes). His world was one of social and upward mobility like his father's (to reference Ross's remark), facilitated by financial improvements and governmental and legal ties. He was far from one of the "youngmen and apprentices of London" that Lilburne championed; nor was he one of the tradesmen or of the immediate family of tradesmen that Hoxby examines.[11] And indeed, his father and he were right in the midst of a world that did not require "labor," steady work hours, or workaday buying and selling on their part. Theirs was a world of middlemen, governed by law and increasingly subject to financial impositions by the crown and the legal entanglements that its pyramidic government created, thereby protecting the "haves." The landlord, the loan provider, the legal intermediary, of necessity, engaged in actions that might embrace conveyances, and certainly some of the Miltons' lands and monies were conveyed.[12] J. Milton French in *Milton in Chancery* details many of these transactions, and we are aware of the problems of father and son in the Rose Downer litigation and those Milton had with his loan to Sir John Cope in 1638, which was not settled until 1659 or after (if indeed it was settled), as just two examples.[13]

It is most interesting and important to note that it was John Milton, the son, who provided the Cope loan on February 1, 1638, a few months before he went abroad, at a time when we cannot be sure where his main residence was—Horton or London. Though he was a man approaching 30, with two university degrees and no work experience, his means of livelihood at this time was what his father provided and whatever monies came to him through the kind of financial arrangements just mentioned. Nothing has been made of this latter transaction—we have no evidence of other such specific transactions on the younger Milton's part alone, although there may have been more—but it surely indicates his own individual usury, not simply as joining his father in moneylending. And as the little evidence we have shows, it continued in 1650, 1651–60, 1658, 1666, and 1674 at least. Who, we might wonder, financed his more than a year's sojourn on the Continent "accompanied by a single attendant" (uno cum famulo)?[14] And especially when he, not his father, had enacted the Cope loan a couple of months before he began that sojourn. (It was for £150 at £3 interest quarterly; he was owed £300 in 1654 because of default after 1641, according to a bill of June of that year.) Some of French's remarks in *Milton in Chancery*, although he avoids any question of illegality on the part of the Miltons, senior or junior, hint at questionable practices in many of these financial dealings. Milton may not have been a "usurer" in the sense of one demanding exorbitant interest or unfair terms, yet he did lend money (even prior to the continental sojourn) and would have to have pursued conveyances of property from which he received rents and interest. His brother, a lawyer, was involved in similar activities, as were his brother-in-law Edward Phillips and later his nephews Edward and John Phillips.[15] Whether or not the conveyances of money, land, or transfer of loans from father to son had even a tinge of fraudulence about them (and some financial actions were taken in the name of father and son), we cannot determine because we do not have enough information about them. Nonetheless, outright gifts—including those attached to observance of a birthday or university achievement—may have provided Milton senior the opportunity to "ensure that the family estate should not be alienated out of the family."[16] Father and son did live off monies that resulted from such sources as cited above: "usury" was not a term distinct from their livelihoods.

The Cross Keys, the property in Ludgate Hill owned by Milton's brother, Christopher, from some time before June 1644, which may have come into his possession around 1636 or so from his father, who had acquired it from John Suckling on July 18/20, 1629. (The property had passed to the poet from his father, also Sir John Suckling, when he died on March 27, 1627. William Barrett of London, the executor of the senior Suckling's will, is likewise acknowledged in Milton senior's indenture.) The purchase price was £560. Part of the premises had been granted to John Murall, a linen draper, and this tenancy continued with a rental charge of £40 a year. Whenever Christopher was given the land with its tenement—perhaps in 1636 (around November?), as William Riley Parker suggests,[17] as a gift upon Christopher's twenty-first birthday—conveyance of some sort took place. Perhaps some ulterior motive existed, if one wants to put a "fraudulent conveyance" label on this action, for in May 1636 Sir Thomas Cotton brought suit against Milton senior in the Court of Requests and again in January 1637. (Apparently the second action was the result of a lack of attention by Milton senior to the first action.) Was there any skirting of taxes or of being sued for money that the father may have avoided? The dates of Cotton's suits with Christopher's birthday occurring in between, if indeed the birthday is involved in such a considerable gift, does give one pause. It is not that Milton's father (and his partner Thomas Bower) did anything illegal in dealings with the Cotton family, but this action, if so timed, could be construed as "fraudulent conveyance" to avoid attachment of monies. The suit was in and out of the courts until dismissed on February 1, 1638, with Milton senior being granted 20 shillings from Cotton "for his costs herein wrongfully susteyned."[18] A gift of such a piece of property to Christopher, even if he was now an adult (he may have received his law degree around this time and probably by around March 1637), may seem unusual to some, but it also suggests that some conveyance of property from father to his other, older son had taken place earlier. (If there had been such a gift made to John and for a twenty-first birthday recognition, it would have occurred in late 1629—a possible impetus for him to think about his lack of "bud" or "blossom"? It could thus have had some influence in his continued three and a half years as a master's student and then his "studious retirement" for five years.)

Later, a different kind of financial convolution appears to interrelate the wheeling and dealing world of John and Christopher when we remember that Thomas Maundy, to whom Milton lent £500 in 1658 (a time when the government was coming apart), put up property in Kensington as collateral, property that abutted land owned by William Hobson, who had bought the Ludgate Hill property from Christopher in February 1654. While Milton may have encountered Maundy through Maundy's work as goldsmith for the Interregnum government, the financial connection might as easily have been effected through the commerce of Christopher and Hobson and Hobson's immediacy of residence with Maundy. Again nothing untoward rears up in these financial transactions, but it all does smack of being much different from an "average citizen" world—rather, it becomes a small world of entrepreneurial friends. We do not know whether Christopher used this property, Cross Keys, as a residence or a part-time residence for his stays in London; he lived in Ipswich from before 1652 and reputedly stayed at the Inns of Court when in town. He may simply have been divesting himself of property in London in 1654, but he had been having difficulty with the Committee for Compounding (that is, the Committee of Parliament for the Composition of Property Owned by Delinquents), who were unsatisfied that he had given them a full accounting of his estate through at least 1652 and perhaps through 1658.[19] The conveyance of property in Ludgate Hill to Hobson appears perfectly legal, and not classifiable as "fraudulent," but it may have been intended to circumvent some financial questions and obligations.

Numerous records that have been discovered indicate that John Milton senior purchased and sold various properties, often acted as go-between in loans from one person to another (at times reinvesting the lender's interest and sometimes being sued for his further actions), and made a number of investments. One example of censurable action lurking in these kinds of dealings is the curious suit brought against him by Dr. Samuel Burton, which, however, was dismissed.[20] Yet the financial and potentially corrupt world in which Milton, the father (and, in some instances, the son), operated rears up. This case initiated by Burton combines one person's use of another person's name in a legal action, double defaults, testimony that people named had never met other people named but between whom some in-person transactions would seem to have been necessary, and accusations that Milton's shop was the locus for payment and that—apparently this is false—he had advised the lender to conceal identity and address. We do not know how many of his father's actions later involved or devolved upon John Milton junior; and we cannot call these actions "fraudulent" or "usurious" (although the general word "usury" is proper here), but they do place the poet-author outside the world of the common man, outside the world of the politically and economically encumbered "people," and into a world in which fraudulent conveyance was not unknown.

In addition to Milton junior's negotiations with the Cope family cited above, sometime prior to February 16, 1649/50 he made a loan of £50 to Robert Warcupp. Extant is a receipt of that date for payment of £5 in interest. The signed document is now owned by the Historical Society of Pennsylvania. Further, Parker remarks, "There is also some reason to believe that he had lent money to the Government ('upon the Public Faith') which he was unable to get back," although he speculates the suggestive evidence refers to Excise Bonds.[21] On May 13, 1651, Milton bought an excise bond of £400 from George Foxcroft (see French, *Life Records*, 3:26–29). Payments of £16 for six months' interest are recorded in 1651 through June 1660. The bond was transferred to Cyriack Skinner on May 5, 1660, and recorded on May 7 (*Life Records*, 4:3417–18). Such a transfer can be called a "conveyance," and in fact both documents are so labeled by the Columbia editors (13:420–21 and 617–18). The word itself is not used in the three transfers recorded (to Foxcroft, to Milton, to Skinner), which instead use "grant assigne & sett over vnto," "transferr and sett over vnto," and "graunt, assigne, transferr & sett ouer unto." Perhaps "convey" is avoided because of its nefarious meaning. In any case, these surviving records make clear Milton's usurial activities, though nothing fraudulent may be attached to the transactions.

2

Further pertinent matters impinging on this discussion of convey and thus on aspects of a scrivener's profession should be remarked upon. In his *Commonplace Book*, under

"De usurâ," (CM 18:162), Milton cites Dante's *Inferno*, canto 11: "usury is a sin against nature and against art: against nature because it makes money beget money, which is an unnatural begetting; against art because it does not work &c."[22] Ruth Mohl dates the entry "1635–1638 (?)"; I have suggested narrowing that to 1637.[23] Milton adds reference to Bernardino Daniello's scholium on Dante's epitome, which the *Complete Prose Works* footnotes (YP 1:418–19): "But to desire that money beget money is a thing illicit, and he who does so offends nature and art, which is the child of nature, by not working and exercising itself; and in consequence it also offends God, of whom nature is a child and art a grandchild." Canto 11 is concerned with violence against a neighbor, and is part of the Seventh Circle of Hell (the first of three concentric rings); the Eighth Circle (the third of the concentric rings) includes the Fraudulent, who commit violence against God by acts against a person whose confidence is not involved and those (like Satan) who commit acts against a person whose confidence is enjoyed (thus involving deceit). Fraud, we are told, is peculiar to humankind, who have the gift of reason, and it is a serious offense against God because human "work" is a reflection of divine "industry," and usury is an "unnatural" use of human industry. The word "fraud" appears 11 times in Milton's prose in its general sense; for example, in *Doctrine and Discipline of Divorce* (1644), in reference to Manasseh's building altars in which he set graven idols (2 Kings 21), "This is the lowest pitch contrary to God that publick fraud and injustice can descend" (YP 2:292).

Milton has two further entries under "Usury" in the *Commonplace Book*, one from John Speed on papal usurers or merchants (Caursini), dated 1639–1641(?), the other from André Rivet, who defends the employment of usury, in the question of its being allowed ("licit"), by a reading of the Decalogue.[24] This is in reference to the eighth commandment, "Thou shalt not steal," and what Rivet construes as a misreading of Jesus' advice: "if ye lend to them of whom ye hope to receive, what thank have ye? for sinners also lend to sinners, to receive as much again. But love ye your enemies, and do good, and lend, hoping for nothing again; and your reward shall be great" (Luke 6:34–35). Milton probably would also have known, at least through Rivet's commentary, that Calvin defended usury. James Holly Hanford assigns the holograph entry of this work by Rivet as "uncertain" and Ruth Mohl repeats the designation.[25] That dating, however, is based on the fact that at CM 18:188 ("Astutia politica" or "Political Adroitness") the last entry citing a different tract by Rivet is in the hand of Jeremy Picard, Milton's amanuensis in the extant second part of the *De doctrina Christiana* manuscript. Picard's employment (also including a number of other items) has been dated circa 1658 through circa 1660, but so little is known about him that questions can be raised about the specific times he worked for Milton, and Milton's rather infrequent continued use of the *Commonplace Book* after around 1650 has not been attended to. (He lost sight in his left eye during 1650 and was totally blind before February 1652.) Mohl dates Milton's holograph entries in the *Commonplace Book* up to 1647 only (as in the range of 1644–47); there are 28 entries by scribes, including 17 from Machiavelli's *Discorsi sopra la Prima Deca di Tito Livio* (in *Tutte le Opere*, 1550). She dates the scribal entries from 1650 through 1667, this latter date resulting from the entry of two items by the amanuensis who produced the extant copy of the first book of *Paradise Lost*. The scribes have been numbered as six (including Edward Phillips) plus an indeterminate number of "Machiavelli scribes," although it is probable that both numbers should be fewer, as I have argued elsewhere.[26]

I rehearse these concerns about the dating and nature of entries because of their relationship with Milton's published work. As Mohl records (YP 1:466–47n10), the citation of Rivet on page 188 of the Yale Prose, concerning

Exodus 1:9–10 from *Commentarius in Librum Secundum Mosis, qui Exodus apud Græcos Inscribitur,* is a direct quotation from the 1651 edition of *Opera,* published in Rotterdam. (Other entries on this page are dated 1639–141[?] and 1642–44[?].) But as Mohl goes on to remark, "he may have used a separate edition here also," and the lack of page numbers (which are included with the first reference to Rivet on page 160 [YP 1]) may be "because the text was easily accessible." Hanford points out that "The entry from Rivet bears a rather striking resemblance to the satirical passage on 'the masterpiece of a modern politician' in *Of Reformation* (1641),... but the similarities may well be accidental. The Commonplace Book entry is unlikely to be as early as 1641."[27] His last statement is clearly the result of its being in Picard's hand and the lack of evidence that Milton may have had an early, separate edition of the work. Whether or not we redate this entry on page 188 earlier (1651? or even earlier—around 1641—as the similarity with the statement in *Of Reformation* suggests), the entry on page 160 in Milton's hand should be dated closer to that from Speed and by 1643, and Rivet's *Commentarius* had been in Milton's cognizance by 1641.

Two matters are noteworthy in this reference to Rivet on page 160: First, there is a line here in Rivet's thinking, and in Milton's consideration of his position, between the lending of money, which is approved and yet which might have the word "usury" attached to it by some people, and usury as the return for such lending when it is a matter of receiving "as much again" (excessive) or when "money begets money" (as when intention in lending is not primarily "charitable"), as Milton's comment on Dante expresses it—that is, lending at high rates of return. We should note that the Latin word simply means "the using of" and "interest" where money is concerned. Were his own financial dealings, as well as his family's, to be considered "usurious" since remuneration of some kind or value was acquired through his services, and his services did not engage "work" in the sense of labor or even through exercise of mind? Is there something hypocritical here or is it just not facing the issue as others—Lilburne's apprentices, perhaps—might? Does the lender's intent or disingenuous justification of his action remove divine disdain? Or is this a psychological vindication of himself and his family from living off the circumstances of others? How "charitable" are these actions, all of these actions, so that they can, for the professedly "moral" and religious, be construed in totally positive terms?

The facts of Milton's life, first, do *not* point to illegalities, nor to fraudulence in actions, nor to any conscious hypocrisy, but they also do *not* paint a picture of what modern labor, or common workers, or believers in a strict "work ethic" would cast as the life of one of the "people," and *not* an epitome of one whose economic and political practices place him in the camp of egalitarianism.[28] Second, the uses of the word "usury" in his writings are informative for us in considering the questions above, and it is interesting thus that these uses of "usury" all date from 1643–45, and that Rivet is cited in these same writings from 1644–45.[29] In the first edition of *Doctrine and Discipline of Divorce* (1643) Milton wrote, "The example of usury, which is commonly alleg'd makes against the allegation which it brings, as I touch'd before. Besides that usury, so much as is permitted by the Magistrate, and demanded with common equity, is neither against the word of God, nor the rule of charity, as hath been often discus't by men of eminent learning and judgement" (34; YP 2:322). This argument comes straight out of Rivet (as quoted before), thus implying a date for the *Commonplace Book* entry as somewhere between 1641 and 1643, but even more importantly for an understanding of Milton's position on "good" usury and potentially "bad" usury—a position that agrees with Calvin and Rivet and disagrees with the popular interpretation of Jesus' words. Other biblical texts that he must have known have pertinency here as well. Exodus 22:25 states as law: "If thou lend money to any of my people that is poor by thee, that shalt not be to him as a usurer, neither shalt thou lay upon him usury." Deuteronomy 15:7–9 admonishes that "thou shalt not harden thine heart, nor shut thine hand from the poor brother: / but thou shalt open thine hand wide unto him, and shalt surely lend him sufficient for his need, in that which he wanteth," and adds, "Beware that there be not a thought in thy wicked heart" and "givest him nought." The Lord's anger with Manasseh (Jer. 15:4, 10) for his woeful boast that "I have neither lent on usury, nor men have lent to me on usury; yet every one of them doth curse me" caps the charitable life that Milton apparently composed for himself (and his relatives). Milton's life does not exhibit usury in the "uncharitable" sense of the word. Nonetheless, an objective reader of his life and these statements will be hard put not to conclude that Milton is really justifying himself and his financial activities (as well as his father's) by finding an agreeable interpretation of a scriptural passage and championing that interpretation, not arbitrating forthrightly on the question of usury—a not very commendable thought. Is the idolatrous view of Milton in need of some adjustment? Is there not hypocrisy here?

Shortly before the aforementioned statement in his argument for divorce, he asserts, "the Christian Magistrate permits usury and open stews, & heer with us adultery to be so slightly punisht...and make no scruple to allow usury, esteem'd to be so much against charity" (33; YP 2:320). The interpretation of usury is continued in *Tetrachordon:*

> And although mans nature cannot beare exactest lawes, yet still within the confines of good it may and must; so long as lesse good is far anough from altogether evil. As for what they instance of usury, let them first prove usury to be wholly unlawfull, as the law allowes it; which learned men as numerous on the other side will deny them. Or if it be altogether unlawfull, why is it tolerated more then divorce? he who said divorse not, said also *lend hoping for nothing againe,* Luk. 6.35. But then they put in, that trade could not stand. And so to serve the commodity of

insatiable trading, usury shall be permitted, but divorce, the onely meanes oft times to right the innocent, & outrageously wrong'd, shall be utterly forbid. (52; YP 2:656).[30]

His view of "charity" is thus also to be remarked. To Parliament he urged approval of divorce law, for "this glorious act will stile ye the defenders of Charity" and will become a "religious" and "holy" "defence" against "the policy of Rome" (*Doctrine and Discipline of Divorce* [1644], A$_4$r; YP 2:232). A year later in *Tetrachordon* (2–3; YP 2:588), he rejected the Old Testament and Moses' law for the New Testament and Christ's love: "The Scripture...also dispenc'd not seldom with it self; and taught us on what just occasions to doe so: untill our Saviour for whom that great and God-like work was reserv'd, redeem'd us to a state above prescriptions by dissolving the whole law into charity." With that dissolution would come, we observe, rejection of usury (when it is "a literall indightment" employed not on a "just occasion") in favor of the charity of love toward one's fellow human being (when it is a "just occasion" and comes "with a greater spirit at the good of mankinde"). But we should also trenchantly observe that he does not explicitly recognize that rejection. "Charity," "the soul / Of all the rest"—"Deeds...Faith...Vertue, Patience, Temperance...Love"—has obliterated usury but not for Milton and his financial dealings.

Milton is a debater, a grown-up student of oratory and rhetoric, using any means to assert his contention and confute others' opposition. We certainly can extract his opinions (at least at the time when he wrote them) from what he argues, and we can look upon those arguments as sincere. Yet we should also admit that in such matters as divorce and "usury" he has a vested interest, a less than totally objective point of view, a psychological need to "prove" his contentions. Most of us, I feel sure, would not have thought of employing the controversy over the interpretation of Luke, chapter 6, in order to analogize it with the controversy over divorce, thereby propounding a kind of compromise. Is this a sign of an issue that bears on his mind?

"Usury" may be "lesse good" but still "far anough from altogether evil"; it may not be "wholly unlawfull," thus, and by analogy "divorce" may not be "good," but it is not "evil" and should not be "unlawfull." Just where do we place Milton as conveyor of money and property in a moral scheme of a work ethic or in some aspect of equity when the components of "republicanism" are considered?

3

Kerry MacLennan, in a reading of the contract with Samuel Simmons for the publication of *Paradise Lost*, posits that, "through its economic terms and its contractual language," Milton "claims rights of intellectual property ownership, and asserts the right to manage, and control, the retail exploitation of his creative production."[31] Her argument gives the lie to the oft-repeated lament, as expressed by Jonathan Richardson, that "the Price for which *Milton* sold his Copy is Astonishing...the Price this Great Man Condescended to take for Such a Work; Such a Work! was Ten Pounds, and if a Certain Number went off, then it was to be made up Fifteen."[32] But what is important in our discussion of "convey" is that MacLennan reports that the contract was different from the standard one. Milton's reads: "That the said John Milton...Hath given granted and aſsigned, and by these presents doth giue grant & aſsigne vnto the said Sam[ll] Symōns his executors and aſsignes All that Booke Copy or Manuscript of a Poem intituled Paradise lost."[33] The standard contract, MacLennan tells us, said, "given granted aſsigned and conveyed." The poet, who had to be well informed about such legal matters, has made it clear that there is no conveyance of property involved, no fraudulent attempt to escape required levies, no nefarious action being undertaken—concepts that often attach to the words "convey" and "conveyance."

It is significant that these words—"convey," "conveyance," "fraud," "fraudulent"—make appearances in Milton's poetry and prose, and thus carry with them connotations that add substance to what is being presented, whether imaginative, as in the poetry, or informative, as in the prose. While Milton's rejection (for that is what it seems to be) of "convey" in this important contract in 1667, as well as the Foxcroft and Skinner bond of 1651 and 1660, removes any hints of potential fraud in future actions regarding the contract, uses of the word "convey" in his writings do carry these connotations. (See chapter 7, where the significance of language and allusion, including "convey" and "fraudulence," is considered.) These negative connotations about "convey" rear up in the use to which the word is used in the epic, implying Milton's rejection, in real life, of the concept of "conveying" because of its subtle, negative meaning: it is a rejection of what might be cast as "usurious" in our modern sense. There is conveyance of property—land, money—but indeed, when Milton finally was paid the money lent to Maundy by Baldwin and Jeremy Hamey in 1665, it was only his loan of £500 that he received back. (Nonetheless, in the intervening years would there not have been some interest payments, although there are no records of such transactions?) Have we in these two instances evidence of a development in thought about activities involving financial gain through contracts and loans, as well as sales of real estate and such, where "conveyance" might occur and "fraudulence" enter?—a "development" that would thus imply a remembrance by an older John Milton junior of what could have raised censure in prior business ventures. Perhaps Milton is exemplifying what he calls "moderation": "it entails insisting upon less than one's full legal rights, or even resigning one's rights altogether" (*De doctrina Christiana*, YP 6:778). Yet the Hameys showed no possibility of their being "poor" or in financial need (such as, perhaps, Maundy might have argued), since one was a physician and the other a London merchant. Thus, this loan, even transferred, does not fit a situation noted when "the loan is made to a poor man, [and] any interest at all is excessive" (YP 6:775), suggesting not a charitable act by Milton but just relief that at last he got his money back without loss, even if without gain—except for whatever financial interest was delivered.

4

To pursue the possibility of development of thought concerning "conveyance," "usury," and "fraud," we should recall what Milton writes in such later works as *Paradise Lost* and *Paradise Regain'd* as well as *De doctrina Christiana*. Book 2 of the theological treatise investigates the worship of God by humankind, and in chapter 14 the specific topic is "More About the Second Class of Special Duties Towards One's Neighbor" (Adhuc de Secunda Specie Officiorum Specialium Erga Proximum) with its discussion of "Commutative Justice" (YP 6:774–78). Milton, following Johannes Wollebius in *Compendium Theologiæ Christianæ*, 2.12, writes: "COMMUTATIVE JUSTICE concerns buying and selling, hiring, lending and borrowing, and the retention and restoration of deposits." The entry notes, "There are various kinds of fraud which are opposed to justice in sale and purchase," records eight biblical proof-texts on "Lending and borrowing," and makes clear that "It is a violation of justice to charge excessive interest on loans, and if the loan is made to a poor man, any interest at all is excessive," citing three proof-texts (YP 6:775–76). The following is directly significant for our discussion:

> There are many conflicting opinions about usury, however,...
>
> Most people agree that usury is not always illicit, and that in judging it we should take into account the usurer's motives, the rate of interest, and the borrower.
>
> As for the borrower, they agree that it is legitimate to take interest from anyone who is well enough off to pay it.
>
> They agree, too, that the rate should square with justice, if not with charity.

> They agree that, where motive is concerned, the usurer should have some consideration for his neighbor as well as for himself.
>
> Given these conditions, they maintain, no fault can be found with usury. (YP 6:776)

But here we have *no* proof-texts from Scripture. The "they" is "Most people," not further identified or delimited, and Milton's words sound like what Rivet (and Calvin) had written on usury, but they also sound suspiciously like self-justification, personal argument to make the kind of usury that Milton and his father (and his brother, his brother-in-law, and his nephews) engaged in defensible and morally upright to God. Yet, "the rate" need not necessarily "square...with charity." Commenting further on "these conditions," he writes, "and they are certainly right about the conditions, for unless they are observed pretty well all business transactions are illicit. Usury, then, is no more reprehensible in itself than any other kind of lawful commerce." The long discussion that follows does cite the Scriptures in justification of certain kinds of lending, but the debater in Milton also pulls out straws to make his kind of usury acceptable to God: "if we may make a profit out of cattle, land, houses and the like, why should we not out of money?...Usury is only to be condemned if it is practised at the expense of the poor, or solely out of avarice, or to an uncharitable and unjust extent; and these conditions apply to every kind of profit-making transaction just as much as they do to usury" (YP 6:777).

Rather than change from (or develop out of) what he wrote about in 1640–45, Milton continues his attitude about moneylending and fraud. However, the dating of *De doctrina Christiana* is far from settled, and it is possible that much that remains in the extant manuscript (particularly in book 2) derives from earlier times, indeed from work first set down during those same years.[34] On the one hand, the treatise shows no development of attitude in reference to usury or to the fraud that might result from it.

On the other hand, the two epics do not associate fraud with the kind of legal matters mentioned above. Instead, fraud is consistently associated with evil, deception, and a conscious attempt to dominate or achieve a boastful position. In the brief epic, Satan employs the word and this concept of "fraud" in addressing his infernal cohorts as the means to ruin Jesus as the nations' "King, their Leader, and Supream on Earth" (*PR* 1.97–99); and the angelic choir places Satan's attempts at temptation as "conquest fraudulent" (4.609). Satan also assigns fraud to God, which he but no other angel would undertake, to ruin Ahab (1.371–76). (Moloch is said to be fraudulent when he influences Solomon to build "His temple right against the Temple of God," 1.401–02.) Such negative associations had earlier been observed in *Sonnet XV* to General Thomas Fairfax, where war can breed only endless war, "Till Truth, and Right from Violence be freed, / And Public Faith cleard from the shamefull brand / Of Public Fraud." In *Paradise Lost* Satan first counsels his fellow fallen angels that the way to defeat God is "by fraud or guile," not by "force," not by provoking "dread new warr," which will not achieve their end (1.643–48). This epitome of Satan's action is iterated by the Son (3.152), the angelic choir (3.692), the narrative voice (4.121), Abdiel (5.880), Raphael (6.555, 794; 7.143), and Satan himself (10.485). The eight uses of the term in book 9—lines 55, 89, 285, 287, 531, 643, 904, 1150 (as well as Adam's assignment of the concept to accuse Eve in 10.871 of "inward fraud")—raise the same association with evil, and thus, by contrast, etch the vast difference for Milton between "fraud" of usury that is approvable and thereby not fraudulent, and usury that is fraudulent.

Aside from justification of his and his family's lives and livelihood in all this discussion of usury and fraud, what we discern is a belief in God, a belief in what is an agreeable interpretation of Scripture that allows for that justification, a separation of what is interpreted as God's disallowance of acceptability of fraudulent usury, yielding, rather, the more extreme assignment of all unacceptable "fraud" (and thus "usury") as evil, the work of the devil. There seems to be no real middle ground, but the potentially hypocritical position of acceptance when certain conditions are not entailed is silently ignored. Although interpretation is at issue (see the discussion of usury above), Milton disavows *his* interpretations as possibly questionable. Citations recorded in the *Commonplace Book* and comments upon them reinforce this reading of Milton as one of the worst kind of Sophist. Under "Lawes," 179 (YP 1:423), he writes concerning Savonarola's parable "that one should obey the spirit rather than the letter of the law"; and from John Speed's *Historie* (1623) that "Lawyers opinions turn with the times for private ends...but thire end is to be consider'd" (1:426); and under "Of Lawes, Dispensations from them, and Indulgences" (1:467), we read: "Dispensations from man-made laws are permitted because of the imperfection of the law-maker who has not provided satisfactorily for all things. Accordingly, they have no place in the laws of God, to whom nothing is hidden."[35] What continues in the concepts related to usury is the self-justification based upon a reading of Paul and the belief in God and God's wisdom as communicated to humankind—but, of course, as humankind wants to interpret it.

Perhaps there has been a change from acceptance of "conveyance" and its possible relationship to "fraud" in biographical circumstances to greater awareness of the negativities that are associated with it. At least as these words are employed in Milton's poetry and prose (from the early 1640s onward) the legalistic connections are eschewed for their moralistic infringements, suggesting the psychological barrier a human being sets up to deny truth about himself and his family and to exploit those negativities, those evil associations where others are concerned, those *truly* uncharitable acts that God would not condone.

Behind any investigation of Milton's attitudes and beliefs in such matters lies his attitude toward the law. God's law, God's mercy and love, replace the Mosaic law and any human-made laws when conflict occurs. The "law" relating to usury is justified, as we have seen, through an interpretation of Jesus' words in Luke, chapter 6. But the legal profession itself held no attraction for Milton. In his poem *Ad Patrem* ("To My Father"), as has often been pointed out, Milton specifically praises his father because

> you did not bid me go
> where the way lies broad, where the field of wealth is easier
> and the golden hope of amassing money glitters sure;
> neither do you force me to the laws and the courts of the
> people,
> so poorly overseen.[36] (68–72; my translation)

And thus notes in the *Commonplace Book* take on a sharper meaning for Milton's world: "Petrarch 'scorns the study of law'" (YP 1:468); and "The King of Hebrews was not free from obedience to the laws [of God]" (1:460).[37] It is clear why we are presented in *Paradise Lost* with Satan's complaint of the "fixt Laws of Heav'n" (2.18) and with Abdiel's honoring "His Laws our Laws" (5.844). "God from the Mount of *Sinai*...will himself / Ordain them [the twelve Tribes] Laws" (12.227–30), but the "grievous Wolves," taking "all the sacred mysteries of Heav'n / To thir own vile advantages" (12.508–10),

> Spiritual Laws by carnal power shall force
> On every conscience; Laws which none shall find
> Left them inrould, or what the Spirit within
> Shall on the heart engrave.   (*PL* 12.521–24)

Jesus in the brief epic, in distinction from Satan's view of God the Father's "new Laws" (5.679, 680, 693) in the diffuse epic, will assert

> The Law of God I read, and found it sweet,
> Made it my whole delight, and in it grew
> To such perfection,...
> I went into the Temple, there to hear

> The Teachers of our Law, and to propose
> What might improve my knowledge or their own.
>
> (*PR* 1.207–13)

Later, Jesus will refute the need for human-made learning, for the Psalms "only with our Law best form a King" (*PR* 4.364). He is speaking about Psalm 1, which in Milton's rendition reads,

> Blest is the man who hath not walk'd astray
> In counsel of the wicked,...But in the great
> Jehovahs Law is ever his delight,
> And in his Law he studies day and night. (1–6)

Three

Milton the Republican

1

A major topic within Milton scholarship in recent years—indeed within most literary discussion and of such great concern in our everyday life—has been the political world. Much of the uneducated name-calling in the popular media has shown ignorance of what words like "conservative," "liberal," "republican," "democratic," "socialist," "communist," "radical," and "revolutionary" mean, and certainly what they entail as concepts. Unfortunately this ignorance rears up among the "educated" as well, who seem determined to make their subject (for instance, Milton or Thomas Jefferson) exemplary of what they cast as one or more of these words. An idea considered aberrant to some people espousing a status quo immediately seems to label that person who so thinks a "radical." But we would do well to heed Barbara K. Lewalski's comment about Milton's construction of himself as "a new kind of author, one who commands all the resources of learning and art but links them to radical politics, reformist poetics, and the inherently revolutionary power of prophesy." That is, Milton is a different kind of radical from the commonplace usage of the word, one of a reformist and oppositional stance, not divided against himself, but requiring positioning within a specific milieu for the time and action which, at that juncture, is being analyzed. Most apt is her reference to *Paradise Lost* 6.122–25, where Abdiel, having defeated Satan's attempt at justification for his revolt, proceeds to defeat Satan bodily: "nor is it aught but just, / That he who in debate of Truth hath won, / Should win in Arms, in both disputes alike / Victor."[1] Not only are logic and reason "choice," but also the warfaring servant of the Bible must at times exercise his might in opposition to those who cite Jesus at every turn. Combine with this a remark by David Loewenstein: "Like the poet whose radical voice remains 'unchanged / To hoarse or mute' in the midst of the evil days of the Restoration, Abdiel will not 'swerve from truth, or change his constant mind / Though single' (V.902–3)."[2] The "radical republican Milton" that Matthew Biberman discusses and describes with a specificity not necessarily inherent in others' usage of either word is an apt designation.[3]

    A major problem in dealing with politics during this period of Milton's life is that it is entwined with the church and religious belief. We are fortunate to have the detailed work of William Haller and Christopher Hill, and many others, which remains informative and basic to any consideration of the issue, although much unequivocal revision has corrected their conclusions. The rise and development of Puritanism during this period, the civil wars and their culmination in the execution of Charles I, and the theocratic rule of Oliver Cromwell and the Council of State establish the seemingly opposed sides of royalism and parliamentarianism. But it is not a simple division, as many important studies have demonstrated over and over again. "Monarchy" is not necessarily evicted by antagonism toward "royalism," for the latter term comes more to mean the backing of Charles, and its "opposition" signifies opposition to that particular king.[4] Adherence to parliamentarian positions does not necessarily mean an approval of Cromwell and the actions of Parliament, and religious schisms develop a myriad of sectarian positions—millenarianism, apocalyptic and quietist beliefs, philosophic stances that smack of numerous heretical ideas and -isms. We will look at some of the changes in the state church that affected Milton in chapter 4, and some of the altered beliefs in the realm of theology in chapters 5 and 6. An important study of the intersection of religion and government is John F. Wilson's *Pulpit in Parliament: Puritanism during the English Civil Wars, 1640–1648*. As Wilson documents, sermons delivered before Parliament, preached by university-trained clerics, frequently argued radical religious ideas and antagonism to authority in statements that looked toward the eschatological and the means of reformation of sinful people (most people, that is) through the work of religious magistrates. He contends that influence from these sermons led to the execution of Charles and the acceptance of the theologic state that ensued.[5]

To John Selden, however, the "contract" (contracts are kept "as long as they like them, and no longer") between Charles and the Long Parliament had ceased.[6] But, N. H. Keeble tells us, "The execution of Charles continued to be regarded with abhorrence by the majority of puritans, and republicanism, the consequence rather than the cause of the regicide, only ever enjoyed minority support. During the 1650s, those whose respect it did command grew disillusioned with the very man who had made it possible, Cromwell." In the 1640s Milton's "support for the New Model Army, the Rump and for Cromwell," Keeble goes on, "was founded in his disillusion at the Long Parliament's abandonment of the principles of reformed Protestantism."[7]

Milton's probably altered attitude toward Cromwell has been debated on both sides of favorable and unfavorable. What emerges is a Milton who had not thought out all of the quirks that governing entails, particularly the inherent opposition to believing in separation of church and state while accepting the theocratic state that involved him in a nondirective, administrative capacity. Instead of relying upon past evaluations, rereading Milton's works can lead to John Rogers's incisive realization: "There may be no pamphlet within this period [1649–60] in which Milton does not assert contradictory positions on the constitution of the ideal political organization," but, Rogers adds, "a pattern of political philosophical development is nonetheless discernible in these treatises." The pattern points to what Martin Dzelzainis proposes (writing with the differences of the two editions of *The Ready and Easy Way*, 1660, in the background): "fundamental continuities in Milton's thought... mean that the radicalism he displays in 1649 [in *Tenure of Kings and Magistrates* and *Eikonoklastes*] is not the altogether unheralded phenomenon it is sometimes taken to be."[8] We move from the vision of a state ruled by the people to one ruled by a Parliament that includes a legislative body chosen by the people, to a Parliament delimited to a specific number of representatives in perpetuity (with some understandable reasoning behind such an outrageous proposal), and then to a federated state with a central rule and various other "commonwealths" (those of the various counties) engaged in a decentralized government.[9] Yet that legislative body and its rulings pursued religiously tinged laws. Is there any question that there has been "conceptual development"? We all engage in such development, correction, improvement, and revision of our ideas, some of which are our most cherished. Continuities exist but so often with elucidation that alters the details, alters it so much so that the execution of choice and the activities of the chosen can have quite different results from those envisaged, just as Charles's monarchy ended and a new formulation began.

Taking a broad perspective on this momentous period in English (and as precedent, world) history, Diana Purkiss, exploring a psychological (Freudian) agenda in investigating the wars, most remarkably views the happenings as Parliament's "beget[ting] a civil society through masculine agency alone..., and it is here that this desire connects most evidently with the need to appropriate the mother's function while repudiating her exercise of it."[10] Gendered overviews (working through assignment of stereotypical attitudes and characteristics) may be meaningful in evaluating these political issues, but the point here is the abandonment of a large section of "the people" by a palliative blindness to their existence. Milton's and others' disregard of the lower class and obliteration of the female half of "the people" carry grave weight in looking at this period and its aftermath, and these issues will be taken up in a moment.

The civil wars broke out in separate confrontations in various geographic spots, partially as a result of bourgeois social and economic concerns as well as religious and political issues, the only ones that most critics seem to have considered. Yet think of the implications in chapter 2 here of a growth of nonroyal, nonaristocratic estates and familial enclaves, and Milton in the midst of such middle-class development. Moving beyond the rogues and vagabonds of the Elizabethan world that included "the underworld," a "lower" class developed accordingly in both number and different kind. By the last quarter of the century social changes, social life, had altered drastically—and debtors' prisons had swelled. The wars attest to a transition from medieval times and feudalism to a capitalistic system that had been gaining momentum for a century and a half.[11] "Revolutionary Independency, as a political force," Andrew Milner concludes, "represented the most class-conscious section of the mid-seventeenth-century English bourgeoisie, that is, those sections which were ultimately prepared to risk a political mobilization of the masses in order to overthrow the feudal state machine and establish a thorough-going bourgeois republic."[12] Selden, opposed to *jus divinum* when applied to the king or to Presbyterian government, nonetheless found "Equity...a Roguish thing": "Equity is A Roguish thing, for Law wee have a measure known what to trust too. Equity is according to ye Conscience of him y^t is Chancell^r." Dependent upon conscience, equity becomes "a term of radical liberty, egalitarianism and experiments with notions of social justice."[13] Mark Fortier has thoroughly examined *The Culture of Equity in Early Modern England*, and, quoting Milton in *A Treatise of Civil Power* (YP 7: 249), indicates that "Protestant equity and conscience [*should*] demand 'a free and lawful debate at all times by writing, conference or disputation of what opinion soever, disputable by scripture.'" Yet an earlier Parliament, as one example, had passed a law "that only hee that had 40^s. p[er] ann should give his voice, they under should bee excluded.... All account Civilly in a Parliam^t.: Women are involv'd in the men. Children in those of 'p[er]fect age.'"[14] This middle-class separation of segments from "the people" and this patriarchal put-down of women as independent people continued; even the Levellers did not advance the franchise for an electorate truly "republican."

2

How we see Milton and how we determine a so-called republican position for him depends upon our definitions of terms, and most importantly what we accept as "the people." A republican state is *not* the same as a democratic state, and thus it is that government expresses the will of its people through their representatives. The term "people" allows for its being a vehicle for a wide range of authority and for some confusion over "equality" or even only over "equity." Milton's explication to Salmasius about "what we wish to understand by the word [name] 'people'" (quid nomine populi intelligi velimus; *Pro Populo Anglicano Defensio*, CM 7:390) is:

> You suppose that you know we mean by *people* only the populace [populi nomine plebem solùm], because 'we have done away with the House of Lords.' Actually it is just this fact which shows that by *people* we mean all citizens of every degree [omnes ordinis cujuscunque cives]. We have made supreme the one assembly of the people, in which the nobles, as part of the people, have a legal right to vote, not indeed as before in their own behalf, but in behalf of the communities electing them. (YP 4:471)

Although one student of Milton has interpreted this to mean "all people," it does not include those not considered "citizens"[15] *legally,* such as the "rabble" or "women," who not only do not assume representation but who do not even vote toward representation. Milton's aim here is to rebut Salmasius (audience and intentionality are always significant!) and thus to declare that not only the House of Lords (one degree or order—*ordinis*—as in the past under the monarchy of Charles I), but also the nonnoble body of persons (the House of Commons, a different degree or order) are both charged with the management of government. The purpose in the statement is simple: the Commonwealth of England is governed by nobles and nonnobles, and that is it.[16] The means of election was not defined by law at this time; procedures varied from county to county and some elections took place at mass meetings. Women and "the dregs of the populace" were not included. Religious and property affiliations did influence such meetings and such selection well into the nineteenth century.

What situations, or circumstances, of properties the term "republican" brings with it, even then, yield different degrees of republicanism. While what Milton writes in rebuttal gives the illusion of something democratic, it is not; yet it coincides with concepts of republicanism through an emphasis on representation by and through unrestricted people. Who represents and who elects the representatives puts a brake on the alleged unbiased act that some commentators have wanted to impose upon Milton's position. Those in "slave" levels were not accepted as "the people" from early biblical times onward, of course; but for Milton surely his dismissal of the "rabble" (the uneducated? the impoverished? the criminal? the *not* "well affected"?) cannot be construed as his acceptance of them as part of these "people." Those who did not own land or have some arbitrary level of financial status were often dismissed from general consideration (politically, governmentally), and although Michael Wilding wishes to deny Miltonic elitism because of acceptance of those in the mechanical trades, there *is* a class attitude that emerges, and consistently women are ignored.[17] In Thomas Corns's words, Milton's "respect for the rights of conscience of the working classes reflects his beliefs in personal freedom and responsibility."[18] We cannot, and we should not, expect Milton to have a current attitude toward classes or women (although such an attitude is very far from being universal even today), but we also should recognize that his position is far from egalitarian, even in the matter of government.

A bourgeois revolutionary, "Milton associates his defence of Cromwell [in *Observations of the Articles of Peace*, 1649] with a recurrent interest in constructing a puritan ruling class in principles other than wealth or ancestry," Corns states. I certainly agree with that view and the point of "a new social formation distinguished by its education and its godliness."[19] But, and this is very important, the words "puritan" and "godliness" exclude Jews and idolatrous Catholics (and thus expose antagonism toward many of the Irish, as Elizabeth Sauer and Mary Fenton show us), and the words "wealth" and "ancestry" reject certain aristocratic classes but not the moneyed dynasties emerging in the middle class. The word "education," with its distinguished associations, smacks of an intellectual snobbery that the "Ode to Rouse" also evinces.

The term "well affected" was commonplace around the time of the Interregnum and the Restoration, and it or "best affected" appears in Milton's tracts and some of the Leveller writings meaningfully.[20] While the term seems to mean only "well-disposed toward" or "well-conditioned toward (mentally)," it is a delimiting term that aligns the representative government and the electorate of that republican government with those who think the same way as the believers in the Good Old Cause, and with those of a middle class in a generally adequate financial and educational status. Perhaps this can be called a "meritocracy," but even if we accept that as a defining label it indicates that "the people" are not the full "populace."

The tracts produced around 1660 are instructive about this point; first in the preface to the Parliament in *Hirelings:* "whether ye will hearken to the just petition of many thousands *best affected* both to religion and to this your return, or whether ye will satisfie, which you never can, the covetous pretences and demands of insatiable hirelings, whose *disaffection* ye well know both to your selves and your resolutions" (YP 7:275; my italics). And, in *A Letter to a Friend:*

> I call it the famous parlament, though not the blamelesse [harmles], since none *well affected* but will confesse, they have deserved much more of these nations, then they have undeserved [YP 7:324–25; my italics, with the reading of the first publication in 1698 bracketed]. If the parlament be again thought on, to salve honour on both sides, the *well affected* partie of the citie, & the congregated churches may be induc'd to mediate by publick addresses & brotherly beseechings. (YP 7:330; my italics)

Or most significantly in "Proposalls of Certaine Expedients":

> that the Elecions of them who shall here after sit in this supreme councell may be of such as are certainly known to have besides their ability, the two qualificacions above named [Liberty of conscience, & the other against a single person & house of Lords], & to the persisting in them shall take their oath, whither they be nominated by the grand Councell, & elected by the *well affected people,* or

> nominated by those of the people & elected by the grand Councell. *The people* also...should be enjoyed by oath to the same two principles. (YP 7:337–38; my emphasis)

Certainly Milton is arguing for a qualified group of representatives and a qualified group of electors, but there is no indication of a full populace or of women to partake in this process, and it is not on the basis of qualification (or competency). Unavoidable is the realization that "the people" are delimited—republican in sentiment but not democratic, not egalitarian, and not even, really, given equity. Some of the language appears in the second edition of *The Ready and Easy Way* and in *Brief Notes upon a Late Sermon*, the first instance in the former and the instance in the latter (YP 7:414, 485) have the same basic meaning.[21] But three other uses in *The Ready and Easy Way* consider how argument for "partial rotation" of a "perpetual senate" (which he proffered in the first edition) may create the defeat of a desirable "well affected" or "best affected" party: "new elections may bring in as many raw, unexperienc'd and otherwise *affected*, to the weakning and much altering for the wors of public transactions....Neither do I think a perpetual Senat, especially chosen and entrustd by the people, much in this land to be feard, where the *well-affected* either in a standing armie, or in a setled militia have thir arms in thir own hands" (7:435; my italics). "But if the people be so *affected*, as to prostitute religion and libertie to the vain and groundless apprehension, that nothing but kingship can restore trade,...because they falsly imagin[ ] that they then livd in more plentie and prosperitie, our condition is not sound but rotten, both in religion and all civil prudence" (7:461–62; my italics).

His argumentative forecast of potential aberration has been the frequent experience of "democracy," of "socialism," of "monarchy," of "theocratic regimes," but as well of "republican" experiments. Yet what should be recognized by Milton's interpreters is that his use of "well-affected" and "people" does not even potentially include "all people" of his nation and ignores constituencies that should be presented and have a voice in choosing their representatives. In addition, he is not totally aware of the problems involved—at the very least because of his intolerance toward certain religious groups, his mental superiority, and his own "masculinist" position. Such personal circumstance is given a different spin by Peter Coleman, who attacks this basically hypocritical conundrum through a focus upon writing (or the author) by positing that part of Milton's argument in *Areopagitica* is "not a liberal argument for the freedom of writers and readers. It is the grievance of the superior man—perhaps the most learned poet in English literature, a scholar who read the Hebrew scriptures daily and wrote some of his best poetry in Latin and Greek—at being judged by his inferiors in scholarship and culture."[22] He concludes that although Milton's purpose was to advance the revolution, the new Reformation, "A fateful error, he tells us, had been to rely on politics and the sword. Reform yourself first, and then perhaps the world." I think it is time that Miltonists stopped excusing Milton's lack of full thought about some issues, his inconsistent or inchoate stands before issues are more fully addressed, and his intolerant positions alongside his seemingly tolerant but biased argument (as in *Of True Religion*, to negate acceptance of Catholics) that so many enumerated sects should be tolerated "as being all Protestants; that is on all occasions to give account of their Faith" (YP 8:422–27). His world is a kind of utopian vision that is blind to the change that is occurring, even when measures are taken to restrict change. There is nothing here that involves revision of class structure or economic reform, which we should realize, given his position on usury, as mentioned in the previous chapter.

3

Changing evaluations of Milton and his thought in the areas of political and social significance present major differences from the past. Elizabeth Skerpan Wheeler epitomizes the change in her study of the early prose, which placed Milton as either "a precursor of modern liberalism, defending freedom of speech (the 'tolerationist' thesis), or a covert authoritarian tyrant, dedicated to the suppression of truly opposing views in defence of a repressive theocracy ('anti-tolerationist')." These positions have been replaced by "historical investigation into the intellectual contexts of Milton's ideas...com[ing] to understand Milton as a classical republican rather than a modern liberal, a person who, following Aristotle, sees the human being as a political animal rather than an individual seeking freedom from the state." Or, "investigation of his social contexts and views on writing...has presented a Milton for whom the whole enterprise of knowledge-making was a collaborative process, an insight that challenges the conventional view of Milton as the epitome of the individualistic, independent author." Wheeler thus offers a Milton "at the nexus of classical republicanism and iconoclastic Christianity."[23] As this statement implies, that reevaluation needs, more clearly than many critics in the past have done, to separate the person from the statement by recognition of the circumstances of writing, the audience (particularly the *male* audience), and the strategies of rhetoric (the aim and means of persuasion in the oration-presentation that Milton learned at school and college), as I have tried to point out a few times in this book. Such reevaluation also calls for a clearer recognition that a poem like *Paradise Lost* is a literary work, a fiction, with characters who *represent* rather than *are* whom they represent. Peter Coleman's position is a big step in the direction of such rethinking about Milton the person and the author, and his view of Milton's changed thought—that one should change oneself, and its corollary that humankind needs to change, not simply the external institution—I have previously argued in looking at *Tenure of Kings and Magistrates* and the philosophic point of *Paradise Regain'd*.[24]

That Milton concedes that "the people" may not "prove faithful to the ideals embodied by leaders like Cromwell and himself" is an important observation by Michael Chappell, and, vying with the frequent presentation of Milton, Chappell states that, "Just as Milton is marginalized as a poet by the masses he distrusts, he in turn marginalizes the masses—the uneducated, the laborers, the merchant classes, the people who need governance no matter whether it be by a king or a Cromwell—in his discourse." Charles Geisst discusses Milton's position concerning "natural political rights": "Rights such as these could only be achieved through the rule of merit by a particular class by virtuous men." Building on this, Chappell sees that "The common people are necessary as the political body, but they are less important than the political head, the leader(s) of the country," thus backing up his contention that Milton obliterated class differences and "replaced them with a single class struggling with a single purpose." Essentially not different in her analysis to what a post-Restoration "fit audience" would interpret, Sharon Achinstein, speaking of the long epic, tells us that he "made the 'revolutionary' content of the poem not an over political statement, but the very process of training readers." His program is directed toward "the element of the ideal, the rhetorical, or the imaginary," with "reflection," as the poem ends of "not gloom at the failures of the revolution, but urgency and optimism."[25] These views of Milton's prose—directly political or only so affinitively—and the political content of his major poetry—so different from the aura surrounding his writing in the past—rest on a rejection of a closed idolatrous reading, on an underlying assumption that Milton would have and did subsume all the intricate components and incertitudes of political and social life that humankind faces in proposing "solutions": these views rest on an argument based on his "unchanging" mind.

So often, particularly in the issues raised in this chapter, Milton's thinking has "developed." It is not necessarily new and different or without seeds in the past that have exploded into specific concepts and idealistic hopes and realistic dampening; instead, his conceptual development has altered his overall attitudes, realizations, a realistic recognition of what may be commonplace, but wrong. Such a realistic acknowledgment extends beyond the social and political, as we shall see in chapters 5 and 6, while at the same time certain matters are *not* faced realistically. The position of women is but one important example. When it comes to politics, women have not taken a different position in Milton's thinking from that which emerges in his life and writing; but, as so many critics have come to realize within the last few decades—and we should recall as just one example Herman's destabilization of the reading of *Paradise Lost*—Milton's thinking has altered or developed substantially, still hampered by his belief in the Holy Scriptures and Paul, but nonetheless with advancement for gender equity. While Eve, as woman, is elevated in both the divorce tracts (when read attentively) and *Paradise Lost* (as has been argued by many commentators), it is a social and familial elevation. It may involve economic and literary improvements for woman, although little attention seems paid by Milton to these areas. Nevertheless, it does not include the political world, any more than the status of woman has changed fully in today's world, even in the boastful Western cultures.

The thesis proposed by Rachel Trubowitz sums up the trends in scholarship: "Milton's shifting, positive and negative representations of the body and nature, his ambivalence about Hebrew scripture, his critique of dynastic kingship's blood-and-soil measure of identity, and his unsettled prose and verse reflect his vision of the new nation and its foundational paradoxes."[26] Milton's readers, it may be suggested, are becoming aware of his uncertainties about political and governmental elitism and lack of attention to major groups of people.

Four

Milton, the Church, and Theology

1

Interrelated, yet separate, for all people are the external world and the internal mind. Much that we do or that occurs for us in life or that concerns us is influenced by that internal mind—our knowledge, our thoughts, our emotions. As these internalities change, if they do for whatever reason, so does that external world in which we find ourselves also change. At times the happenings outside ourselves have their toll on our knowledge, certainly, and then on our thought, attitudes, and emotions. In the realm of religion there is a similar bifurcation: discipline and doctrine—the externals that are related to the practice of religion, the church, and the internals of belief that involve the dogma of theology on which a church would be based. We have raised the matter of Milton's clerical career—his being "church-outed," his rejection of life as a minister—and we have noted his skepticism of the Trinity as conceived and expressed in an orthodox way. In this chapter I will begin to reengage these issues. First, I attempt to understand Milton's position on the church, on what becomes his "church" upon being "church-outed," and accordingly what might be described as his religious consciousness. This "visible" church eschews the external discipline that had developed in the state church but remains as "THE WHOLE MULTITUDE OF THOSE WHO ARE CALLED FROM ANY PART OF THE WHOLE WORLD, AND WHO OPENLY WORSHIP GOD THE FATHER IN CHRIST EITHER INDIVIDUALLY OR IN CONJUNCTION WITH OTHERS" (YP 6:568). It is, for Milton, interrelated with "internal worship," what may be called the "invisible" church.[1] Second, in succeeding chapters, I look at such theological issues as the Trinity, the virgin birth, the Son, transubstantiation and the Real Presence, and accordingly what can be suggested as Milton's theological position; that is, what relates to Milton's "internal worship." These have been basic and argumentative issues for commentators, who have not been in much accord at any time over when his career decision became realized, or what label to apply to his theological position, and therefore how to read *Paradise Lost* and whether indeed he was the author of *De doctrina Christiana*. These matters have led to questions about his church-going and his burial site, and to his place in the philosophic alterations that were emerging in the latter part of the seventeenth century. The externals changed for Milton during his lifetime but so did the internals, except that godly belief still remained. His mind and the world it produced for him changed, like anyone else's would, yet a constancy remained in his belief and faith in God that can be construed as delineating his "unchanging mind."

Much of the disagreement among critics—the contradictory readings of Milton's work, the attitudes toward him as a person—has been the result, I suggest, of the critic's own position coming up against what she or he recognizes as stridently opposite (*not* apposite) in Milton's writings. It may be a nonacceptance that a person may have differences of opinion about God and God's ways toward humanity, and thus about the origin of life, the astronomical world (should we not say "worlds"?) surrounding us, the future—whether divine or infernal, whether there even is an afterlife for a mortal—and the like. Some credit only orthodox positions without explanation or modification attached, and some may acknowledge the substance of only certain aspects of orthodoxy and heretical thinking, but not those unaccepted by the critic. That Milton may fall in between these extremes has not been considered by either kind of critic. The specious argument against Milton's authorship of *De doctrina Christiana* is a case in point: the questions that have arisen since the discovery of its manuscript (from, for example, Thomas Burgess's opinion onward) through more current times with the arguments advanced by William B. Hunter result from those readers' finding Milton's "beliefs" different from theirs—unorthodox statements of theological matters.[2] Such critics exhibit a kind of idolatrous attitude, as suggested in chapter 1, that Milton is never wrong, is never unsure, is always of constant mind.[3]

Two contrasting examples of this kind of inadequate reading resulting from the clash of ideologies tell us much about Milton's critics' positions. First, at the end of the war in heaven in *Paradise Lost*, the poem reads:

> When the great Ensign of *Messiah* blaz'd
> Aloft by Angels born, his Sign in Heav'n:
> Under whose conduct *Michael* soon reduc'd
> His Armie, circumfus'd on either Wing,
> Under thir Head imbodied all in one.   (6.775–79)

The lines indicate that the faithful angels (who have been "circumfus'd," that is, diffused in surrounding positions) as a group are led back ("re-duc'd") by Michael to assume again position in heaven under God. But additionally the lines, metaphorically, poetically, even graphically reprise the concept that God is One and at the end of time all will return to Godhead so that God will once again be All in All: "And when all things shall be subdued unto him, then shall the Son also himself become subject unto him that put all things under him, that God may be all in all" (1 Cor. 15:28). *Creatio ex Deo* underlies the significance of the lines, and line 779 specifically presents the angels as being made "smaller" ("reduc'd") so that they become the "body" ("imbodied") to the "Head" (God), who again becomes "all in one." This important biblical text and concept first appears in the poem when God the Father, addressing the Son, foretells the end of time in book 3:

> Here shalt thou sit incarnate, here shalt Reign
> Both God and Man, Son both of God and Man,
> Anointed universal King
>
> ....
>
> When thou attended gloriously from Heav'n
> Shalt in the Sky appeer,
>
> ....
>
> Then all thy Saints assembl'd, thou shalt judge
> Bad men and Angels,
>
> ....
>
> Then thou thy regal Scepter shalt lay by,
> For regal Scepter then no more shall need,
> God shall be All in All.   (3.315–41)

The concept, the belief, underlies the last line of the poem spoken by a character, that is, Eve, who iterates the protevangelium: "By mee the Promis'd Seed shall all restore" (12.623). The prominence of the biblical text and its substance in Milton's thought is evidenced by repetition in the poem and placements of it.

But this reading of the passage in book 6 has not sat well with critics who, apparently, find such graphic representation of the concept irreligious; who ultimately ignore that we are reading a literary work, not a theological treatise; who find some kind of blasphemy, it would seem, in such expression. This cannot be the Milton they love. Nor should such a literal reading of 1 Corinthians be countenanced. Additionally, there may be a nonacceptance of Milton's belief in *creatio ex Deo* rather than *creatio ex nihilo*. Part of the problem for such critics may be their (and, it would seem, most people's)[4] reading of Genesis 1:1–2: "In the beginning God created the heaven and the earth.... And the Spirit of God moved upon the face of the waters." But the verb "moved" implies sexual activity;[5] and the verb "created" does not settle a question of what is "nothing" if it is not the substance of God.[6] For Milton it is a matter of faith that God exists and created the world: he attempts offering an explanation that provides an analysis that can be "logical" to the mundane mind but one that also seeks an understanding to the thinking person beyond acceptance of a miracle on faith alone. He proclaims a continuing belief in God and his omnipotence, but the perspective view of creation and the afterlife when God will be All in All is not unmodified or unexplained orthodoxy.

The Milton of *Paradise Lost* and *De doctrina Christiana* is nonorthodox—a "heretic" in some people's vocabulary through such a display of heterodoxy.[7] However, it is important to comprehend Milton's definition of heresy, albeit in an argument to disengage Socinians and Arminians and others from the appellation. Such schismatic groups

> may have some errors, but are no Hereticks. Heresie is in the Will and choice profestly against Scripture; error is against the Will, misunderstanding the Scripture after all sincere endeavours to understand it rightly.... But so long as all these profess to set the Word of God only before them as the Rule of faith and obedience; and use all diligence and sincerity of heart, by reading, by learning, by study, by prayer for Illumination of the holy Spirit, to understand the Rule and obey it, they have done what man can do. (*Of True Religion*, 6; YP 8:423–24)

68   *The Development of Milton's Thought*

We should heed this concept as we think about Milton's theological positions. We may not accept this definition of "heretic" and may continue to make "heresy" congruent with "nonorthodoxy" (or "heterodoxy"), but a Miltonian should acknowledge what Milton seems to believe and credit and its possible—probable—difference from others' beliefs. It should not be a matter of who is right and who is wrong.

We cannot determine when Milton abandoned "creation from nothing," if he indeed had believed that explanation of creation at one time as we might imagine he did because of its common acceptance. Therefore, we cannot determine when he accepted "creation from God" and the implications of the *substantia* of God as the source of all created things. Earlier references to creation point to neither specifically; for example, see stanza 12 of *On the Morning of Christs Nativity*. Even the citation of 1 Corinthians seems not to occur before its inclusion in *Paradise Lost* and *De doctrina Christiana*, not that Milton would not have known it, but perhaps he had not pondered the implications in this biblical "foreknowledge" that he (perhaps) later found. Do we have change in this instance? development of concept? We do read incertitude in the statement given in note 4 above, and interestingly he does not pursue what God did prior to the creation of the world, but rather calls anyone who asks such a question "a fool; and anyone who answers him is not much wiser" (YP 6:299).

A different example of a problem in critical reading, secondly, is the matter of Arminianism, both because of what it points to for a Milton not simply iterating the doctrine of Jacobus Arminius, and because it illustrates the misappropriation of a label that critics seem always ready to make. An idea associated with Arminius concerning salvation (which is different from that of Calvin and some adherents of the state church) would seem to be the point of

> And I [God the Father] will place within them as a guide
> My Umpire *Conscience*, whom if they will hear,

> Light after light well us'd they shall attain,
> And to the end persisting, safe arrive. (*PL* 3.194–97)

Yet just before this God refers to a Calvinistic principle of election, which Arminius accepted but modified, as does Milton:

> Some I have chosen of peculiar grace
> Elect above the rest; so is my will:
> The rest shall hear me call, and oft be warnd
> Thir sinful state. (*PL* 3.183–86)

The rejection of absolute predestined election as the only means to salvation and a recognition that there are good people in this world who deserve salvation sounds logical to many people who would expect this of a merciful God. Does this make Milton "an Arminian," or does it tell us only his agreement with an Arminian principle? There is a world of difference between the stereotyping that calling him an Arminian misassigns and speaking of his agreement with one of its principles. The problem is not different from that created by all kinds of stereotyping: racial, ethnic, religious, nationalistic. Milton, like Arminius, rejects Calvin's "irresistible" grace, for example, and here because, shall we say, he realistically knows that some will resist grace: "my [God's] day of grace / They who neglect and scorn, shall never taste;...none but such from mercy I exclude" (3.198–99, 202). Thus, we would *not* call him a Calvinist although he is "calvinist," as was Arminius. But while other general points of likeness with Arminian thought, for instance toleration or liberty of conscience, can be seen, the view of reprobation accepted by Arminius is rejected. Milton writes that "the cause of reprobation, which is followed by punishment, must, if it is to be just, be man's sin alone, not God's will.... This reprobation lies not so much in God's will as in their own obstinate minds, and is not so much God's decree as theirs, resulting from their refusal to repent while they have an opportunity" (YP 6:195). The actions of Adam and Eve at the end of book 10 and beginning of book 11 are a demonstration of his point in opposition to Calvin and to Arminius.[8]

James Holly Hanford's discussion of Milton and Arminianism blurs the distinction that I believe must be acknowledged.[9] "That Milton was Arminian rather than Calvinistic may clearly be seen in his definitions of all the crucial theological terms which were in controversy"; an accurate statement, but an implication of Milton's being an Arminian is created, particularly when he does not record Milton's disagreement with Arminian reprobation, for example, and when in his previous paragraph he twice cites "the Arminian."

"Just when Milton took his leave of Calvin and orthodoxy is not certain," Maurice Kelley tells us, and he points out that *The Doctrine and Discipline of Divorce* (1644) and *Areopagitica* (1644) are questionable toward Arminius. Yet what seems a tacit acceptance of the Arminian position in the latter work indicates that "if Milton had not consciously and openly accepted Remonstrant doctrines by the time of *Areopagitica,* he had at least taken a position that would logically develop into the Arminianism advanced in the *Christian Doctrine*" (YP 6:82).[10] We cannot call Milton validly either *an* Arminian or *a* Calvinist, although adjectival forms of both are in order. Milton surely has changed in some basic theological principles, and that would seem to have come about through a conceptual development as he analyzed election, free will, reprobation, sin, and its source, salvation and God's grace.

2

Aside from a realization that he was not well suited to be a preacher that Milton's letter in the Trinity Manuscript to an unknown friend reveals, the church itself of which he would be a minister had altered in ways he did not approve. Theological concepts were also in flux and were surely matters of concern while he was at university. Chapters

5 and 6 note some of these pertinent tenets that may also have had an effect on Milton's determination of career and rejection of active ministry. But the alteration in the discipline in the church, the administration and views of its administrators, particularly William Laud, loom large in this decisive change of mind. In his study of Milton's divine vocation, John Spencer Hill examines the "evolving self—awareness and deepening vocational tone in the prose works" as well as the changing concepts of Milton's writing from 1625 to 1660—the ministerial, the poetic, and the prophetic.[11] A conspicuous turning point, as Don M. Wolfe (in Yale Prose, volume 1) and Hill point out, was the 1640 *Constitutions and Canons Ecclesiasticall* produced by Archbishop William Laud.[12] As a "turning point," however, this publication really only makes clear what had happened to the church and some of the changes that attempted to return to an earlier discipline, which, to those who *should* have been analytic, was not approvable by many. The intrusion of politics into the religious document was surely one major canon that Milton would have rejected. Yet on this issue one must wonder just how much Milton realized about the church during his university years, for he twice signed the subscription book (1629 and 1632),[13] when one looks at the 1612 *Canons* (which were maintained and repeated through publication): realities seem to have taken a number of years finally to impress themselves on him. The planks of the 1640 *Canons* that are cited here already existed in substance in earlier promulgations of canons and in various visitations from archbishops and bishops.

The 1640 *Canons* assert:

> THE most High and Sacred order of Kings is of Divine right, being the ordinance of God himself, founded in the prime Laws of nature, and clearly established by expresse texts both of the old and new Testaments. A supream Power is given to this most excellent Order by God himself in the Scriptures, which is, That Kings should rule and command in

their severall dominions all persons of what rank or estate soever, whether Ecclesiastical or Civill, and that they should restrain and punish with the temporall sword all stubborn and wicked doers. (YP 1:987)

The oath required to prevent change in doctrine or in government would also be summarily condemned:

I A. B. Do swear, That I do approve the Doctrine and Discipline or Government established in the Church of *England,* as containing all things necessary to salvation: And that I will not endeavour by myself or any other, directly or indirectly, to bring in any Popish Doctrine, contrary to that which is so established: Nor will I ever give my consent to alter the Government of this Church, by Arch-bishops, Bishops, Deanes, and Arch-deacons, &c. as it stands now established, and as by right it ought to stand. (YP 1:990-91)

This is the kind of thing that "church-outed" Milton as he expressed it in 1641/42, after joining the assault on episcopacy to which the SMECTYMNUUANS, including his former tutor Thomas Young, contributed most notably.

The "Root and Branch" petition to abolish episcopacy was presented to Parliament on December 11, 1640 (published in 1641),[14] in response to the *Canons* of 1640 and spoke for "a reformation in Church-government, as also for the abolishment of Episcopacy." Charged are such as the evils of the prelates and their dependents, "The great increase of Idle, lewd, and dissolute, ignorant and erroneous men in the Ministery," who by being "zealous of Superstitious Ceremonies...may live as they list, confront whom they please, preach and vent what errours they will, and neglect preaching at their pleasures, without controule" (YP 1:978-79). Plank 10 is significantly accusative: "The publishing and venting of Popish, Arminian, and other dangerous Bookes and Tenets, as namely, that the Church of Rome is a true Church, and in the worst times never erred in Fundamentals, that the Subjects have no propriety in their Estates, but that the King may take from them what he pleaseth, that all is the Kings, and that he is bound by no Law, and many other, from the former whereof hath sprung." The church itself—the turning of the Communion tables, the placing of images and crucifixes, and bowing before them—and its liturgy "framed out of the Romish *Breviarie Ritualium* Masse-book," the "Prophanation of the Lords day" through the reissuance of the Book of Sports (in 1634), as well as Charles's Scottish wars (YP 1:979, 980, 981, 983) are all evils requested of the High and Honourable Court of Parliament to redress. The upshot was the impeachment of Laud on December 18, 1640; with articles for the impeachment passed on February 24, 1641; imprisonment in the Tower on March 1, 1641; and execution on January 10, 1645. The revisionist argument of recent years that has attempted to ameliorate Laud and his actions is well challenged by Andrew Foster, who describes the "coherent programme relating to Church and state" that developed in the 1630s, through a rise in Arminianism that "stressed different attitudes towards God, to the nature of worship and to the sacraments."[15]

What the above indicates is the turning point for Milton of engaging public church and political activity with the "Postcript" to Smectymnuus's *Answer* in March 1641, *Of Reformation* in May 1641, *Of Prelatical Episcopacy* in July 1641, *Animadversions* in July (September?) 1641, *Reason of Church-Government,* written in late 1641 and published in early 1642, and *Apology to Smectymnuus* in April 1642 (dates being those generally accepted). The rejection of career as a practicing minister had already been determined; I have argued that its rejection was starting to occur with his last years at Cambridge and was final by mid-1637 when he took steps to employ his talents for God's (and his countrymen's) glory through creative literature.[16] Impetus for his "tardie moving" and his "belatednesse" (as he expressed it in the manuscript letter) may have been, in personal and psychological terms, the death of his mother on April 3, 1637, and the notorious imprisonment and mutilation of William Prynne, John Bastwick, and Henry Burton in June through the Laudian controls over the church. His divine vocation, as Hill argues, encompasses the employment of those authorial talents in such prose tracts as those just cited as well as poetic endeavors.[17] Milton's mind has indeed been changed in terms of career and in terms of vocation, while the unchanging element of faith in and duty to his God remains.

During Milton's years at Cambridge issues against trends in the state church were extensively debated, particularly through such arguments (against Arminianism, which was seen as creeping into the church) as Richard Montagu's *A Gagg for the new Gospell? NO: A New Gagg for an Old Goose* (1624). "The several errors imputed to the PROTESTANTS, by this *Gagger,* [are] so many Lyes," among them *"That only Faith iustifieth: and that good workes are not absolutely necessary to Saluation"* (140). Montagu counters that "faith without Charity does not iustifie: for the greatest Faith that can be, without it, is nothing" (145). That concept, long afterward, seems to echo in Michael's final words to Adam concerning "Charitie, the soul / Of all the rest" (12.584–85).[18]

Such trends continued and intensified as Milton began his "studious retirement." The "Orders Agreed on by the General Vestry of St. Bartholomew Exchange, London, 1633" (on June 2, 1633)[19] sets forth certain aspects of church discipline that Milton rejects later but that must have aided in turning him from active ministry in a church no longer "his": "All our communicantes which weare to receue the holly comunian; that they did receue it reuerently kneeling one theire knees according to the cannones and whear as it hath bine heiretofore propounded to make a decent frame about the comunion table as in diveres churches in this citty: to the end the communicantes might come to the table and receue the holly sacrament kneelinge" (no. 4; 82).[20] Laud had set up the collations for bishops and places soon after he became archbishop. Metropolitan visitations of 20 dioceses in the southern province occurred from 1634 to 1637, and his "Metropolitan Articles for Lincoln Diocese, 1634" derived from Archbishop George Abbot's earlier order and influenced later orders by various bishops.[21] Bishop William Juxon's Articles for the London Ministry, 1635, concurs: "2. That a mynister cannot with a safe conseynce, administer the sacrament to any but to those that kneele.... 7. That bowing att the name of Jesus is a pious ceremony. 8. That bowing before the altar is lawfull.... 11. That the Church of Rome is a true Church and truly soe called." Bishop Richard Bancroft of Oxford's articles for ordinands is similar. "Bishop William Juxon's Injunctions [to the clergy] for Barstable Deanery, London Diocese, 1637" (September 5, 1637) maintains a like discipline: "1. To bowe at the name of Jesus. 2. The communion table to be rayld.... 5. To stand up at the gospell the creed and *Gloria Patri.*"[22]

By 1640 the *Canons* that replaced those of 1612 also produced *Articles to be enquired of within the diocesse of London.*[23] Included under article 2, "Concerning the Church, the governement, authoritie, and discipline thereof," is the question of plank 5, which surely would have been abhorrent to John Milton the Christian republican and the new schoolmaster: "Is there any who doth affirme or teach, that the kings maiestie hath not the same authoritie in causes ecclesiasticall, that the godly kings had among the Iewes, and Christian emperours in the primitive Church"; and under article 6, "Concerning schoolmasters, parish clarkes, and sextens," we can imagine what the reaction of the new schoolmaster would be: "Either in publicke school or private house, but such as be allowed by the bishop of the diocesse, or other ordinary of the place under his hand and seale... doth he teach them any other grammar than that which was set forth by King Henry VIII and hath since continued?" (planks 1–2).[24] These church visitations had been plaguing many ministers for a number of years with their prescriptions for the church and their emphasis on *The Book of Common Prayer* (which was to be read in surplice and hood—remnants for one like Milton of the Roman Catholic Mass), the required observations daily of "his maiesties instructions," the ornaments and accoutrements, and dress, the prescribed readings and holidays and fast days. "[Doth] he [the minister] deliver the bread and wine to every communicant severally, and kneeling...? Doth he use the signe of the crosse in baptisme, or baptize in any bazon [basin], or other vessell, and not in the usually font...?"[25]

Laud's *A Speech Delivered in the Starr-Chamber*, was readily available to one such as Milton who was concerned with the way of the church as it was moving in the 1630s.[26] Here the argument that he was plotting to alter the established religion and to bring in popery (14, 26) Laud listed as "Innovations charged." Among other "innovations" that Bastwick, Burton, and Prynne are reported to have "charged" Laud with are: 1. "last yeeres Fast was enjoyned to bee without Sermon in London, the Suburbs, and other infected places" (16–17); 2. the appointment of Wednesday as the Fast-day (19); 6. "Lady Elizabeth and her Princely Children are dashed (that's their phrase) out of the new Collect" (25), and 7. "who art the Father of theire Elect and of their seed" is "charged in the Preface of that Collect, which is for the Prince and the Kings Children" (27); 8. the change of the word "In" to "At" in "At the Name of Iesus every knee shall bow" (29); 11. "the reading of the second Service at the Communion-Table, or the Altar" (this involves reading of prayers before and after Communion) (41); 12. "bowing, or doing Reverence at our first coming into the Church, or at our nearer approaches to the Holy Table, or the Altar," which is construed as worshipping "the Holy Table, or God knowes what" (43). This last point leads Laud to argue that *"Idolatry* it is not, to *worship God* towards His Holy Table" (48); rather it is "true *Divine worship."* He thus accepts "divers *Ceremonies"* like bowing and '*adoring* at the Sacraments [but note that it is 'adoring at,' not 'adoring'], kneeling, standing up at the Gospell," all matters that had early been accepted by Bishop John Jewel.[27]

Innovation 13, like the preceding, may strike today's religionist as less than grave, yet such external matters loomed large in the antagonism toward Laud: "the placing of the holy Table Altar-wise, at the upper end of the Chancell, that is, the setting of it North and South, and placing a Raile before it, to keepe it from prophanation, which Mr. Burton sayes, is done to advance and Usher in Popery" (51). The final charge, number 14, is particularly significant since it raises the question of interpretation: "*forged a new Article of Religion, brought from Rome...and have foisted it...into the beginning of the Twentieth Article of our* Church" (64), the reference being to the 1628 printing:

> The *Clause* (which they say is *forged* by us) is thus: *The Church*, (that is, *The Bishops, as they expound it*) *hath power to decree Rites and Ceremonies, and Authority in matters of Faith*. (The word is *controversies* of *Faith*, by their leave.) *This Clause* (say they) *is a forgery fit to be examined, and deeply censured in the Star-chamber. For 'tis not to be found in the Latine or English Articles of* Edw. 6. *or* Q. Elizabeth, *ratified by Parliament*. (65)

Finally, on p. 74, Laud states: "these *Ministers* are *punished*...for preaching *Schisme* and *sedition* not [for] *Vertue* and *Piety*."

Did Milton agree with these three challenges to Laud's controls and the interpretations they offered of Laud's actions in 1637? Milton's actions abroad and in the early 1640s suggest yes. Did Bastwick, Burton, and Prynne preach schism and sedition in Milton's view, or were they exhibiting their virtue and exemplifying their piety? These matters had been swelling during the twenties and thirties, and perhaps the catalyst of what the virtuous and pious might suffer at the hands of the church discovered or firmed up

Milton's drift from active ministerial service in the state church that it had become. Did Milton not fully recognize what had happened to the discipline of the church? Was he not, during his university years, truly conscious of what he, as a minister in that church, would be doing? Did he not attend to political implications? Why was not the difficulty with his tutor William Chappell a warning flare? or the treatment of Thomas Young exiled to Hamburg? With the forties the episcopal problem publicly emerged among those who were and continued to be practicing members of the state church. A result was a church split into episcopal and nonepiscopal persuasions, and the fifties brought intolerance under Cromwell toward those believing in episcopacy, only to lead to a strident Parliament after the Restoration that returned to episcopacy and antagonistic action against Dissenters of all kinds.

These externalities of religion, this unacceptable discipline of the church, and the accompanying alteration of career into divine vocation that did not include ministerial presence find a "changed" Milton in the 1630s and 1640s. It is not surprising, therefore, to discover a Milton beginning to question—even, perhaps, questioning to the point of modification—the doctrine, the dogma, of his religion, a subject to be pursued in chapters 5 and 6.

Before Laud's beheading on the scaffold on Tower Hill on January 10, 1644/45, he related the history of the "troubles" and of his trial, and contended that "As for 'circumstantials' [such as *Quid?* (what a man believes), *Ubi?* (place, here involving denial 'that Christ took our flesh'), *Quibus auxilis* (help to man in believing and obeying), and *Quando* (when Christ will come, except that he has already come)], it seems these men [Parliament] have forgotten, or never knew, that many times 'circumstantials' in religion do quite destroy the foundation." In rebuttal of the last (*Quando*), Laud raises the question of how Christ is present in the sacrament (the Eucharist; see chapter 6 here for discussion) and professes that *"ens et verum,* 'being' and 'true,' are convertible one with another. And everything that hath a being, is truly that being which it is in truth of substance; but a right or an orthodox Church I never said it was, either in doctrine or manners." Such a position, it proffers, negates the erroneous basis for Parliament's judgment: "an endeavor in me to subvert the laws of the kingdom" and "a like endeavor to alter the true Protestant religion into Popery."[28]

What had been going on from the end of the sixteenth century through the 1630s had been the "progressive" actions of the Puritans and countermovements by the "conservative" ecclesiastical authorities. That is, Puritans, those who desired a continued reform from Roman Catholicism, argued for further reformation despite the many so-called reformations experienced from the mid-sixteenth century onward. There was much—external and internal, disciplinary and doctrinal—that remained of Roman Catholicism in the state church for Puritans, especially "idolatrous ceremonies."[29] For one example—and a rather lesser one, at that—David Cressy affirms, "Puritan controversialists found less to argue about in the Order for Burial of the Dead than in many other services in the Book of Common Prayer, but that did not stop them finding fault with unreformed burial customs. Their main area of complaint concerned traditional cultural activities that preceded the actual interment of the body, but the formal religious burial service also drew godly criticism." And he points out a variety of practices that Puritans found offensive in their "view of popish abuses yet remaining in the English church," which is attached to the 1572 *Admonition to the Parliament*. This document also objected to "ecclesiastical vestments, the font, the sign of the cross, private baptism, and permissive attitudes to emergency baptism by women"; these "were all 'abominations' left over from popery."[30]

In view of the objections and actions and changes that preceded Laud's elevation to archbishop, some of which are sketched above, Kenneth Fincham therefore asks, "Why then were Laud's policies so much more controversial?"

> Here great weight is attached not just to Laud's intemperate zeal, but also to the appointment of George Abbot to succeed Bancroft as Archbishop of Canterbury in 1611.... James I allegedly bowed to pressure from his favourite, the Earl of Dunbar, and chose Abbot, a churchman obsessed with popery but indulgent towards puritans. Thus during Abbot's 22 years in office the pass was sold to the puritans, and only on his death in 1633 could William Laud attempt to reimpose neglected discipline and ceremonies. His government provoked a puritan backlash, and after 1640 both he and the episcopal order were eliminated.

Fincham modifies this statement, however, as not really satisfactory because of complexities in each of its various parts, and with the important critical argument putting theological issues (rather than only the discipline of episcopacy and church services) back into importance.[31]

For us, attending to Milton's position in all of this accusation and counteraccusation, the significant realization is that those matters that he would have objected to and did object to had existed well before 1640, and indeed before 1637; that the issues were well discussed in his years at Christ's College when he was planning on a clerical career; and that a placement of him in any absolute terms is fraught with uncertainty (to the point of error as in labeling him an Arminian). He might be called a moderate Puritan, but obviously "moderate" subtends a wide range of differences. Such a range also exists because of social and economic, and thus cultural, status: Milton, as I argue in chapters 2 and 3 here and elsewhere, was far from being "one of the people." I think the best we can do in labeling is to call him a "Protestant" (which term places him as an anti-Roman Catholic but perhaps also anti-certain sectarian positions), who emphasized the Scriptures, believing them the Word of God, and who professed a closeness between God and the individual without intervention from others, stressing the "paradise within" and the inculcation of the attributes of the Christ (as depicted in the example of Jesus in *Paradise Regain'd*) and thus "the inner light": finally, a "church of one," as it has previously been called.

FIVE

Theological Concerns, Especially the Trinity

1

In the epistle prefacing *De doctrina Christiana*, Milton indicates that he realized he could "not depend upon the belief or judgment of others in religious questions" and that "the only authority...was God's self-revelation, and accordingly I read and pondered the Holy Scriptures themselves" (YP 6:118). The statement accepts God's "writing" of the Bible through God's various "messengers" and recognizes the need to return to the words of the Bible themselves ("an earnest study of the Old and New Testaments in their original languages"). The substance of the Bible "should derive...from the word of God and from that alone, and should be scrupulously faithful to the text" (120). Implied is the misinterpretation possible through not examining the original language of a text, and the possibility that, "measured with greater strictness against the yardstick of the Bible," not only "interpreters" but even a "messenger" may not be presenting "the word of God and...that alone."[1] He is well aware that "many of the views [he has] published are at odds with certain conventional opinions," but he urges that his "readers will be sympathetic, and will avoid prejudice and malice" (YP 6:121). His hope has, of course, not been granted by his readers who, shocked that some of those views oppose "conventional opinions"—such as concepts of the Trinity and the relationship of God the Son to God the Father, the concepts that those readers accept—have impugned Milton for his conclusions and some have even rejected his authorship of the treatise as a result.

It is difficult to know with full confidence when what appears in the manuscript of the treatise was written or perhaps rewritten and altered, but the content of the preceding paragraph does point to a possible development of attention to and thought about issues that the Bible and commentators upon it may have exacted from his college days through to the Restoration period (since *De doctrina Christiana* has often been assigned to the years 1658–60 and beyond). Milton believed in the Scriptures as the word of God and thus as Truth ("The Writings of the prophets, the apostles and the evangelists, since they were divinely inspired, are called THE HOLY SCRIPTURE" [YP 6: 574]). This removed the Apocrypha and the Pseudepigrapha from inclusion as Truth, as note 1 here makes clear. Such a definition demands the acceptance of what is written as Truth (for example, Matthew 1:23, "Behold, a virgin shall be with child, and shall bring forth a son, and they shall call his name Immanuel, which being interpreted is, God with us"); as Truth despite the problem of inappropriate commonplace translation (for example, the Latin reference in a Hebrew text in Isaiah 14:12, "How art thou fallen from heaven, O Lucifer, son of the morning!"); as Truth *if* its source be a bona fide prophet, apostle, evangelist (not, for example, the questionable "John" of books 1, 2, 3 John, placing those books into doubtfulness as to Truth); and as not necessarily Truth when a belief is *not* attested to by its being explicitly written in the Bible (some apocryphal materials may thus receive approbation by coincidence with the Holy Scriptures). Commentators may disagree with a conclusion that Milton offers, but we should attend to his reasoning and admit our own position on a question that may color our response to Milton's thought.

The problem of biblical interpretation in terms of its narrative use in such a fictional work as *Paradise Lost* is the burden of Lawrence Rhu's study of traditional exegesis in the poem. Citing most specifically James L. Kugel's *Traditions of the Bible,* Rhu demonstrates that "narrative demands force upon Milton's fundamental conviction in the 'all-sufficiency' of Scripture" a contradiction in "Milton's emphatic rejection of tradition...when we appreciate the exegetical dimension of early retellings of stories from the Bible."[2] As the following discussion indicates, for Milton we find three contrasting concepts underlying both his fiction and his religious beliefs, concepts that Milton scholars have not really acknowledged although they appear in the foundation of his exegesis in *De doctrina Christiana*. First, as often repeated, Milton believed in Scripture and accepted it, despite the lack of "reality" in some of its "legends." Second, he used and accepted certain translations, and thus traditions developed from such translations, particularly in identifications (which are *not* typological); such metaphoric reading opposes the Hebraic language and apparent reference and time element but is nonetheless unquestioned exegesis. Third, he rejected traditional beliefs that are not explicitly stated in Scripture.

The text of Matthew 1:18–25 presents the birth of Jesus Christ in language that calls Mary, his mother, a "virgin" and alludes to her virginal state even after that birth when Joseph "took unto him his wife: and knew her not till she had brought forth her firstborn son." Mark makes no mention of this; Luke 1:26 and following reprises the foretelling of the birth, 2:4 and following talks of the birth, all in generalized narrative; and John 1:9–14 alludes only to the Word's being made flesh.[3] Through Christian typology of the Old Testament Isaiah 11:1 and Micah 5:2 have been elicited as prophesying the birth of Jesus, and the birth is referred to in later books of the New Testament. There are no references to any of these texts citing the birth in Milton's prose except for *De doctrina Christiana*, although a few uses do allude to the birth. In the treatise the texts present the birth as well as significances that do not cite virginity. The "spirit of God" or the "holy spirit" is the focus of *De doctrina*, YP 6:283, where Matthew 1:18, 20, and Luke 1:35 appear; of Micah 5:2 Milton comments that it "refers to his [the Son's] works, not his generation" (YP 6:210). Matthew 1:25 is cited to join his argument of the primacy of the "Son of God": the "Son of man" is "in the same sense" the "*first born* of Mary" (YP 6:303). There is also ambiguity introduced concerning the readings of his "opponents" of Matthew 1:23 (which "does not prove that the person they are going to call Immanuel is necessarily God, but only that he is sent by God" [YP 6:241]).

In two discussions in *De doctrina Christiana*, the orthodox belief in the birth of Jesus and acceptance of his mother as the Virgin Mary underlie what is written: 6:293 and 6:427–29. In the first, an attempt to define the Holy Spirit, he writes:

> The announcement made to Mary and Joseph in Matt. i. 18, 20 and Luke i. 35, that the Holy Spirit was the author of that divine conception, is not to be understood as referring merely to the person of the Holy Spirit. For we have agreed that, in the Old Testament, either God the Father himself or his divine power is signified when the Spirit of God or the Holy Spirit are [sic] named. Mary and Joseph had heard nothing at that time of any other Holy Spirit, and indeed to this very day the Jews do not acknowledge the person or divinity of the Holy Spirit. Accordingly in

both the passages quoted πνευμα is without the usual article. If that is not enough evidence, in Luke the angel is quite explicit in what he says...that is, the Son of the Father, unless we choose to imagine that there are two Fathers, one Father of the Son of God and the other Father of the Son of man.

Milton's tortured prose is, of course, his attempt to refute nonorthodox interpretations of the language presented in these two verses. While it moves beyond an orthodox reading of the Holy Spirit (the subject of the discussion, and which we will pursue in a moment), it does exhibit an orthodox reading of the birth with no modification or elaboration.

In the other passage in *De doctrina,* YP 6:427-29 (in a chapter dealing with Christ the Redeemer), Milton divides the Incarnation into Jesus' conception and Nativity. The former has the Holy Spirit as the efficient cause—and we have looked at this in the immediately preceding paragraph—and "The aim of this miraculous conception was to evade the pollution of Adam's sin." This is a major statement and evaluation of the reason it is called a virgin birth. It interestingly predates the concept of the Immaculate Conception, although the Bible and Milton do not mention Anne at all (see my note 24 in chapter 1). Milton and other seventeenth century writers do not explain the evasion of "the pollution of Adam's sin" by anything like later Catholic dogma. The prophecy of the birth, Milton points out, is found in Micah 5:2 and Isaiah 7:14 and 11:1, and narrated in Matthew 1:18 and Luke 1:42, 2:6, 7, 22. He accepts the miracle of this birth narrative and does not raise any question of the reality of birth as humans know it: the Holy Scriptures have presented this miracle and he, in faith, accepts it. This point is of major importance in understanding Milton's positions in *De doctrina Christiana,* and lies at the heart of critical dissension about his presentation of the Trinity and the Holy Spirit. The consideration of a "realistic" point in the matter of birth in the relationship of God the Son to God the Father and thus within the Godhead, however, does arise and has been the major contention in calling Milton a heretic and an Arian.

Belief in the virgin birth undoubtedly always existed for Milton and did not change because it is attested in the Holy Scriptures. There would seem to be no conceptual development here and no examination of this miracle since it is not questioned. There has been some discussion provoked by some of the interpretations surrounding the biblical verses (such as those concerning the Holy Spirit); that "clarification" has yielded disagreement with what may, in the past, have been simply assumed without modification. But it is not a clarification of the virgin birth since none, on faith and the authority of the Holy Scriptures, is needed.

On two occasions in the prose Milton alludes to the virgin birth, implying its theological importance, but to poke fun at the recipient of his argument in almost blasphemous terms. In *Apology Against a Pamphlet* (YP 1:940), he attacks the "Romanish" liturgy advanced by such as the author of *A Modest Confutation:* "if we imagine that all the godly Ministers of England are not able to new mould a better and more pious Liturgy then this which was conceav'd and infanted by an idolatrous Mother: how basely were that to esteeme of Gods Spirit, and all the holy blessings and priviledges of a true Church above a false?" (Of course, we must constantly remember in all these uses of "true" and "false" that I have quoted from Milton there is nothing inherent in something like "faith" or a "church" that is either "true" or "false" but one's attitude, one's belief, one's acceptance or rejection of whatever it is.) Even more pointed is the accusation against Charles I's and his adherents' "divine" posturing of the monarch:

> He ought then to have so thought of a Parlament, if he count it not Male, as of his Mother, which, to civil being, created both him, and the Royalty he wore. And if it hath

bin anciently interpreted the presaging signe of a future Tyrant, but to dream of copulation with his Mother, what can it be less then actual Tyranny to affirme waking, that the Parliament, which is his Mother, can neither conceive or [sic] bring forth *any autoritative Act* without his Masculine coition: Nay that his reason is as Celestial and life-giving to the Parlament, as the Suns influence is to the Earth: What other notions but these, or such like, could swell up *Caligula* to think himself a God. (*Eikonoklastes,* YP 3:467)

It is probably difficult for religious people to accept such near blasphemy, but one way of looking at this is as such an assertion of unquestioned belief in God, in his miracles, in the account of the Bible, that anything that implies an infringement upon it (such as the "divinity" of Charles as the Christ or as David the King, both appellatives being frequent in the war of words over him and particularly over *Eikon Basilike* and William Marshall's frontispiece) is fair game for lampooning.

2

Belief in the orthodox view of the birth of Jesus Christ and of the Virgin Mary appears often in the poetry. Such belief is evident in the 1629 Nativity ode and in the 1660s and 1670s *Paradise Lost* and *Paradise Regain'd*. In the early poem, he writes, "the Son of Heav'ns eternal King, / Of wedded Maid, and Virgin Mother born"[4] and "see the Virgin blest, / Hath laid her Babe to rest" (3, 237). In the longer epic, there are the Father's words of the Son: "And be thy self Man among men on Earth, / Made flesh, when time shall be, of Virgin seed, / By wondrous birth" (3.283–85); Michael's reprise: "A Virgin is his Mother, but his Sire / The Power of the most High" (12.368–69); and Adam's apostrophe, which we can surely assign to Milton's own constant belief:

> O Prophet of glad tidings, finisher
> Of utmost hope! now clear I understand

> What oft my steddiest thoughts have searcht in vain,
> Why our great expectation should be call'd
> The seed of Woman: Virgin Mother, Hail,
> High in the love of Heav'n, yet from my Loyns
> Thou shalt proceed, and from thy Womb the Son
> Of God most High; so God with man unites. (12.375–82)

The brief epic, introducing Mary as a character and narrating the Son's life just prior to his ministry and anointing as the Christ,[5] presents a number of unequivocal acceptances of this miracle: from Satan's report of God's "This is my Son belov'd, in him am pleas'd," and his interpretation, "His Mother then is mortal, but his Sire, / He who obtains the Monarchy of Heav'n" (*PR* 1.85–87); to Satan's lie (for that is what it is when his earlier statements are remembered), "Then hear, O Son of *David*, Virgin-born; / For Son of God to me is yet in doubt" (4.500–501). Satan proceeds to allow that Jesus is "The Son of God" in some "degree or meaning," but so is he and all men "Sons of God." Between these two sites in the narrative of *Paradise Regain'd* are included such definite and positive statements of the birth as the Father's words, 1.132–40; the Son's, 1.238–39; Mary's, 2.66–67; and, of course, Satan's, 2.135–39 and 3.152–55.[6]

I think the point should be clear: Milton believed in the virgin birth, referred to it often and without incertitude, and this concept would seem to be maintained throughout his lifetime, an example of the "unchanging" mind resultant from faith and faith in the Holy Scripture. In contrast the reference to the Latin "Lucifer" which Isaiah 14:12 and following provides appears in the poetry and prose usually in metaphoric terms, being a naming rather than a belief in the existence of Satan and the evil that he is. The identification is accepted metaphorically since it is supposedly in Holy Scripture,[7] and the equation of Lucifer with Satan derives from the falling of the "Morning Star," the sun, the "carrier of light." Provided is a literary but morally significant message. In *Paradise Lost* the citation is specific and one of the first descriptions of Satan:

> If thou beest he; but O how fall'n! how chang'd
> From him, who in the happy Realms of Light
> Cloth'd with transcendent brightness didst outshine
> Myriads though bright. (1.84–87)

The identifying equation occurs in a few places:

> At length into the limits of the North
> ...came...*Satan* to his Royal seat
> High on a Hill, far blazing,
> ....
> The Palace of great *Lucifer* (5.755–60)

> Know then, that after *Lucifer* from Heav'n
> (So call him, brighter once amidst the Host
> Of Angels, then that Starr the Starrs among)
> Fell with his flaming Legions through the Deep
> Into his place (7.131–35)

>   the rest were all
> Farr to the inland retir'd, about the walls
> Of *Pandæmonium*, Citie and proud seat
> Of *Lucifer*, so by allusion calld,
> Of that bright Starr to *Satan* paragond. (10.422–26)

It is Raphael who specifically transitions Satan into the Morning Star, which is the sun:

>   for great indeed
> His name, and high was his degree in Heav'n;
> His count'nance, as the Morning Starr that guides
> The starrie flock, allur'd them, and with lyes
> Drew after him the third part of Heav'ns Host. (5.706–10)

The Morning Star as the sun is seen in "Song: On *May Morning*" ("Now the bright morning Star, Dayes harbinger, / Comes dancing from the East"). Again in the Nativity ode Lucifer is the sun, but now to be contrasted with the Son (playing upon a most frequent pun):

> The Stars with deep amaze
> Stand fixt in stedfast gaze,
>   Bending one way their pretious influence,

> And will not take their flight,
> For all the morning light,
>   Or *Lucifer* that often warn'd them thence...
>   ....
>   The Sun himself with-held his wonted speed,
>   And hid his head for shame,
>   As his inferiour flame,
>   The new-enlight'n'd world no more should need;
>   He saw a greater Sun appear
>   Then his bright Throne, or burning Axletree could bear.
>   (69–74, 79–84)

The punning message sets up the opposition of the truly radiant "only begotten" Son of God and a son of God of "inferiour flame." It also underlies the continuance of lines 135–36 of book 7 of *Paradise Lost* quoted above: "and the great Son returnd / Victorious with his saints." The contrast between the fallen star (Lucifer, Satan) returned "Into his place" and the true sun (the Son of God) returned to "this High Temple" is presented as in existence from before humankind's existence. As the stanzas above from the Nativity ode indicate, the conflict between the Son of God and Satan, presented as a metaphor by the sun, who rises *but falls*, exists fairly early in Milton's writings. Faith in the Son and, behind this image, his brief fall in the Crucifixion, only to arise eternally (unlike the diurnal sun), is maintained through *Paradise Regain'd* 1.194, when "*our* Morning Star then in his rise" (my emphasis) conquers all temptation and thwarts Satan and disengages the physical sun from the taint of Satan.

The two verbal references to the sun in this poem appear at the end of the storm in book 4, when the "patient Son of God...stoodst / Unshaken," and "Thus pass'd the night so foul till morning fair / Came forth with Pilgrim steps" (4.420–27). "Thunder chas'd the clouds, and laid the winds, / And grisly Spectres, which the Fiend had rais'd / To tempt the Son of God with terrors dire" (4.429–31). Satan, fallen and inhabitant of hell, has become "The Prince of darkness" (441) whose realm is that metaphoric night that

Jesus has nullified. "And now the Sun with *more effectual beams / Had chear'd the face of Earth, and...To gratulate the sweet return of morn;...this joy and brightest morn"* (432–39; my emphasis), allowing the Son to "walk[ ] on a Sunny hill" (447). (Perhaps we remember the final line of *At a Solemn Music* as we read lines 438–39: "To live with him, and sing in endles morn of light.")

The three occasions of "Lucifer" in the prose exemplify again the metaphor for Satan and his evil, and place this biblical Truth in a quite different category from that of the virgin birth. To lampoon the prelates (particularly, in this case, John Williams, Bishop of Lincoln), for their lack of "sure foundation in the Gospell," Milton, in *Reason of Church-Government,* reminds them, "For *Lucifer* before *Adam* was the first prelat Angel, and both he, as is commonly thought, and our forefather *Adam,* as we all know, for aspiring above their orders, were miserably degraded" (YP 1:762). In *Areopagitica* it is the Court of the Star Chamber that is the object of the affront because of its [her] enactment of "this *authentic* Spanish policy of licensing books" "for which she is now fall'n from the Starres with *Lucifer*" (YP 2:569–70). And of course Charles (erstwhile "Christ" and "David the King") is queried about "that supreme title," "*Gods soverantie,*" which he "doth...contest with God": "God bids us *Be subject for conscience sake,* that is, as to a Magistrat, and in the Laws; not usurping over spiritual things, as *Lucifer* beyond his sphere" (*Eikonoklastes,* YP 3:501–02).

3

In contrast to both of the prior matters—the virgin birth and the metaphoric use of the Old Testament identification of Satan/Lucifer/Morning Star—the issue of the Trinity has proved difficult to resolve and make understandable to students of Milton. Milton's reason for the problem should be clear: he believes in the Scriptures; the Scriptures do *not* refer to a Trinity or to the Spirit as part of the Godhead except by interpretation of 1 John 5:7. Therefore, can this basic tenet of Godhead be accepted and catechized by the Christian with certainty? Repetition of a tenet by people, even the church, does not produce fact. At issue is not only the lack of direct statement, but also the text of 1–3 John has long been suspect and cast as spurious even by Eusebius, and thus is put into doubt. Even Erasmus omitted 1 John 5:7 from his Greek New Testament as spurious (although later editions inserted it). Surely such a theological "fact" would be in evidence, is Milton's point, in Scripture that has canonical authority (see *DDC*, book 1, chap. 30),[8] but it is not to be found. Many writers on Milton and the Trinity seem not to pay attention to the preceding, or their own belief is so strong that they do not understand the point that Milton advances as significant for *his* belief. It should not be a question of right or wrong, but in discussion of Milton and his work it should be a matter of what he believed and why.

There was an alteration of concept for Milton concerning the Trinity from 1629 to 1659 or so, but it is a different alteration of thought from that which even those who remember such early references as "Trinal Unity" have viewed it. When he wrote *De doctrina Christiana*, Milton was not "anti-Trinitarian" but was grown up enough to question whether the lessons of youth and tales about all aspects of life have substance. (For youngsters, is the existence of Santa Claus or Martians any different? For adults, is the possibility of a virgin birth or a reincarnation of some sort that different religions propose still "truth"? For Milton, the virgin birth *is* truth because it appears in the Holy Scriptures; reincarnation is not.) Behind that awakening we see a Milton—living like the rest of us—who had at times assumed that what everyone said about such matters was truth but who at other times—later on—came to wonder whether indeed such is truth—particularly when that which holds doctrinal truth for him does not allege this fact. While a ministerial career had early been his future, such unorthodoxy for a Christian minister in a visible church of God—even only as uncertainty—would be the height of hypocrisy.

That Milton accepted the Trinity early (as the Nativity ode shows) may result from what is commonplace belief, and from what his religion (and parents and teachers) taught him. The quotation from *Of Reformation* quoted above in chapter 1, note 20, indicates a continuance of belief through 1641 at least. But at a later age he would confront, among other matters that childhood prescribed, the question of this miraculous concept—one God in three persons. In discussing *De doctrina Christiana* critics have generally not attended to this human development of the mind and intellect.[9] Milton's discussion of the Spirit and the Spirit of God "remove such a Spirit from any standard concept of the Holy Spirit as the Third Person of the Trinity, even with such affinities to the Son, in whom the Spirit is, or with the Father, of whom it exists. There is a seemingly 'trinal' relationship, but the Spirit is not a person and not of the Trinity" (139). (We cannot be sure when these thoughts were entered into the treatise, but possible work on it beginning in the mid-1640s could entertain its consideration from that time forward.)

The text of Matthew 28:19 ("baptizing them in the name of the Father and of the Son and of the Holy Spirit") has also been raised as a biblical statement of the Trinity;[10] this verse is cited 12 times in the treatise (for example, YP 6:271, in the examination "Of the Son of God," chapter 5). The following chapter, "Of the Holy Spirit," discounts the Holy Spirit as a person and its appearance as a person in that biblical text: "Ultimately, 'spirit' can mean the actual person of the Holy Spirit, or its symbol.... Clearly this was a symbol: a sure pledge, as it were, of that promise which is fulfilled in Acts ii.2–4, 33:...Matt. xxviii. 19" (YP 6:285–86). "But no one teaches us more plainly what the nature, source, and functions of the Holy Spirit are than the Son of God himself:...Thus the Spirit is called the Spirit of God, the Spirit of the Father, and even the Spirit of Christ....As a result of all this we have Matt. xxviii. 19:...I John v. 7"

(286–87). The nub of Milton's argument—raised because he does not find explicit recognition in Holy Scriptures of a Trinity as orthodoxly stated—is:

> the Holy Spirit, unlike the Son, is nowhere said to have submitted himself to any mediatorial function. He is nowhere said to be under an obligation, as a son is, to pay obedience to the Father. Nevertheless he is obviously inferior to both the Father and the Son, inasmuch as he is represented as being and is said to be subservient and obedient in all things.... Moreover the Spirit is frequently called the Spirit of God and the Holy Spirit of God, Eph. iv. 30. And as the Spirit of God is actually and numerically distinct from God himself, it cannot possibly be essentially one God with whom whose Spirit it is. (288)[11]

Reprising this verse from Matthew, Milton remarks, "Here, it is true, three persons are enumerated. But there is not a word here that establishes the divinity or the unity or the equality of the three" (293), and further, "The baptism of Christ was accomplished by a more solemn form of words... though, as a matter of fact, it is nowhere recorded that the apostles ever used this formula" (551).[12]

In the two epics there is confusion that has not been attended to by readers of Milton's use of "Spirit"—whether reference is to the Spirit of God or to the created Holy Spirit just discussed. *Paradise Lost* 1.17 addresses "Thou O Spirit" who with "mighty wings outspread / Dove-like satst brooding on the vast Abyss / And mad'st it pregnant" (20–22), without further specific designation. It is not "the Holy Spirit" in the sense of the "Holy Ghost," for this Spirit is addressed as "Thou from the first / Wast present"—which can mean only God, the Spirit of God, not the "Holy Spirit" that is the subject of *De doctrina Christiana*, for that "Holy Spirit" was "created" after the Son and by the Father. In the reprise in book 7 of the creative action in book 1, we are told that "Darkness profound / Cover'd the Abyss: but on the watrie calm / His brooding wings the Spirit of God outspred" (233–35), which leads to creative action. Indeed, throughout *Paradise Lost* Milton avoids reference (at least direct reference) to the Holy Spirit. Rather, "the Spirit," "The Spirit of God," "the Spirit of Grace" (7.514, 519, 525), as typical usages, do not refer to the Holy Spirit. This Spirit, the Spirit of God, allows no concept of Trinity in the poem. While the creational action of this Spirit might imply God the Father only, it takes on a kind of extended understanding of the Spirit of God as being jointly God the Father and God the Son, for, as the Argument to book 7 indicates, it is the Son who is sent to effect the Creation in that book.[13]

But an impediment arises with the Spirit's being "Dove-like," for it is the Third Person of the Trinity, the Holy Spirit, who is usually associated with the descent of the dove, based on Matthew 3:16 ("And Jesus, when he was baptized, went up straightway out of the water: and, lo, the heavens were opened unto him, and he saw the Spirit of God descending like a dove, and lighting upon him"), Mark 1:10 ("he saw the heavens opened, and the Spirit like a dove descending upon him"), Luke 3:22 ("and the Holy Ghost descended in a bodily shape like a dove upon him"), John 1:32 ("And John bare record, saying, I saw the Spirit descending from heaven like a dove"). Luke, in the translation, is most specific. We have already remarked that the Spirit is said to be *in* the Son. The first citation of the Spirit in the poem (in book 1 as quoted above) thus could seem to include the Son because he is specifically delegated as a surrogate for the Father in book 7. Problems, as noted before, constantly adhere to the expressions of "God" and "God the Father," which are so often employed interchangeably—by Milton as well as many others—but the Son would not be included as the Spirit that made the abyss pregnant. The greatest difficulty, though, lies in the "Spirit of God," who becomes a separate entity, not the Father per se, although it is only the Father *of* which it is: it is not the Holy Spirit.

We are in the realm of a mystery in which language and logic do not necessarily unite. The confusion in language and idea and logic is not solved by Milton in his usages any more than it is by others who employ such "standard" epithets.[14] *Paradise Lost* 11.611 equates "Maker" and "his Spirit" ("Unmindful of thir Maker, though his Spirit / Taught them"), partaking of the same possibility that the Son effects the "making" by the Spirit. Yet ambiguous is

> but from Heav'n
> Hee to his own a Comforter will send,
> The promise of the Father, who shall dwell
> His Spirit within them, and the Law of Faith
> Working through love, upon thir hearts shall write,
> To guide them in all truth, and also arm
> With spiritual Armour, able to resist
> *Satans* assaults. (*PL* 12.485–92)

The Spirit seems to be only the Father, and humankind is to be guided by his Truth, but the "love" through which the law of faith will work surely extends this Spirit to the Son. The Comforter, according to the *Confession of Faith*, is the Holy Spirit. The arming with "spiritual Armour" to resist Satan, which is also part of God's "guidance," implies the Holy Spirit, whose province of justice is thus offered to humankind. It cannot be without significance that this armor is "spiritual." We have here a triunal conception: if there had ever been a Holy Spirit in the poem, he has been obliterated from it. Still, succeeding lines citing "The Spirit of God," "the Spirit within," the "Spirit of Grace" in *Paradise Lost* 12.518–26 sound only to be evoking the Spirit of the Father.

All of the above suggests that Milton may at one time have believed in the Holy Spirit (Holy Ghost) as part of a triunal representation of the Godhead but that by the time he was completing *Paradise Lost* his position had changed to that presented in *De doctrina Christiana*. The position of the Son in the aforementioned discussion of the Spirit (the Spirit of God) looms up as not being part of that creative Spirit except as delegate from the Father. While the Spirit may be "in" the Son, the Spirit of God is essentially only the Father. This mystery produces only confusion in attempting to offer a "realistic" logic to account for the spirit who effects the birth out of the abyss, the birth of Jesus and the dove that descends on the Incarnated Son. It demands acceptance on faith.

Paradise Regain'd complicates the issue. What "Spirit" is intended in 1.8 ("Thou Spirit who ledst this glorious Eremite / Into the Desert"), 1.31 ("in likeness of a Dove / The Spirit descended"), 1.189 ("One day forth walk'd alone, the Spirit leading"), and 1.282 ("The Spirit descended on me like a Dove")? In 1.282–83 there seems to be a distinction between "The Spirit" and "my Father"; and 1.462 ("And sends his Spirit of Truth henceforth to dwell / In pious Hearts") should refer to the Father only. But most telling is that the Holy Spirit is associated with the descent of the dove,[15] and God recounts Gabriel's announcement to Mary "that on her should come / The Holy Ghost" (1:138–39). The Spirit seems to be both the Father and the Holy Spirit, but not, logically of course, the Son. Has Milton fully thought out such conundrums created by usage? None of this supports a Trinity, but it does suggest that the triunal concept that I advance here in my pondering of Milton's analysis in *De doctrina Christiana* lies in the background.

There seems to be accord with what Milton says about or implies about the Holy Spirit in the noncanonical Apocryphon "The Martyrdom and Ascension of Isaiah," a Jewish-Christian account thought to have been written in Rome during Nero's reign (CE 36–68). "In fact...the Holy Spirit, from the outset, appears as an angel, never as wholly divine, perhaps to suggest his tertiary status among the divine persons."[16] He is separated from the Son, his "glory" is surpassed by the Son, and he worships the Father.

Milton's position on the Holy Spirit and thus on the orthodox Trinity is heterodox: it does not accept the Holy Spirit as a person; it does not accept the Holy Spirit, therefore, as a member of an orthodox Trinity; it does accept the Holy Spirit as *of* God the Father and *in* God the Son; it is not generated as is the Son but it is also not created in the same way that the angels and others are created; it remains a mystery, but is accepted as existent for it is recorded in Holy Scripture. What seems to arise (but Milton is not this explicit) is God, who is God the Father, the Son, and the Spirit of God who at times is the Holy Spirit, who at other times is a distinct created being. A triunal relationship is presented but one that is most unorthodox. His conclusion in the chapter on the Holy Spirit is:

> Although the scriptures do not tell us explicitly who or what the Holy Spirit is, we need not be completely ignorant about it, as this much may be understood from the texts quoted above. The Holy Spirit, since he is a minister of God, and therefore a creature, was created, that is, produced, from the substance of God, not by natural necessity, but by the free will of the agent, maybe before the foundations of the world were laid, but after the Son, to whom he is far inferior, was made. (YP 6:298)[17]

This conclusion may have superficial likenesses to others' ideas about the Godhead, but it is certainly *not* Arian or Socinian.[18] Milton's "Holy Spirit" is in accord with the *Confession of Faith* (plank 4): "we believe that the *Church* on earth is sanctified and *instructed* by the *Holy Ghost*, for he is the true comforter, when Christ sendeth from the Father, to teach the truth, and to expell darknes from the vnderstanding of the faithfull." This triunal concept is made clear by Michael as *Paradise Lost* moves to its conclusion in lines 485–92.

The Interpreter's Bible writes of 1 John 5:7:

> this verse in the KJV is to be rejected (with RSV). It appears in no ancient Greek MS nor is it cited by any Greek father; of all the versions only the Latin contained it, and even this in none of its most ancient sources. The earliest MSS of the Vulg. do not have it. As Dodd (*Johannine Epistles*, p. 127n) reminds us, 'It is first quoted as a part of 1 John by Priscillian, the Spanish heretic, who died in 385, and it gradually made its way into MSS of the Latin Vulgate until it was accepted as part of the authorized Latin text.[19]

This rejected verse and its relation to the subject at hand is then explained: "The mention in the true text (v5.8) of the *three witnesses* which *agree* naturally led to an interpretation along trinitarian lines." The three witnesses are cited for the redemptive meaning of the Incarnation, not as a statement of an orthodox Trinity in this latter verse—"And there are three that bear witness in earth, the spirit, and the water, and the blood: and these three agree in one"—thus unifying holy inspiration, the rite of baptism, and the rite of the Lord's Supper.

4

Students of Milton have not been happy with this unorthodox reading of the Holy Spirit and Trinity, for it makes Milton theologically unacceptable to those who do believe in an orthodox Trinity. As I said before, surely we should not say that he is right or that he is wrong: we should accept that this is his opinion and his explanation of how that opinion was derived. Those who accept an orthodox Trinity do so on faith; Milton's faith in this matter extends only so far. He was, of course, living in a time when such theological issues were being questioned, revised, and altered (1) into faithful acceptance without modification or explanation, (2) into faithful acceptance with modification and explanation akin to Milton's, and (3) into full rejection of the mystery of Trinity. During the sixteenth century the many attacks on the papacy and thus on Catholicism itself theologically resulted in a question between "person" and "essence" (or "substance"). There is one divine essence, it was argued, and the persons of the Trinity are constituted by the internal relations of generation and procession (or spiration) with that essence. "Apart from these relations there is only the One Divine Essence." Accordingly, Scripture became "the one and only primary authority in matters of belief. Paul, not Augustine, was to be followed on justification, grace and faith."[20] Geoffrey Nuttall's full investigation of *The Holy Spirit in Puritan*

Faith and Experience confirms the recovery of the doctrine of the Holy Spirit after the religious and philosophic break-up of the Middle Ages. The "centrality of the doctrine of the Holy Spirit," what is called "the age of the Spirit," leads to the catchwords "halcyon days" among the radical Puritans of the 1630s and 1640s.[21] Interestingly Milton does not use "halcyon" in prose or poetry, but his attention to the Spirit of God as well as to the "creation" of the Holy Spirit surely reflects his contemporary world. As Nuttall points out, in *Animadversions* (YP 1:703) Milton argues an apposite concept (here, to counter the Remonstrant's defense of episcopacy):

> in a *Protestant* Nation that should have throwne off these tatter'd Rudiments long agoe, after the many strivings of Gods Spirit, and our fourscore yeares vexation of him in this our wildernesse since Reformation began, to urge these rotten Principles, and twit us with the present age, which is to us an age of ages wherein God is manifestly come downe among us, to doe some remarkable good to our Church or state, is as if a man should taxe the renovating and re-ingendring Spirit of God with innovation.

Unfortunately the sixteenth and seventeenth century generally applied the label "Arian" to any alteration of strictly orthodox belief—the Trinity and the status of the Holy Spirit or of the Son especially—but to continue calling Milton an Arian thereby is simply ignorance. This labeling, this stereotyping misleads, misrepresents what his beliefs on such issues had developed into since the 1620s and through the 1640s. Particularly in relationship to literary works such as *Paradise Lost* and *Paradise Regain'd*, the stereotype and its rebuttal have created readings denying such *literary* metaphorization as that of "Under whose conduct *Michael* soon reduc'd / His Armie, circumfus'd on either Wing, / Under thir Head imbodied all in one" (*PL* 6.777–79).

Philip Dixon writes, "It is difficult to decide the nature and extent of Milton's alleged heresy in regard to the

Trinity"; "Milton perceived the teaching of the ante-Nicene Fathers to be the true teaching of Christ and his Apostles. The understanding of that teaching, which again it must be stressed was not strictly speaking Arian, lent the subordinationist tone found in his writing," yet "by the time that the *Treatise* was written Milton's Arianizing is clear." That latter word, though here it is *not* a labeling, does disservice to Dixon's otherwise well-informed research. He posits that the seventeenth century was "*the* key time as far as the loss of trinitarian vitality is concerned" and that Milton's examination of the questions "displays many of the criticisms of the radicals of the 1640s and 1650s that were to receive a fresh impetus in the controversies of the 1690s: lack of intelligibility; absence of scriptural warrant; detraction from the worship of the true God; a corruption produced by the Roman Church; the assumption that truth and clarity are closely related." In the eighteenth century, Trinitarian discussion, especially that involving the Holy Spirit, was neglected (largely a result of "enthusiasm" and the rise of manifestation replacing revelation).[22]

As the seventeenth century closed, such discussions as Herbert Croft, Bishop of Hereford's *The Naked Truth; or, The True State of the Primitive Church* (1675), argued that "simple acceptance of the doctrine of the Trinity was sufficient and further expansion of this belief unwise." "The Attributes of God...all these must be confessed to be *Mysteries,* not above our Reason, but above our Capacity," pronounces the Protestant against the Papist, according to Edward Stillingfleet's scenario in 1687, and thus instancing eyes and ears, he encourages "examining the sense of those certain Notions of visible things which God and Nature have planted in us; otherwise we are not dealt with as Reasonable Creatures. And therefore we must use those Faculties God hath given us, in reading and comparing Scriptures, and examining the sense that is offered by such Notions which are agreeable to the nature of things." The Papist accepts church authority and needs not Reason, but nonetheless alleges Trinity on the basis of three things:

"Scripture, Reason, and Tradition."[23] (We observe here the influence of rationalism in the Protestant's argument that will lead to the Enlightenment of the next century as well as a relationship with manifestation. Milton's analysis of the Holy Scriptures is part of this path toward the Age of Reason, and while he would question tradition, Milton accepted "Scripture, Reason," and found them lacking in proof of an orthodox Trinity.) With Milton's position we should compare the statements of such theologians as John Owen:

> The Doctrine of the Trinity...declares, as we said, that *this God is one, the Father, Son, and Holy Ghost;* that the *Father is this one God, and therefore is to be believed in,* worshipped, obeyed, lived unto, and in all things considered by us as the first cause, Soveraign Lord, and last end of all: That the *Son, is the one true God,* and therefore is to be believed in, worshipped, obeyed, lived unto, and in all things considered by us as the first cause, Soveraign Lord, and last end of all. And so also of the Holy Ghost.

It is a sign of the confusion that orthodox believers experienced when they read "that *the Father is this one God"* and then "That the *Son, is the one true God."* The comment on the Holy Ghost suggests a difference and some uncertainty. Nonetheless, for Owen, "The summe of this Revelation [various cited biblical "Testimonies"] is, that the Holy Spirit is an eternally divine existing substance, the Author of Divine operations, and the Object of Divine and Religious Worship.... The summe is, that the Holy ghost is a *divine distinct* person, and neither meerly the power or vertue of God, not any *created Spirit* whatever" (90, 94).[24] In 1714 Daniel Whitby admonished investigation of the mystery in *A Dissuasive from Enquiring into the Doctrine of the Trinity; or, The Difficulties and Discouragement Which Attend the Study of that Doctrine.*[25]

Prior to the Council of Nicaea (AD 325), at which the Nicene Creed was developed and adopted, the Trinity was not a part of orthodox thought. With the concept of mystic numbers and observation of the "natural" presence of three (as in a human's head, torso, and limbs, or the insect's head, abdomen, and thorax) the postulate of Pythagoras (before the Christian era) that "The whole universe [is] a harmonious world-order dependent on arithmetical relations" had strong effect in developing triunal thinking before the council met.[26] Numenius (late second century) anticipated Plotinus's Neoplatonism of the three ultimate principles (that is, three gods): "The Absolute Good (the Pythagorean Monad), the Demiurge (or Intelligence), and the Sensible Universe (or World Soul)" (Ferguson, *Encyclopedia*, 821). Expressed as "three divine hypostases (entities)—God, Mind, and Soul" (929), Plotinus proffered the further elucidation that God, "who contains within himself the divine ideas and constitutes the intelligible universe," produced the mind, from which emanates the soul (the principle of life and growth). "Soul, or Nature, animates and contains within itself the whole of the physical universe" (929). Early Church Fathers both rejected and expanded upon such philosophic thought, Tertullian (ca. 160–ca. 240) arguing that "*Substantia* had its precise Greek equivalent in *hypostasis*, which easterners would soon be insistently applying to the three!" (1144), and Augustine advancing, "The Godhead of the Father, the Son, and the Holy Spirit is one, their glory is equal, their majesty co-eternal" (1144). Tertullian was the first to employ the word "trinitas": "The three *personæ* were three not in their basic quality or power but in 'grade' or 'sequence' (*gradus*), 'aspect' (*forma*), and 'manifestation' (*species*). The Spirit issues from the Father through the Son" (1144).

Milton's study of the church fathers, such as Eusebius and Tertullian, is recorded in the *Commonplace Book* in entries dated 1637–39, a most important time, of course, for Milton's decision and action concerning a career, his sojourn to the Continent, and the beginning of his school teaching. Edward Phillips's report of the students' reading of religious treatises—implication places this in the earlier

1640s, prior apparently to 1646, when Phillips seems to have left his uncle's home—suggests continued attention to the church fathers and religious treatises and the elementary beginning of what became *De doctrina Christiana*. During these school-teaching years (1640–48) Milton did turn to "educational" writing (aside from *Of Education* in 1644): *Accedence Commenc't Grammar, Artis Logicae Plenior Institutio, History of Britain,* and *A Brief History of Moscovia*. The religious treatise may have joined these educational endeavors.

But most important in establishing a context for Milton's rethinking of his theological concepts at this time was, I suspect, *The Confession of Faith* by Cyril Lucaris (also referred to as "Lucar" and "Loukaris"), patriarch of Constantinople, and reactions to it.[27] There were also such movements as that in which John Biddle was immersed, which brought rebuttals particularly as the 1640s progressed. In his Biddle's *A Confession of Faith Touching the Holy Trinity, According to the Scripture* (1648) is a furtherance of what is labeled Socinianism. On May 2, 1644, Biddle had expressed his personal confession of faith to the royalist magistrates of Gloucester that there is one infinite and almighty essence called God; thus, there is only one Person in essence, but Jesus Christ through his being united to that only Person is truly God.[28] Lucaris, on the other hand, has not been mentioned in connection with Milton, to my knowledge,[29] yet his attempt to unite Calvinist views of predestination and justification with Catholic doctrine was notorious on the Continent and known in England, causing his condemnation by Eastern Orthodox synods in 1638 and 1642 (as well as in Kiev in 1640) and his assassination in June 1638.[30] The issue continued in the Eastern Orthodox Church up to the Synod of Jerusalem in 1672 (also called the Synod of Bethlehem since it was held in the Church of the Nativity there).[31] This Synod also condemned Lucaris and explicitly rejected his teachings. It defined orthodox dogma for the Eastern church, rejecting doctrinal variations of reformers and asserting orthodoxy. It differs from the Western church in the role of love and grace, and opposes Lucaris's assigning the means to justification and salvation to faith alone. Unlike Protestant reformations, it affirms seven mysteries, which are not simply symbolic, affirms Christ's sacramental presence, and accepts the deuterocanonical books of the Old Testament in distinction from the Protestant shorter version.

Perhaps written in 1621 in Greek, *The Confession of Faith* of the Eastern church ascribed to Lucaris[32] shows Calvinist influence in its acceptance of predestination and justification, and asserts positions on the Trinity, transubstantiation, and the virgin birth. Giovanni Diodati, the uncle of Milton's friend Charles, whom he visited in 1639 in Geneva, was instrumental in dispatching the Reverend Antoine Leger to Constantinople as chaplain to the Dutch embassy there, and Leger soon afterward sent the manuscript of *Confessio Fidei* to Geneva.[33] Diodati caused it to be published in Geneva in 1629 in Latin, and a considerable addition dated January 1631 appeared in a Greek version in 1633. There were various editions in Latin, Greek, and French on the Continent in the ensuing years (as well as that in English by William Raitt, entitled *A Vindication of the Reformed Religion, from the Reflections of a Romanist,* 1711). But most significantly for our discussion, it was also published in March 1629 in England (at the end of the translation is printed: "Dated in Constantinople, in the Moneth of March, 1629"): *The Confession of Faith of...Cyrill, Patriarch of Constantinople...Written at Constantinople, 1629,* the English text being followed by a Latin text.[34]

This early edition would be the one read by English clerics in the 1630s, 1640s, and 1650s, unless they perused the Greek or Latin versions. The first statement in this edition is: "We belieue *one God* Almightie and Infinite, three in persons, The *Father, Sonne and Holy Ghost,* The Father vnbegotten, The Sonne begotten of The Father before the World, consubstantial with The Father: the Holy Ghost proceeding from The Father by The Sonne, hauing the same essence with The Father and the Sonne: we call these three persons in one essence the *Holy Trinity* euer to be blessed, glorified, and to be worshipped of euery creature." The similarity of "the Holy Ghost proceeding" with Milton's position in *De doctrina Christiana* is striking, even though Milton nowhere refers to Lucaris or this document.[35] The Lucarian text implies a difference between "begot" and "proceed"; "consubstantial" for the Son with the Father separates the Holy Ghost from either of them; and the timing of existence of the three is that which Milton argues. The term "proceeding" is subject to various interpretations, but it does seem to be distinguished from "begot" in the *Articles of Fayth* (1562) and *The Confession of Faith* of the Westminster Assembly (1649 onward). The Thirty-Nine Articles cite that there is but one true God, "And in unitie of this Godhead there be three persons, of one substance, power, and eternitie, the father, the sonne, and the holy ghost." "The Sonne which is the worde of the father, begotten from euerlastyng of the father, the very and eternall GOD, of one substaunance with the father." "The holy ghost, proceedyng from the father and the sonne, is of one substance, maiestie, and glory, with the father and the sonne, very and eternall God." *The Confession of Faith* iterates that "The Son is eternally begotten of the Father; the Holy ghost eternally proceeding from the Father & the Son."[36]

Lucaris's agreements and disagreements with standard concepts of the state church is the burden of the second part of Thomas Smith's important orthodox dissertation in 1680, *An Account of the Greek Church, as to Its Doctrine and Rites of Worship*. He talks of "*that great man* Cyrillus Lucaris" (in the dedication to Henry, Lord Bishop of London) and writes "against the furious assaults of her [the Church of England's] restless enemies, the

Papists on the one hand, and the Giddy *Sectaries* on the other (who doth agree in the same designs of pulling down the Hierarchy, and overturning the Government, in order to her more effectual ruine)." In reference to "The Third Person of the glorious *Trinity*," Smith observes confusedly that the Greeks "acknowledge the Holy Spirit to be of the same substance with the Father and the Son, to be *God* from eternity proceeding from the essence and nature of the Father, without beginning, and to be equally adored. Likewise they acknowledge, that He is the Spirit of the Son, and that He is sent, poured out, and given by the Son." Smith refers to the Eastern church's position with and after the Synod of Jerusalem.[37]

The authority of the Bible is attested in Lucaris's *Confessio Fidei* by the following, which, with the statement from the 1629 English version of his *Confession of Faith*, indicates that the "author" is God through the agency of his Holy Spirit: "We belieue the *Holy Scripture* to be giuen by God, to haue no other Author but the Holy Ghost, which we ought vndoubtedly to belieue.... Besides, we belieue the *authority* thereof to be aboue the authority of the Church."[38] This last comment is, of course, of major moment for many Protestants of the Reformed sects and certainly for Milton. "*The Church on Earth may erre, taking falshood for Truth.*" The difference between "discipline" and "doctrine" is fundamental. The precedence of the Holy Scriptures is clearly in agreement with Milton's belief, though others, such as adherents of the Church of England, as Smith was, differ on the position of the church's authority.

Lucaris's *Confession of Faith* accepts God's predestination of humankind, "without having in any wise regard to their works," and such election is through divine mercy. His acceptance of Calvinist concepts is repeatedly evident: we are governed, he affirms, by God's Providence and we should not "curiously pry into [it], as being above our comprehension." "[A] *man is iustified by Faith*, and not by workes...[but W]orkes must not be neglected," for they are "necessary means, and testimonies of our faith." Milton was to write: "JUSTIFICATION IS THE JUDGMENT OF GOD, FREELY GIVEN, BY VIRTUE OF WHICH THOSE WHO ARE REGENERATE AND INGRAFTED IN CHRIST ARE ABSOLVED FROM SINS AND FROM DEATH THROUGH CHRIST'S ABSOLUTELY FULL SATISFACTION, AND ARE ACCOUNTED RIGHTEOUS IN THE SIGHT OF GOD, NOT BY THE WORKS OF THE LAW BUT THROUGH FAITH" (YP 6:485), and "GOOD WORKS are those which WE DO WHEN THE SPIRIT OF GOD WORKS WITHIN US, THROUGH TRUE FAITH, TO GOD'S GLORY" (YP 6:638). This accords with the position of Richard Montagu, whose *A Gagg for the New Gospel?* led to numerous arguments at Cambridge and rebuttals (during Milton's time at Christ's College). For Montagu, "only faith justifies and good works are not absolutely necessary for salvation." Further, for our attention to Milton's possible acquaintance with the text, the *Confessio* summarily states, "We belieue that the man created by God, fell in Paradise, because neglecting the Commandement of God, he yelded to the deceitful counsell of the Serpent: from whence sprung vp originall Sinne to his posterity, so that no man is borne according to the flesh, who doeth not beare this [the t is upside down] burthen, and feele the fruits of it in his life."[39]

The significance of having a Bible in the vernacular for all people was an immediate result of such concepts, and thus Leger's announcement to the Company of Geneva in March 1629 that a new edition of the New Testament in modern Greek was underway (actually not published, though, until late 1638) points to a text in better accord with non-Catholic views. That text, published in Geneva by P. Aubert, has parallel columns of the ancient and the modern Greek, and a preface by Lucaris, who allegedly read the proof (he was murdered in June). Diodati, in the meantime, had translated the Holy Scriptures into Italian in 1632 and sent a copy to Lucaris, who acknowledged the gift in a letter dated April 15, 1632. In this letter Lucaris refers to *his Confessio*.[40]

In other words, the connections between Diodati and Lucaris were significant. The publication of the controversial

Confession of Faith in English in 1629 when Milton was embarking on his graduate studies as a ministerial student, the contrary development of the state church under Laud in the 1630s, and Milton's stay for about a month in Geneva, visiting Diodati, a year after the notorious strangling of Lucaris, a time when Milton was on the Continent and frequently in doctrinal discussion with those favoring Catholicism and denouncing Protestantism—all of these may have contributed to Milton's awareness of such theological concepts. It seems unbelievable that Milton would not have known about Lucaris and his *Confession of Faith*; it is at least possible he had read it impressionably. The verses that Milton wrote in Cerdogni's album, which we looked at in chapter 1, may indeed have sprung to mind in such a venue as Geneva, in remembrance of such recent events, and after such experiences as he had had in Italy. Beneath such potential familiarity with these issues from 1629 through 1639 and his studies in the years from later 1639 through the 1640s exists a developing alteration of thought concerning the Holy Spirit and the Trinity. Lucaris's work and the positive and negative responses it received may have contributed to Milton's rethinking of these significant theological concepts during the 1640s.

Six

Theological Concerns, the Son, and the Divine Presence

The most notorious theological concern that has flooded Milton scholarship is the relationship of the Son to the Father, the Son as God, leading to the Arian label for his thought and, in counterdistinction, to the positing of a subordinationist classification.[1] As we have seen with the significant concepts of the virgin birth and the Holy Spirit, Milton, accepting the word of Holy Scripture, believed in the virgin birth without any modification but rejected the Holy Spirit as a member of an orthodox Trinity because of the lack of citation in Holy Scripture. A modification in the understanding of the Holy Spirit is thus advanced, and the lack of citation of a Trinity in Holy Scripture removes its orthodox concept from his belief.[2] The Holy Spirit "is a spirit, in the sense in which that term is correctly applied to the Father and the Son" (*De doctrina Christiana*, YP 6:281); it "is a minister of God, and therefore a creature,...

created, that is, produced, from the substance of God, not by natural necessity, but by the free will of the agent" (6:298). The Holy Spirit is created *from* the Father after the *generation* of the Son *in* whom it exists and is thus inferior to the Son.³ Quite clearly the Son has a totally different status from that of the Spirit, for the Son is attested to by Holy Scripture over and over again. Therefore, there is absolute and explicit belief in the Son as the Son of God and thus as part of the Godhead. However, reality of language steps in for Milton in this case, which it does not in the miracle of the virgin birth (an indication that Milton does accept miracles or mysteries): that is, a father exists *before* a son, and as a son he is "inferior" to his father. (This position, this thought was not unique to Milton, of course.) While some wish to label this subordinationism — and in analogy it extends to the relationship between husband and wife as Paul and Milton view it⁴ — it derives from the reality factor that the words "Father" and "Son" demand: "the Son existed before the creation of the World, but not that his generation was from eternity" (YP 6:206) since he could not exist before the Father existed. Milton does not adopt the matter as the mystery that orthodox believers do — a view collapsing time into a "moment," as it were, with classification that nonetheless does not imply (and is not used with any sense of) precedence or inferiority in even this one exceptional case. Orthodoxy on this issue ignores the language for Milton; he thus casts God as one being who is two persons (a variation of the Trinity as three persons indivisible), a statement that can be accepted only on faith in such a miracle. But as Dixon remarks, for Milton, "The Father alone is the *ens*" (103).⁵

1

What is the operative thought that emerges at least later in Milton's career? How does this position — which still encompasses a "miracle" — relate to others' fairly contemporary thought within Milton's experience? *The*

Confession of Faith, and the Larger & Shorter Catechism avows that "There is but one only *a,* true, and true God *b:* who is inf[i]nite in Being and Perfection *c,* a most pure Spirit *d,* invisible *e,* without body, parts *f,* or passions *g,* immutable *h,* immense *i,* eternal *k,* incomprehensible *l,...* In the unity of the God-head, there be three persons, of one substance, power, and eternity; God the Father, God the Son, & God the Holy Ghost *o.* The Father is of none, neither begotten, nor proceeding; the Son is eternally begotten of the Father *p,* the Holy Ghost eternally proceeding from the Father, and the Son *q.*"⁶ The meaning of "begotten" and of "proceeding" causes difficulties: "begotten" in reference to the Son is for Milton "generated from," and "proceeding" in reference to the Holy Spirit is different and suggestive of "created by" the Father from his substance and yet related to the Son. (The creation of the Holy Spirit is, however, different from the creation of the angels and all else.) As I have pointed out previously, Milton differentiates *generatio* and *creatio* in *De doctrina Christiana* as he should.⁷ Translations have not paid attention to Milton's specific and differentiating language, and readers should not depend upon translations. "Generatio est qua Filium ex decreto suo genuit Deus unicum. unde et Pater primario dicitur" (CM 14:178): the Son is *generated* from the Father, who thus is called "Father" because of such generation. The Son is *not created*. For Milton, unlike Kersey's Arian, the Son *is of* the same substance as the Father. The Father remains the same as the being of God, thus accounting for Milton's and the generally interchangeable usage of "God" and "Father." The Son is a derivation from the Father as a separate person (see also the quotation from Tertullian in note 1), which Milton expresses in *Of Prelatical Episcopacy* as: "The Father is the whole substance, but the Son a derivation, and portion of the whole, as he himselfe professes because the Father is greater then me" (YP 1:645).⁸ Though employed in a different context, the separation of Father and Son in terms of Godhead underlies *De doctrina Christiana:* "THE VISIBLE

CHURCH IS THE WHOLE MULTITUDE OF THOSE WHO ARE CALLED FROM ANY PART OF THE WHOLE WORLD, AND WHO OPENLY WORSHIP GOD THE FATHER IN CHRIST EITHER INDIVIDUALLY OR IN CONJUNCTION WITH OTHERS" (YP 6:568)

The employment of "begotten" (and its forms) in the translations of *genuit* (and its forms) has created much of the problem.[9] (The expression "eternally begotten" would seem to mean "always existent," without any thought of the time difference between the existence of a father and of a son.) The word "proceed" (and its various forms) as used by theologians, Milton writes, as well as "emanate," has been read to mean such procession ("breathing") of the Holy Spirit from the Father and the Son ("spirari idcirco a patre et filio spiritum," CM 14:356, 358), but who would be so bold as to make this assertion ("quis hinc ausit statuere")? Of course, one answer to Milton's question (and he undoubtedly knew this) is the Westminster Assembly's *Confession of Faith* (see chapter 5). And another, I would suggest, is Lucaris's *Confessio*. Rather, Milton argues that "these words [proceed and emanate] relate rather to the mission than to the nature of the Spirit" and that the Son too is seen "either 'to go forth' or 'to proceed' from the Father" (CM 14:359), the sense of which he equates with the usage in "'to live by every word that proceedeth,' or 'goeth forth from the mouth of God,' Matt. iv. 4." Thus, the Son does not proceed from God in the sense of a creation, and he is not begotten in the sense of a creation, either. The listing of proof-texts in discussing the *generatio* of the Son in the Columbia Milton (14:180, 182, 184), all employ a version of that word when the Son is the subject (*not* when "omnis rei creatæ" is discussed), but the translations in Columbia and the Yale Prose, even in the proof-texts, incorrectly record "begotten" (or some version of it).

Lucaris, importantly *if* indeed his *Confessio* had early influence, writes: "*the Holy Spirit proceeds from the Son essentially and internally and as to his subsistence.*" "The

Holy Spirit proceedeth from the Father by the Son" (199), and "the manner of Generation, whereby the Son subsists, is distinct from the manner of the Procession of the Holy Spirit."[10] The similarity between Lucaris's understanding and Milton's is certainly noteworthy.

The problem of meaning in language is particularly important in *Paradise Lost*.[11] The origin of the rebellion in heaven, according to Milton in the epic—and motivation was necessary literarily for his extended fictive account of what was considered truth as given so briefly in the Holy Scripture—and thus of the war in heaven, the expulsion of the rebellious angels, the Creation of the world and Adam and Eve, and the ensuing need for the Incarnation, lies in God the Father's words to the heavenly host, drawn from Psalm 2:

> This day I have begot whom I declare
> My only Son, and on this holy Hill
> Him have anointed, whom ye now behold
> At my right hand; your Head I him appoint.   (5:604–07)

This is, of course, not "generation": the Son has existed prior to the angels, prior to Satan (a point that readers of the psalm forget about the merchant and his son and the kings of the earth when they read it as typology—or rather as identification); the Son *is* God and has existed well before this specific point in the poem. God the Father has "exalted" his Son (prophetic of his role as Messiah), who by all accounts did not exercise any position prior to this time.[12] Milton does not pursue what God the Father, God the Son, the Holy Spirit, or Satan or any of the angels did prior to this time: he is not the "fool" he identifies in *De doctrina Christiana* (YP 6:299). The motivation bypasses the differences of "Son" and "sons" of God; it does not stand up under real analysis because there is no realistic, logical answer to the underlying question—except a belief in God and his ways, including miracles. Critics of *Paradise Lost* keep forgetting that it is a fiction and that its basis is belief in something that is not delineated in all points of conception. A major problem with criticism of Milton's position (whatever it is) is the critic's opposed or at least different position from his. And critically what the critic reads as theological theory in the poem is read as exactly what Milton himself believed.

It is clear that in both *Paradise Lost* and *De doctrina Christiana* there is a separation of the Father and the Son, although the assignment of "subordinationism" may be overstating Milton's position. Milton is most clear that the Father is God and that God is the only God. In chapter 5 on the Son he states,

> According to the Son's clearest possible testimony, the Father is that one true God from whom are all things.... Christ therefore agrees with all God's people that the Father is that one and only God....[citing Jer. 3:9]. In this passage Christ, as God wished him to be known and worshipped by his people under the gospel, is firmly distinguished, both by nature and title, from the one God Jehovah. Christ himself, then, the Son of God, teaches us nothing in the gospel about the one God other than what the law had taught us already [referring to the first commandment]. He asserts everywhere, quite clearly, that it is the Father....If the Father is Christ's God and our God, and if there is only one God, who can be God except the Father? (YP 6:214–25)

Milton repeats the point in the next chapter on the Holy Spirit: "It follows that he who sent both the spirit of his son and his Son himself, and upon whom we are taught to call, and upon whom the Spirit himself calls, is the one God and the only Father" (YP 6:280). Milton further contends the separation of the Christ and the one God: "Jesus Christ, or, *the anointed*, is the Son of God. He is, therefore, not one with nor equal to God, who anointed him" (297). It thus is also clear why Milton calls God the Father God and delimits the Son as God, although in delegation from the Father he joins what is considered the Godhead. There is a similarity here in thinking with the vision of

Isaiah in the apocryphal Ascension of Isaiah. As Labriola recounts that nonorthodox book, "The Son of *Paradise Lost* is thrice begotten literally, not metaphorically: first as divine, second as angelic, and third as human." The first begetting refers to the Son's generation from the Father from beginning of time and before any creation or kind of creation. (The significance of recognizing this, as I have suggested, alters some people's reading of Psalm 2 and of Milton's use of it in book 5 as the hinge of the narrative and Satan's jealousy.) The second begetting refers to the Son's angelic being, and Labriola relates this to the passage in book 5 (that is, Milton's employment of Psalm 2, and thus more meaningfully to the Son's angelic, rather than divine, status as superior to the created angels). The third begetting, of course, recounts the Incarnation.[13]

I think that the above makes clear why labeling Milton a subordinationist is misleading. The parallel with Adam and Eve may also be recalled, concluding that Milton views both as humankind—the two hand-in-hand—but the male, created first and in God's image, is in a superior position, for the female was created second, from the first, and in God's image through the male's: "Hee for God only, shee for God in him" (*PL* 4.299). I have previously called such a position "masculinist." As we look back on Milton's earlier work and then on *Paradise Lost*, this attitude seems to be expressed, but then, as Herman argues, as we proceed to read the epic we find a shift in the attitude toward woman, an attitude of love such as the Son, the Christ, also exemplifies. This conceptual development accords, it will be seen, with Michael Bryson's argument that observes God's (the Father's) "tyranny" but argues that the true "kingship," with its charity and love, of the Christ (the Son) is the ideal to be sought.[14] The strong, rather unyielding attitude of the Father—a masculinist view stereotypically—is ameliorated by the merciful and loving nature of the Son—a view often associated with woman.

2

A matter that has bothered some critics is Milton's apparent non-church-going and his burial at St. Giles, Cripplegate, where his father had been buried and in the vicinity of his last residence. That is, they point out his lack of church involvement, as far as we know, and his unorthodox beliefs that *we* know could have denied him burial at the church. But, of course, we do not know that church authorities would have been aware of his beliefs, for his published writings were not read as unorthodox. His subordinationist position, as it has been called, is seen as a heresy although it is *not* Arian or Socinian, despite similarity as to the relationship of the Son to the Father; both classifications would indicate beliefs that Milton absolutely did not accept. It is similar to the problem of calling him an Arminian and even a Calvinist. acceptance of certain ideas does not make such labeling cogent. Indeed, part of the problems that the state church underwent lie in some people's acceptance of Calvinism while others were only Calvinistic, and of certain concepts of Arminianism.[15] But Milton continued to believe in the Godhead, to accept the ways of God, to maintain a basic Protestant position, and to view God the Father in a capacity that equates "God," just as so many other people did and do. He does not employ the word "Father" in his delineation of God in chapter 2 of *De doctrina Christiana*, "De Deo," in the treatise as a separate person; the word appears eight times only in scriptural quotations or in one reference.[16] In chapter 3 (YP 6:166), on divine decree, Milton writes, "God's first and most excellent SPECIAL DECREE of all concerns HIS SON: primarily by virtue of this he is called FATHER," followed by proof-texts, which lead to: "From all these quotations it appears that the Son of God was begotten by a decree of the Father" (167). The translation is inaccurate—again—for the word is *genitum* and should *not* be translated as "was begotten." As Maurice Kelley notes (YP 6:166 nn42, 43), Milton is laying the foundation against the argument of the Son's eternal generation and for viewing the texts as a metaphorical generation of the Son. Such citation and reference—and such mistranslation—continues in chapter 4 on "Predestination," which only God—that is, God the Father—enacts. The first sentence of this chapter uses the phrase "by which God," and this is explicated: "BY WHICH GOD: meaning, of course, the Father. Luke xii.32: *it was your father's pleasure;* similarly whenever mention is made of the divine decree or plan" (YP 6:173). On page 179, after citation of John 3:16 ("God loved the world so much that he gave his only begotten Son, so that everyone who believes in him may not perish"), we read that even for Judas, "it is said not only that he was elected...but also that he was given to Christ by the Father." (And again "only begotten Son" is wrong, although it is also the reading of the Geneva and King James Bibles: Milton's words "filium suum unigenitum dederit" refer to the Son's singular generation, not his exaltation. Milton gives a Latin translation of the Greek, but of course the translation of the original Greek in the above Bible is also wrong; the word is μονογενησ [*monogenes*], which means "only generated.")

Milton did not renounce his belief and faith in God; he maintained a Protestant position, albeit different from that of others attending church services, and his published writings do not lead to interpretation of heresy on his part. That is, of course, on the basis of *his* definition of heresy to understand his belief about himself and his allegiance to God (see chapter 4). He has not made a "choice profestly against Scripture," and he emphasizes understanding it "rightly" (which, of course, the orthodox will not accept as "rightly"). He has set his interpretation of the Word of God before his reader "as the Rule of faith and obedience." "The rule of faith," he asserts in the preface to chapter 5, "De Filio Dei," that he will "state quite openly what seems to [him] much more clearly deducible from the text of scripture than the currently accepted doctrine. [He does] not see how anyone who calls himself a Protestant or a member of the Reformed Church, and who acknowledges the same rule of faith as [he], could be offended with [him] for this, especially as [he is] not trying to browbeat anyone, but [is] merely pointing out what [he considers] the more credible doctrine" (YP 6:203). He adds, "I take it upon myself to refute, whenever necessary, not scriptural authority, which is inviolable, but human interpretations" (204). Thus, most simply we may say that Milton believed in God; that he recognized a division between God the Father and God the Son both through the logic that a father must precede the existence of a son and through a metaphoric understanding separating thought (Word) and action, and truth and mercy. Thus, God, or rather God the Father, has omnipotence, omniscience, and omnipresence, and it is the Father who knows and states the Truth. But specific action is delegated to God the Son, who metaphorically is exalted over all created things, and who thus enacts the Father's power, knowledge, and presence. To achieve righteousness in humankind and effect its eschatological return so that God will be All in All, the Incarnation of the Son occurs, and after the man Jesus has demonstrated to humankind the means to righteousness through obedience and faith, the Man/God has been anointed the Christ and is he "whom provident God himself has sent...and who bring[s] joyous messages from heaven, and who teach[es] the way which leads beyond the grave to the stars." (I am, of course, citing Milton's 1627 *Elegia Quarta* to Thomas Young, who is also a minister of God's Word. God the Son is central to *Paradise Lost*, and as Man/God to *Paradise Regain'd*.)

Clearly Milton remains a devout believer in God and there is no reason for withholding burial at St. Giles. That he did not, apparently, attend services—or at least as far as we know, though perhaps he did on occasion?—underscores his (and general Protestant) belief that *sola scriptura* and close association of the Christian and his God, without intermediary of any sort, was proper and the true sign of devotion.

Various unorthodox beliefs that fall into a wide-ranging concept of Protestantism do not fall under Milton's definition of "heretic," as he tells us in *Of True Religion*: "But here the Papist will angrily demand, what! Are Lutherans, Calvinists, Anabaptists, Socinians, Arminians, no Hereticks? I answer, all these may have some errors, but are no Hereticks" (YP 8:423); specifically, "The Lutheran holds Consubstantiation; an error indeed, but not mortal.... The Arian and Socinian are charg'd to dispute against the Trinity: they affirm to believe the Father, Son, and Holy Ghost, according to Scripture, and the Apostolic Creed" (424). It is clear that Milton, at least, does not consider his beliefs "heretic," although there may be some agreements with Calvinists, Anabaptists, Socinians, Arminians, and Arians. But this does raise the question of the Trinity (discussed above in chapter 5) and transubstantiation (which follows below) since it involves concepts involving the Christ and extensive argument during Milton's lifetime (as well as before and after). The matter of consubstantiation for Milton we can dismiss: it is an argument to oppose Catholic transubstantiation, proposing a combination (or coexistence) of the body of Christ with the bread and wine of the sacrament of the Eucharist or Lord's Supper, yielding an equation of the wafer's having the same nature, or the same substance or essence, as the body and blood of Christ. Thus, it differs from the single presence of the body and blood through a changing of the substances in transubstantiation.

3

The Catholic belief in transubstantiation of the Eucharist at Mass by the priest who is enabled to change the substance of the bread and wine into the body and blood of Christ was long debated before Milton's time. It is a subject we must pursue in an examination of Milton's concepts about the Son, his Incarnation and anointing as the Christ. Most discussions assign the basic argument against transubstantiation to begin with the statements of Huldrych Zwingli (1484–1531), the Swiss "reformer" of Roman Catholicism and critic of the papacy. He viewed the sacrament of Holy Communion as a commemorative service, a symbolic remembrance of God's sovereignty and Providence, and thus of humankind's dependence on the Godhead. Such a position led to a rejection of transubstantiation and, thereby, the Real Presence of Christ in the Eucharist partaken by a communicant. Much was made of the inference that such transubstantiation would make partaking of the Eucharist a corporal "eating" of Christ. Transubstantiation and the Real Presence are distinct concepts, although some medieval writers seem to unite them through what had been advanced through Aristotelian substance and accident. The concept of transubstantiation arose from the text of Matthew 26:26–28, "And as they were eating, Jesus took bread, and blessed it, and brake it, and gave it to the disciples, and said, Take, eat; this is my body. / And he took the cup, and gave thanks, and gave it to them, saying, Drink ye all of it; / for this is my blood of the new testament, which is shed for many for the remission of sins."[17] The occasion was "the first day of the feast of unleavened bread," that is, Passover, and was subsequently called the Lord's Supper. Zwingli interpreted "This is my body" as "This signifies my body," and to "eat" as to "believe" in Christ.

Significant for reformational views was the text of 1 Corinthians and Paul's statement that such partaking of the bread and wine was "in remembrance of me." As a Protestant, and as an anti-Catholic, Milton undoubtedly accepted this understanding of the Lord's Supper from childhood onward. Influences in college (1625–32) from teachers, reading, and general atmosphere of belief would affirm such a view. In *De doctrina Christiana*, book 1, chapter 28, "Of the External Sealing of the Covenant of Grace," Milton discusses the Lord's Supper (YP 6:552–55), citing the text above and those given in note 17, and stating, "THE LORD'S SUPPER *commemorates* the death of Christ

Theological Concerns, the Son, and the Divine Presence 123

by the breaking of bread and the pouring out of wine: both are tasted by all present, and the *benefits* of his death are thus sealed to believers" (my emphasis). The words presented in the Bible

> show us quite clearly that the mere flesh is of no use here any more than it was in feeding the five thousand: also that not teeth but faith is needed to eat his flesh: also that what he gave was the heavenly and spiritual bread which had come down from heaven. It was not the earthly bread, which had been born from the virgin and which, had he merely given his flesh, he would have given, but a bread which was, so to speak, more heavenly than the manna itself, and which *he who eats shall live for ever.* (YP 6:553)

Some of those words and images are the same as those used by other writers on the subject, including Lucaris. He immediately lampoons the papists' belief, quipping that, "if this were so, even the most wicked of the communicants, not to mention the mice and worms which often eat the eucharist, would attain eternal life by virtue of that heavenly bread."[18] The Catholic "monstrous doctrines" turn "the Lord's Supper into a cannibal feast," although "cannabalism [is] utterly alien to reason, common sense and human behavior."[19] Indeed, he even becomes rather scatological by pursuing what he construes as the realistic outcome of Catholic interpretation: "if we eat his flesh it will not remain in us, but, to speak candidly, after being digested in the stomach, it will be at length exuded" (YP 6:554). His images and tone hardly seem commendable in a serious religious discussion and in a text for the edification of his readers (perhaps those thought of as readers of *The Art of Logic, The History of Britain, Brief History of Moscovia, Accedence Commenc't Grammar*). Has Milton confused his audience for that of, say, *Colasterion?* Do we have some suggestion of composition over time and with the remnants of an earlier time? Do such remnants join with the invasive remarks in book 1, chapter 10 of the treatise in diverging into divorce? Has attention to actual publication simply been inadequate, perhaps not really pursued, in days after the Restoration?[20]

Milton's "reformed" view understands the Lord's Supper as meaning "that Christ will dwell in us and we in him" (YP 6:554), a variation of Saint Hilary's "These things being taken and drunk cause Christ to be in us and us in Him."[21] The bread is a type of manna; the blood, a type of "the water which flowed from the rock" (citing 1 Cor. 10:3–4). We can relate this concept to his paraphrase of Psalm 114; it is a "figure of speech...where the relationship between the symbol and the thing symbolized is very close" (555). Milton is certainly not alone in his thinking about this subject, as is clear from a glance at a few contemporary authors. The opposition to Catholic belief in the Real Presence of Christ in the Eucharist at the Mass (that is, the "bodily" presence) existed throughout Milton's lifetime, not simply emphasized during the Interregnum, as has sometimes been alleged. For one example, the work of William Forbes, who died in 1634 and was Bishop of Edinburgh, was published from manuscript in 1658. Citing Zwingli in his discussion, he wrote, "Christ is present in the Eucharist only by the contemplation of faith; that there is no place to be given here for a miracle, since we know in what way Christ is present to His supper, viz. by the quickening Spirit, spiritually and effaciously; that sacramental union consists wholly in signification, &c." "The opinion of those Protestants and others seems most safe and most right, who think, nay, who most firmly believe, that the Body and Blood of Christ is truly, really, and substantially present and taken in the Eucharist, but in a way, which is incomprehensible to the human understanding and much more, beyond the power of man to express; which is known to God alone, and not revealed to us in Scripture." This last statement likewise attests to the questioning of Revelation that was occurring at this time (see chapter 9 for discussion). Forbes argues that there is no proof in Scripture, none given by the church fathers, nor by Protestants: "spiritually" is not rightly explained, nor can it be perceived by the senses.²² The question becomes one of interpretation, and the terms "real" and "presence" take on different meanings from those of Catholic dogma.

Other references by Milton include quotation of the text from Matthew in *The Doctrine and Discipline of Divorce* (YP 2:325) and the following of the Greek church in Moscovia (YP 8:492), where the Eucharist is received in both kinds;²³ that is, where both the wafer (bread, host, the body) and the wine (the blood) were offered. Communion of the transubstantiated Eucharist (the "both kinds" of the Western Catholic church) and as communion in remembrance that Christ died for humankind and thus to "feed on Him in thy heart by faith, with Thanksgiving" (as in the "one kind," that is, the symbolic wafer of Reformed religions).²⁴ Montagu had also labeled this act of the priest "*That monster of monsters,*" and goes on to say, "This is my body. *Which we deny not, either in words or sense. The very body of Christ really received in the Sacrament of the Altar, is warranted by those formall words of Institution,* This is my body: *but not* per modum Con, *or* Trans, *or any other like. It is not said, this is my body corporally; eaten orally; there carnally; conceiued of grossely,*" followed on the next page with a citation of Saint John Chrysostom's translation: "You must conceiue of me spiritually." Joseph Mede's beliefs (and ridiculing) would have been known to Milton, we would suspect: "I must tell you also some of the *Miracles* and *Lies* for laying the foundation of *Transubstantiation,* and thence advancing the *Idol of the Mass.* . . . These wonders and other the like of apparitions of *flesh* and *blood* began not till about the end of the eighth-hundredth year."²⁵

Laud, in defending himself from charges of "a like endeavour to alter the true Protestant religion into Popery," seems to hedge somewhere in between the two kinds. He writes under the "circumstantial" *Quando* that the question of how Christ is present in the sacrament is a "bare circumstance of *quomodo*" (that is, "in what manner?"). He offers the argument that Rome differed from Protestants only in "circumstantials," not "about fundamentals," "for the foundations of Christian religion are the Articles of the Creed, and the Church of Rome denies no one of them."[26] Most adherents of the state church (at the very least) and the Puritans would not have condoned such an argument. His basic position, however, seems not to oppose that of the *Confession of Faith*, although his language of defense would raise uncertainties and does not state an outright rejection. It strikes one frequently as pettifoggery. Chapter 29 of the *Confession*, "Of the Lords Supper," reads:

> Our Lord Jesus, in the night wherein he was betrayed, Instituted the Sacrament of his Body & Blood, called the Lords Supper, to be observed in his Church unto the end of the world for the perpetual remembrance of the sacrifice of himself in his death; *the sealing all benefits* thereof unto true believers, their spiritual nourishment, and growth in him, their further ingagement in, and to all duties which they owe unto him, and to be a bond and pledge of their communion with him, and with each other, as members of his mysticall body.[27]

The elements are called body and blood, or bread and wine, but "albeit his substance & nature they still remain truly and only Bread and Wine, as they were before." We should note "benefits" here, which is the word Milton employed (*beneficia*).[28]

Transubstantiation "is repugnant, not to Scripture alone, but even to comon sense & reason; overthroweth the nature of the Sacrament & hath been, & is the cause of manifold Superstition; yea of gross Idolatries." The "Worthy receivers" are blest "inwardly by faith, really and indeed, yet not carnally and corporally, but spiritually, receive and feed upon Christ crucified, and all the *benefits* of his death. The Body and Blood of Christ being then, not corporally, or carnally, in, with, or under the Bread and Wine, yet, as really, but spiritually, present to the faith of Believers in the Ordinance as the elements themselves are to their outward senses."[29] Acceptance of the *Confession of*

Faith by Milton on this issue, generally at least, is patent.

But Lucaris's "Protestant" view, if indeed his *Confessio* had effect upon Milton's thinking, may have been most important: it does not hold to the Greek belief in both "kinds," as Milton noted for the Eastern Orthodox Church in his history of Moscovia; rather, it advances a Calvinistic reading. After citing Paul's words and relating the Eucharist to the Last Supper, Lucaris speaks of it as "a *true and reall presence* of Christ our Lord, but yet," he continues, "such a one as *faith* offereth to vs, not such as deuised *transubstantiation* teacheth. For we belieue, the faithfull doe eate the body of Christ in the Supper of the Lord, not by breaking it with the teeth of the body, but by perceiuing it with the sence and feeling of the soule, sith the body of Christ is not that which is Visible in the Sacrament, but that which *Faith spiritually* apprehendeth, and offereth to vs."[30] Smith, reviewing the Synod of Constantinople and its rejection of Lucaris, says, "Thus the people communicate in both kinds; which is the express doctrine and constant practice of the *Greek* Church" and "As to the moment of Consecration, in which the Symbols become and are made the Body and Bloud of *Christ*, 'tis certain that the *Greeks*, herein following the authority of several eminent Writers of their Church, do not hold this Divine Mystery to be perfected and consummated by or after the pronunciation of those words, *Take, eat, this is my Body.*"[31] The vagueness and word-playing in the matter of "both kinds" is clear from the statement from the Synod of Jerusalem in chapter 17 of their *Acts and Decrees:* "Eucharist accepts...the true real presence of our Lord Jesus Christ, but not in any material form, as in transubstantation"; "For we believe the Faithful that partake in the Supper eat the Body of our Lord Jesus Christ, not by perceptibly pressing and dissolving the communion with the teeth, but by the soul realising communion."[32]

The later years of the seventeenth century as well as the early years of the next saw the dissension between Catholic and non-Catholic in tracts trying to balance the two positions, to advance the Protestant position, or to refute the non-Protestant "kind." William Atwood (formerly "Anonymous"), in *A Seasonable Vindication of the Truly Catholick Doctrine of the Church of England: in Reply to Dr. Sherlock's Answer to Anonymous his three Letters concerning Church-Communion*, asserts (using Romans 14:23) that "He that doubted is damned if he eat, because he eateth not of Faith; for whatsoever is not of Faith, is Sin." To William Payne in opposition to Catholic justification: "It is hereby declared, that no Adoration is intended, or ought to be done, either unto the sacramental Bread and Wine there bodily received, or unto any corporal presence of Christs natural Flesh and Blood; for the sacramental Bread and Wine remain still in their natural substances and therefore may not be adored, for that were Idolatry to be abhorred of all faithful Christians."[33] In his dialogue between a Protestant and a papist, Stillingfleet stresses tradition, which accepted the Trinity, but transubstantiation is not acceptable, for it is not "ancient." The papist counters that it was not questioned until "rash Reason attempted to fashion the unlimited Miracles and Mysteries of God." In turn, citing Saint Ambrose, the Protestant replies, "*that the Body of Christ in the Sacrament, is a spiritual Body, or a Body produced by the Divine Spirit;* and so he parallels it with *that spiritual food, what the* Israelites *did eat in the Wilderness:* And no man will say, that the *Substance* of the *Manna* was then lost."[34] In a full exposition of the topic, Anthony Horneck, Chaplain in Ordinary to William and Mary, in *The Crucified Jesus*, explains that "*It's the Lord's Supper, because the Lord Jesus is Meat and Drink in this Feast;* Meat *indeed*, and Drink *indeed, as the expression is, John 6, 11...Spiritual Meat and Drink....It's the Lords Supper, because the nourishment and strength it affords or yields, is by the influence of the Lord Jesus.*" Horneck states the Protestant position, akin to what Milton wrote, as quoted above: "the Bread is a Symbol, a Figure, a Sign, a Representation, and a Memorial of Christ's Body, which was offer'd for the Sins of the World."[35] The subject of the

Eucharist has been treated frequently in ensuing years, right up to the present moment.[36]

The basis for belief in transubstantiation has been traced to age-old attempts at explaining phenomena in life experience, and answers thus have led to mythic postulations. Van der Leeuw concludes that "transubstantiation must be considered as a theoretically grounded reversion to the more primitive aspects in the sacraments." It is related to "the *epiclesis* [which] was intended to invoke the Lord's spirit into the food.... In this way power-stuff, changed *ad hoc*, was substituted for the real presence of the Saviour in the Eucharist, equally in the elements and in the sacrificing community, equally in the past (the redemptive history), in the future (*maran atha*), and at the present moment."[37] The concept of sacrifice points to a mythological basis in the ceremony, one older than the event commemorated. To Jung, the

> bread symbolizes the visible manifestation of the divine numen [the spirit presiding over a place or thing] which dies and rises again, and wine the presence of a pneuma [breath] which promises intoxication and ecstasy. The classical world thought of this pneuma as Dionysus, particularly the suffering Dionysus Zagreus, whose divine substance is distributed throughout the whole of nature. In short, what is sacrificed under the forms of bread and wine is nature, man, and God, all combined in the unity of the symbolic gift.[38]

That the Eucharist represents a sacrifice and specifically the sacrifice of the Passion, including the Crucifixion, was not advanced by Justin Martyr (middle second century CE) but by Irenaeus (later second century). In other words, such dogma as derived from the Bible (like that surrounding the Holy Spirit) has developed through interpretations, often conflicting, by formulators of religious thought over a number of years. The reason for the statement, "The sacrifice is, in fact, explained by, and identified with, the effects which it produces upon the worshippers," is thus understandable.[39]

4

We have a Milton whose belief in these matters has not changed over time, a Milton whose emphasis on faith in Godhead sees the concept of the Eucharist through symbols, as a figure of speech, as a symbol (the signifier we might say) that is virtually the thing that is symbolized (the signified). He interprets the Bible, in agreement with other Protestant authors but not with reliance upon them—perhaps, however, with influence from them in his earlier years. The Real Presence of the Christ is denied in the Eucharist, but a Divine Presence of a different sort is there. The terms have often been interchanged, but for Milton there is a definite difference between "Real" and "Divine" here. Milton is often concerned with the presence—including the omnipresence—of the Godhead. But again, language—"presence"—becomes a problem. The Eucharist has been called a commemoration of and representation of the Passion, on which basis Rudolf Otto thus asserts, "Christ's Eucharist does indeed include what is called a real presence.... What is present is the most numinous *fact* in the world's history, the fact of Golgotha."[40] His word "real" is not the Catholic use of carnally "Real" in this case; what Otto's attempt at concord does may confuse the issue. His "real" implies true, cogent, significant. Yet the word "presence" has the same denotation as existence and whereness, but it does not equate bodily presence. It is symbolic, present in its spirituality, in its representationalism. But most importantly the Catholic "presence" in the Eucharist is *not* related to God's omnipresence: it is, in fact, in major disagreement with Martin Luther, who had rationalized the Real Presence through the "ubiquity" of God. Reformed sects also did not accept ubiquity; Laud, among others, saw this as a doctrinal error.[41] The subject of ubiquitarianism (assigned to Lutheranism during these years) equates it with the proposition that "Christ is present in the eucharist in body as well as in spirit, and that his body is not therefore confined to one place, but can be everywhere (*ubique*)."⁴² Thus, the omnipresence that without adequate thought would be read in "ubiquity" does not exist for Catholics or for those of Reformed persuasion. The presence (whether carnal or spiritual only) of Christ in the Eucharist should not call to mind this accepted attribute of God; it does not occur in the Eucharist because God "can be everywhere." (In fact, although the term "omnipotence" is Latin, "omnipresence" and "omniscience" are medieval Latin and enter English vocabularies only in the early seventeenth century.)

For Milton the term and concept of "presence" is most important. Michael Lieb defines it as "involv[ing] a witnessing of the manifest 'glory' of God, a beholding of the 'blessed count'nance,' as it is accommodated to the sight of man, a conversing with God, and, by implication, a 'walking' with him, as his 'footstep' can be 'traced' from 'place' to 'place.' " There is emphasis on "place" and "Shekinah," God's "Dwelling Presence," but no sanctity should be assigned to "these narrow bounds confin'd / Of Paradise or *Eden*", as Michael admonishes Adam.⁴³ In *De doctrina Christiana* Milton's statement of this attribute is "that God is PRESENT EVERYWHERE," and he refers to Psalm 139: 8, 9; Proverbs 15:3; Jeremiah 23:24; and Ephesians 4:6. Kelley footnotes *Paradise Lost* 11.336–37, 7.588–90, and 7:517–18 (YP 6:144). Alerted by elaborations of the meanings that this concept of omnipresence had brought forth from religious writers, Milton warns: "Our ideas about the omnipresence of God, as it is called, should be only such as appear most reconcilable with the reverence we ought to have for him" (YP 6:144). Such a statement castigates not only Lutheran "ubiquity" and the Catholic "bodily" presence in the Eucharist, but some Reformed clerics' loose employment of the term, and others who deny any presence whatsoever.

Of the latter people who "err most gravely, who argue that 'Christ is not really in the Eucharist, by weak reasonings such as these;' 'Christ is in heaven, is circumscribed in place &c., therefore He is not in very deed, or really present in the Eucharist,'" Forbes maintains that "the mode of the presence,...we hold should be altogether left to the infinite wisdom and power of God." He believes in "the presence," but "the manner of the presence" is not defined anymore than in "baptism the blood of Christ washes us."[44]

In addition to the references cited above from Lieb and Kelley, we should remember Psalm 114, "and at the presence be agast / Of him that ever was, and ay shall last" (15–16); *Paradise Lost* 8.311–14: "Here had new begun / My wandring, had not hee who was my Guide / Up hither, from among the Trees appeer'd, / Presence Divine"; *Paradise Lost* 10.144–45: "To whom the sovran Presence thus repli'd, / Was shee thy God"; *A Treatise of Civil Power* (YP 7:257): The "churchmen, who...never cease calling on the civil magistrate to interpose his fleshlie force; an argument that all true ministerial and spiritual power is dead within them: who think the gospel...cannot stand or continue, supported by the same divine presence and protection to the worlds end"; and *Hirelings* (YP 7:318): "our Saviour; who hath promisd, without this condition, both his holy spirit and his own presence with his church to the worlds end." Special attention should be paid to *Paradise Lost* 11.335–38, which Kelley cites:

> *Adam,* thou know'st Heav'n his, and all the Earth,
> Not this Rock onely; his Omnipresence fills Earth,
> Land, Sea, and Air, and every kind that lives,
> Fomented by his virtual power and warmd.

These uses emphasize the presence of God, and extend to "our Saviour" through his church, in Milton's thinking. While the people of Dan in *Samson Agonistes* ignore their role in God's "plan to the worlds end," even as Samson had in his former misconceived actions, they are aware of the hidden God whose Divine Presence is everywhere (just as Michael reminds Adam of his "virtual power"). Such Divine Presence exists for Milton in the Lord's Supper, not through anything carnal, not because of God's omnipresence, but through his "glory," through that faith—Milton's and "Worthy Receivers'"—in the Godhead and in remembrance of Christ's sacrifice, inwardly and spiritually, which it manifests. The sacrifice is remembered and commemorated, not reenacted, in such Protestant thinking.

There have been some references to God's glory in remarks cited before. The "concept of *summa gloria* or *divinæ gloriæ*" as "reminders both of God's grandeur and of his ultimate removal from the realm of human comprehension" lies in various texts of the Bible, especially Ezekiel and Revelation, as Michael Lieb analyzes the concept. The Hebrew term for "glory" is *kabod:* it points to a God (as in chapter 2 of *De doctrina Christiana*) as a "deity...at its most fearsome, awesome, and essentially threatening as a mode of representation. It is God at his most 'glorious,' but it is also God at his most secret, mysterious, and 'inconceivable,'" Lieb continues. John Rumrich's full discussion of *The Matter of Glory* in *Paradise Lost* further explicates that twofold meaning in the term *kabod*, the "sensible manifestations of his majesty through his creatures" and God's "*Divine Essence*" as seen, for example, in his mercies. Rumrich most significantly relates this double meaning to Milton's earliest poems, the translations of Psalm 114 and of Psalm 136.[45] In discussing the attributes of God, Milton states that "The flower" (indicated through the verb *efflorescit*) they create "is that supreme excellence of God, by virtue of which he is truly perfect and truly blessed in supreme glory, and through which he is most justly and deservedly the supreme Lord of all things, as he is often called" (YP 6:151). We can understand, thereby, the double meaning of *kabod* given here and understand how the concept of the Lord's Supper, for him, points to the remembrance (for humankind, it seems, needs the constant reminder of God and his deity and relationship with his true servants) of both God's divinity (glory) *and* God's mercies toward his creatures.[46] Although he does not discuss transubstantiation, Rumrich points us to Milton's belief that "by faith in Christ man can gradually be 'transformed'": "The same glory that appears in the revelation of light out of darkness in creation shines in the face of Christ, and versions of that glory shine in the faces of all unfallen and redeemed creatures."[47]

Milton's faith exists from the beginning; on such issues as God's glory and God's omnipotence, omniscience, and omnipresence, *and* God's "mercies," his is an unchanged mind. Yet one can see a development of intensity, of recognition of others' thoughts and what he found unacceptable in them, of a need for change in others, not only in religious matters but political matters as they include religion as well. Alongside Psalm 114, *Paradise Lost*, *Paradise Regain'd*, and *Samson Agonistes*, as well as a work like *Tenure of Kings and Magistrates*, demonstrate that intensity, that need for transformation in humankind, the development of mind that goes beyond his own faith. Yet, as Achsah Guibbory remarks, "Milton speaking through Samson and the Son absolves himself of the responsibility of transforming 'the people.'" His apparent lack of public worship was provoked, I suggest, by "the impossibility—of Milton's imagining in 1671 what form true rites of worship might take," as Guibbory concludes. "The desire to integrate external and internal, to connect body and spirit in worship, which characterized ceremonialist ideology and shapes Milton's representation of Edenic love, is at odds with fear that the body will pull down the spirit, distract it from God—the fear that drives the puritan rejection of ceremony."[48]

SEVEN

Conceptual Reflections in Milton's Poetry and Prose

For the reader and scholar of literature the words and images employed to communicate the meanings, experience, creation, and enjoyment of that literature are extremely important—they are the very elements constituting any reading or analysis. I have in previous chapters paid attention to words and images and the specific concepts that are carried within their usage. We receive pictures that supply connotative realizations, leading the reader to more than surface, denotative meaning. Some of those pictures provide allusions to other words and depictions and situations, sometimes other writing, other happenings, and sometimes, thereby, deeper meanings. Allusion may lead us to things that lie outside the writing we are reading; they may be sources the author is echoing, consciously or unconsciously.[1] But allusion may also lead us to the fuller text by being self-referential, by internal allusion, cued often by repetition, echo, prolepsis. The word or image with its conceptual connotation adds meaning with each echoing occurrence,[2] perhaps alters meaning that has been misinterpreted (often deliberately intended by the author), becomes witness to the author's composition and artistry and intended conception to be communicated or to be made ambiguous (destabilized, to recall Peter Herman's significant description in chapter 1), at times to undermine and even oppose what the reader would first have concluded.

This chapter first looks at a different kind of conceptual development: the alteration of meaning ("concept") in a literary work through allusion and particularly through internal allusion. It is not that the essence of the concept has changed but that the reader's understanding of the concept may change, and it may move into the realm of uncertainty, even fallibility. Second, specific words, including some treated earlier, are shown to bear connotations that have often been unacknowledged (or not recognized at all), adding to or altering concepts that otherwise would seem to be delimited in many readings of Milton's work.

1

We are all aware of an author's using allusions to other authors and works in order to achieve a depth of meaning and context well beyond the denotation of the words or their specific appearance in the author's text. At times the meaning or context is iterative; at other times it yields additional knowledge or sets up irony or satire or even paronomasia. It may serve particularly to link events and thoughts across a period of time, thus stressing likenesses and differences. Critical arguments have been lodged against things like variora that point out only the existence of an allusion, but, to repeat myself, "The fault...lies in the lack of attention that has generally been paid to such citations by those who have made them....

Most commentators have simply cited a source because of a language similarity, or at least they do not generally go beyond simple citation."[3] But while allusions as sources are important, so is self-allusion, internal allusion within a work.

The first words of *Paradise Lost* take us immediately to the Bible, for example, the reader not even being required to understand them as biblical, for they state common and much-repeated lore:

> Of Mans First Disobedience, and the Fruit
> Of that Forbidden Tree, whose mortal tast
> Brought Death into the World, and all our woe,
> With loss of *Eden*.

Recalling the common and much-repeated lore about the Fall of humankind through its disobedience of breaking God's one prohibition by eating the fruit of a particular tree in Eden, the reader may immediately think of "apple" and "Eve" and "sin." Recalling the usual Bible translation, near its beginning in chapter 3 of Genesis, another reader may remember further that the text specifically cites the woman's quoting God as admonishing them not to eat or even touch it "lest ye die," and, of course, the role of the serpent is elaborated upon. But as we read those first four lines of the poem carefully we understand that this is only "Man's" *first* disobedience, and we recognize that Milton is punning in talking of a *mortal* taste since that adjective ("of man," human) derives from the Latin for death. Significantly Milton says "Man's disobedience," meaning obviously humankind's (as the word is used in chapter 1 of Genesis: "in the image of God created he him [Man]; male and female created he them"). Later on in the poem we see that Eve's eating of the fruit brings sin, and Adam's eating of the fruit establishes death. The opening lines unite Eve and Adam in the Fall as breaking the prohibition but they also stress (as we read on) what will be Milton's view of the Fall within the poem (a somewhat different view, let it be observed): it is through Adam's (generically, man and woman's) tasting of the fruit that death enters humankind's world. Of Satan's rebellion in heaven the narrative voice had said (prior to the account of the Fall itself), "to such evil brought / By sin of disobedience" (6.395–96), and it is Eve's act of first disobedience that ushers sin into humankind's world, but only, we are told, with *"signs of woe,"* not knowing that she was "eating Death" (9.783, 792). The woe and the death have not yet been established; Milton's internal referencing, echoing, and allusion express more fully the story and ideas that the proleptic statement opening the epic might proffer the reader. And, we ought to admit, this deeper reading corrects what might have been an incomplete reading, a somewhat inaccurate reading—that is, a prejudiced reading of what the Bible may imply or at least as it has been understood: Eve as the cause of the Fall, Woman as agent of Man's Fall, the genderization of humankind into good and evil. John Donne, of course, referred to this ubiquitous misconception when he wrote, "Must I, who came to travaile thorow you, / Grow your fixt subject, because you are true?" ("The Indifferent," 17–18). The two-stage Fall is delineated in book 9, with the more significant cause being the man's succumbing to the temptation of "Femal charm," "not deceav'd," with the popular accusation against woman being the burden of Adam's diatribe in book 10—after the Fall has been completed.

When Adam engorges the fruit, "not deceav'd," the woes of Nature are detailed:

> Earth trembl'd from her entrails, as again
> In pangs, and Nature gave a second groan,
> Skie low'rd, and muttering Thunder, som sad drops
> Wept at *compleating* of the mortal Sin
> Original.   (9.998, 1000–1004; my emphasis)

I cannot overemphasize the word "compleating": the sin is complete only with Adam's partaking of the fruit, disobeying God, but doing so not deceived at what he is doing, as Eve had been by the serpent. (While these words are spoken by the narrative voice, they offer a concept that Milton himself, at least, had to have entertained.) The death that is encased in Eve's act causes the garland of flowers Adam has prepared to give her to drop and fade, just as she to him is "Defac't, deflowrd, and now to Death devote" (9.901). And so he resolves "to Die" and "t' incurr / Divine displeasure for her sake, or Death" (9.992–93). With *his* eating of the fruit, "Death" has been brought "into the World, and all our woe": the mortal sin has been completed with Adam's nonfraudulent but willful act of disobedience.

Returning to those first four lines we should now be struck by the realization that Milton is urging that "Man's" first disobedience is not simply Eve's act but Eve's and Adam's acts. Generations of biblicists have been wrong, according to his thinking: it was not Eve's act, resulting from deceit by the serpent, that established the Fall, but the joining of Adam's act, through willfulness, not through deceit, that completed that momentous Fall. To redeem this state of affairs for mortal Man, humankind must wait "till one greater Man / Restore us, and regain the blissful Seat" (1.4–5). The reference immediately says to the average (or Christian) reader, Jesus, Son of God, but what is to be understood is that Jesus combines those attributes that "Man" in Genesis 1 defines: "male and female created he them." These attributes—male and female—will be delineated in two lines notoriously interpreted by those wishing to cast Milton as a misogynist: "For contemplation hee and valour formed. / For softness shee and sweet attractive Grace" (*PL* 4.297–98). The lines become a chiasmus (see comment in chapter 5, note 4). That is, "contemplation" (the mind) is to "attractive Grace" (the mind and soul) as "valour" (strength and courage, the body) is to "softness" (the body), creating a chiasmus. The "one greater Man" will encompass the whole being of Man, humanity, male and female, as created in the image of God. The chi, X, depicted here states that the Son as the Christ represents contemplation (the mind), valour (bravery of body), softness (Christ's mercy), and "attractive Grace" (God's love).

That sense of unity of male and female is, as has often been pointed out, made physically clear by the hand-in-hand image throughout the poem (as well as the disunity through the separation of hands), and of course in the phrase "wedded Love" (4.750). The hand-in-hand image describes two different persons joined as one entity, a reflection of the two persons of God who is one. The two verbs in line 5, "Restore" and "regain," are subjunctives, indicating that there is uncertainty of such restoration and such regaining of paradise, for while the Son provides for the salvation that will occur for such as Ezekiel or Elijah, it will not occur for the sons of Belial or a Nimrod, whose actions determine their fate.

Allusion takes many forms, and I employ the concept as discussed by John Hollander, who demonstrates the way this concept may be acoustical or allegorical, schematic or metaphorical, or metaleptic. But we should also be wary, as John Leonard points out, that at times the allusion (both literary and historical) may be erroneous: was it a simple mistake, a purposive mistake to create irony, perhaps, or a psychologically revealing one?[4] The gaffe in *Areopagitica* of having the palmer accompany Sir Guyon to the Cave of Mammon (*Faerie Queene* 2.7.2) has resulted in many comments on Milton's error (the palmer did not proceed to the Cave of Mammon). The most significant, I think, is Ernest Sirluck's note that Milton has missed the point of Spenser's allegory: while it can be read to mean that Man does not need reason (the palmer) to resist the temptation of wealth, he does need reason to resist "the bowr of earthly blisse" represented by Acrasia's bower, which follows the encounter with Mammon (*Areopagitica*, YP 2:516 and n108). Or there is the amazingly nondoctrinal and most illogical last line of *At a Solemn Music*, given three times in Milton's holograph in the Trinity Manuscript, where God is presented as joining in the palmers' and harpers' singing before God's throne (Rev. 7:9–10, 14:2–3).

Milton is sometimes very subtle in his use of allusions and particularly in his echoes, proleptic passages, and internal allusion. Lines 602–07 of book 7, following the recitation of the six days of Creation and the Son's return to heaven, are truly interesting in this regard (the reader should read very carefully):

> Great are thy works, *Jehovah*, infinite
> Thy power; what thought can measure thee or tongue
> Relate thee; greater now in thy return
> Then from the Rebel Angels; thee that day
> Thy Thunders magnifi'd; but to create
> Is greater then created to destroy.

The contrast in book 6 and book 7 between the defeat and destruction of the rebellious angels and their being doomed to hell and the creation of a new world peopled with innocent creatures—fish, fowl, beasts, humans—is strongly and validly and *unavoidably* recorded in the heavenly host's words. But note that we are here seeing another reprise of the contrast between the strength of the male, needed to defeat these insurrectionists as in the Son's victory in book 6, and the compassion and birthing of the female as in the relenting opportunity for obedience offered through this creation in book 7 and in the creation of humankind to demonstrate its obedience.

Perhaps there is someone who read my quotation just now who recognized that I did *not* present exactly what Milton wrote. The poem does not read "in thy return / Then from the Rebel Angels"; it reads "in thy return / Then from the Giant Angels." Milton's word "Giant" is, first, a parodic insult. They are not giants: they are insignificant pygmies, trivial puppets, diminished things. (The ending of book 1 echoes.) But the word is, as well, an allusion supplying added significance and meaning that evokes prior usage, application, and resonances—developing a historical though mythic panorama linking all such giants, all such rebels, together as descendants of Satan and his cohorts. The Giants of the Earth were the sons of Ge or Gæa, the Earth, who revolted against Zeus in Hesiod's *Theogony* (line 185), assaulting Olympus, and seen as a savage race of men by Homer (*Odyssey*, 7.59), leading to the reading of the myth as a description of the constant fight of civilization against barbarism. The gods, however, can defeat the giants only with the help of a mortal; this is Herakles, who thus is seen as a type of the Christ, and the myth thus as an analogue of the revolt of Satan against God and the defeat of the rebel angels by the Son. The myth has other facets that are repeated in other epics as well as *Paradise Lost*, and we might compare George Sandys's comment on Ovid's *Metamorphoses* (1.151–55): "Pherecides the Syrian writes how the Divels were throwne out of heaven by *Jupiter* (this fall of the Gyants perhaps an allusion to that of the Angells) the chiefe called *Ophioneus*, which signifies Serpentine: having after made use of that creature to poyson *Eve* with false ambition."[5]

Not only does Milton subtly allude to this myth and its Christian interpretations here, but he likewise points to a reprise of *Paradise Lost* 6.640–67 and its biblical source. Here the hurling and uprooting of land, which Hesiod among others reports of the Giants, reinforces the Christian message, equating the rebel angels with the Giants of the Earth:

> Thir Arms away they threw, and to the Hills
> ....
> Light as the Lightning glimps they ran, they flew,
> From thir foundations loosning to and fro
> They pluckt the seated Hills with all thir load,
> Rocks, Waters, Woods, and by the shaggie tops
> Uplifting bore them in thir hands. (*PL* 6.639, 642–46)

But God turns the table on "the rebel Host":

> coming towards them so dread they saw
> The bottom of the Mountains upward turn'd,

> Till on those cursed Engins triple-row
> They saw them whelm'd, and all thir confidence
> Under the weight of Mountains buried deep,
> ....
> That under ground they fought in dismal shade;
> Infernal noise.   (648–52, 666–67)

The classical references are, first, to the piling of Mount Pelion on Mount Ossa by the Giants, and, second, the burying of the bodies of the Giants under volcanoes, such as Mount Etna. The equation with hell is clear. The typological reading invokes Revelation 6:14–16 with its aggregate of all who oppose God and his righteousness:

> and every mountain and island were moved out of their places. And the kings of the earth, and the great men, and the rich men, and the chief captains, and the mighty men, and every bondman, and every free man, hid themselves in the dens and in the rocks of the mountains; and said to the mountains and rocks, Fall on us, and hide us from the face of him that sitteth on the throne, and from the wrath of the Lamb.

This, some readers of the Bible know, is an echo of Hosea 10:8: "The high places also of Aven, the sin of Israel, shall be destroyed:... and they shall say to the mountains, Cover us; and to the hills, Fall on us." Even more significantly, Luke 23:30 reports that at the Crucifixion, Jesus said to the bewailing and lamenting women to weep for themselves and their children and their barrenness, and "then shall they begin to say to the mountains, Fall on us; and to the hills, Cover us." But those who know their *Paradise Lost* well have also heard its variant, which notes, not mountains and rocks, but natural vegetation. Adam laments his disobedience whereby they "Good lost, and Evil got," the result of their "foul concupiscence" thus:

> O might I here
> In solitude live savage, in some glade
> Obscur'd,
> ....

> Cover me ye Pines,
> Ye Cedars, with innumerable boughs
> Hide me, where I may never see them more.
>   (*PL* 9.1084–86, 1088–90)

The interlocking allusions and echoes lead to readings placing the events and persons of the epic into a continuing panorama of mythic and biblical lore, setting up comparisons and contrasts that in turn amplify and alter our inference of what we state as John Milton's message and beliefs and artistic achievement in this work. And particularly thinking of some recent criticism on Milton and his epic, we should reconsider the concepts of gender and gender recriminations.[6] The ideas readers draw from the epic seem to be in flux as concepts are developed and variously encountered, yet there is a continuance of the same moral and theologically loaded image that epitomizes the guilty person's attempt to escape retribution through hiding and secrecy, and the unavoidable omnipresence and omniscience of God.

There is, however, another comparative point that Milton's text will have evoked in the reader's mind in the previously cited passages. In book 1 the "Giant" rebels, now in hell, build Pandaemonium and enter in:

> Behold a wonder! they but now who seemd
> In bigness to surpass Earths Giant Sons
> Now less than smallest Dwarfs, in narrow room
> Throng numberless, like that Pigmean Race
> Beyond the *Indian* Mount, or Faerie Elves.   (1.777–81)

The passage makes clear that "Giant" status is only the egocentric view of Self. It tells us much about Satan and the other fallen angels in the very first book of the epic, and the alleged devolution of Satan is with the reader from the beginning. Milton's playing unfairly as we proceed through the full text, culminating in the serpentine creatures the devils become in book 10, has contributed to the view that Milton was of the devil's party. Yet he has not advanced Satan as hero if we read the text carefully. The seeming devolution of Satan as the epic continues has two functions: first, to chronicle the recognition of his and his companions' declining positive view that they present to themselves of themselves, and second, to reorient the reader's inadequate and superficial awareness of the "hunderds and...thousands trooping" into "the spacious Hall," "Thick swarm'd, both on the ground and in the air, / Brusht with the hiss of russling wings. As Bees," a "thick...aerie crowd Swarm'd" (1.760–76) that will be metaphorized (as well as metamorphized) as "hissing through the Hall, thick swarming now," then "issuing forth to th' open Field...a crowd / Of ugly Serpents...the dire hiss renew'd,...exploding hiss,...rould in heaps, and up the Trees / Climbing, sat thicker then the snakie locks / That curld *Megæra*" (10.522–60). What is changed is external form; what remains unabated is the internal being of "incorporeal Spirits [who] to smallest forms / Reduc'd thir shapes immense" (1.789–90).

Most appropriately the reference to Megæra, one of the Furies, reminds us of the retribution that all those who are jealous will experience, underscoring the jealousy of Satan and the fallen angels toward God and especially toward God the Son. The uncertain generation of the Furies (or Erinyes) cast them as daughters of Gæa (the Earth) and Erebus (Darkness, a son of Chaos), or of Nyx (Night). The visit of Satan to Chaos and Old Night in book 2, aside from all that has been written about this episode, is significant to someone knowing the mythology surrounding the three Furies. We can analyze Satan psychologically as attempting to get revenge on God, such as he is trying to prepare for (although it should be the other way around, were God not God), because, ironically, it was his jealousy, his constant anger (Allecto), and his "murdering" of Man (Tisiphone) that has now led to his (and his fellow devils') fate as serpentine creatures. The daughters descendant from Chaos and Old Night have led to his situation; psychic eradication (though impossible) leads him to seek revenge on God, who "provoked" such feelings, which have led to his state of hell and in hell, through use of the like forms of "Fury" avengement—jealousy, anger, and the "murder" of Adam and Eve and their descendants. The episode in book 2 is ultimately a kind of prolepsis of what will come to pass in book 10, where the Furies effect their vengeance upon the fallen angels.

The multiplicity of the foregoing interlocked allusions was triggered by that one word "Giant," where a word like "rebel" would have delimited the passage in book 7 to only the war in heaven. Similarly it is but one phrase—"nothing loath" (9.1039)—that tells us much about the heritage of Milton's poem and its striking influence on one later author's consciousness, its reappearance informing the later author's reader of, as in this case, what he is really saying as well as suggesting a psychological analysis of the literary characters and the event that is happening—*and with a good touch of the psychic self of the author.* I refer here to the passage in book 9 shortly after Adam has eaten the fruit and

> displaid
> Carnal desire enflaming, [when] hee on *Eve*
> Began to cast lascivious Eyes, [and] shee him
> As wantonly repaid; in Lust they burn.   (9.1011–15)

Adam asserts, "Much pleasure we have lost...now let us play...With ardor to enjoy thee," and seizes her hand, "and to a shadie bank, / Thick overhead with verdant roof imbowr'd / He led her nothing loath" (1022–39). Eve, that is, does not draw back and is indeed eager to "play": she is in no way loath to enjoy *him*. As I have pointed out elsewhere, John Cleland in *Memoires of a Lady of Pleasure* (1747–48)—a novel we know as "Fanny Hill"—writes of Louisa, who is led to a couch by a young lord (with a group of voyeurs around the hall): "The girl, spreading herself to the best advantage, with her head upon the pillow, was so concentered in what she was about" that the others' presence "seemed the least of her care and concern." The fiction that she is inexperienced, that it is the young lord only who is sexually anxious, that *he* is seducing *her* is exploded by those two words: she goes "nothing loath." We pick up on the graphic description of "spreading herself to the best advantage." The allusion creates a linkage over time that calls all such "seductions" types of the incipient Fall of humankind, but it also iterates the commonplace that Cleland would appear to subscribe to that it was Eve who was the enticer: woman, the cause of man's damnation.[7]

That there is change in the physicality of sexual intercourse and especially attitudes toward it between pre- and post-worlds (book 4 and book 9) is fundamental within a reading of the poem. It causes the narrative voice to divide so-called love relations between man and woman as those between "wedded Love" and "Harlots, loveless, joyless, unindeard" as well as "Court Amours." (The lines seem to emerge from what would be considered the male's experience.) Is this Milton? Does Milton firmly believe this, without any intervening concessions? If it is Milton, does he ever alter this view of the sexes—that woman is either faithful wife or whore, man is faithful husband and at times unfaithful "client"? The emphasis here on "our mutual help / And mutual love" (4.727–28) and the helpmate, mutuality, conversation (and loneliness without such "conversation") in the divorce tracts would appear to supply a positive answer to the first two questions and no certain answer to the last. But what can be inferred is a devaluation of the male from an exalted archetype through Adam's actions and lack of faith and a recovery of the female through Eve's ascendant charitableness. These developed concepts suggest a "changed" mind, but with a continued trust in God as well.

3

I began this chapter with the first lines of the epic; I now turn to the last lines and a significant internal allusion that I suspect few readers of *Paradise Lost* have observed. Adam and Eve leave Eden with "The World...all before them"; their place of rest is for them to choose; they go with "wandring steps and slow"—that word "wandring," however, having the double meaning of uncertainty and of potential error, even sinfulness in those steps. We like to think that they will heed the Providence that is their guide and that they will hear Conscience, as the Father speaks of it in book 3, so that "Light after light well us'd they shall attain, / And to the end persisting, safe arrive" (3.194–97). *But* subtle Milton has, a few lines before Adam and Eve leave Eden, informed us that they go not only with Michael's admonition and the promise that Eve's seed "shall all restore" and especially with God's Providence, but they also go with Satan near at hand, so that indeed where they choose their place of rest may result from those "wandring" steps. The scene of their departure is described thus:

> on the ground
> Gliding meteorous, as Ev'ning Mist
> Ris'n from a River o're the marish glides,
> And gathers ground fast at the Labourers heel
> Homeward returning.   (12.628–32)

Not only will Adam and Eve and their progeny be laborers (as part of the punishment detailed in book 10), not only does the mist gather around the laborer's heel (we remember that in the protevangelium the serpent will bruise the heel of the Promised Seed), and not only are they attempting to return "home" ("thir [late] happie seat," "the blissful Seat" of line 5 of the poem), but Satan will be near at hand as that "Ev'ning Mist" tells the reader attuned to internal allusion. When Satan first enters Paradise in book 9,

> There was a place,
> Now not, though Sin, not time, first wraught the change,
> Where *Tigris* at the foot of Paradise
> Into a Gulf shot under ground, till part
> Rose up a Fountain by the Tree of Life;
> In with the River sunk, and with it rose
> Satan involv'd in rising Mist, then sought
> Where to lie hid.   (9.69–76)

The rising mist near the Tree of Life, "involving" Satan with its sense of "enfolding,"[8] has been a metaleptic plant for us to recall when the setting of the Fall is presented in book 9, and then later as the result of that Fall proceeds and the expulsion from Eden occurs. Satan will avoid "the vigilance" of the watchful "flaming Ministers" "thus wrapt in mist / Of midnight vapor glide obscure" (9.156–59); "Like a black mist low creeping" (180) he finds the serpent. (There is almost an oxymoronic insinuation of the river, the mist that is Satan, and the flaming ministers, like the "burning lake" that begins the poem from which Satan had risen.)

Note the repetition of the word "glide" but a lack of a substantive that is said to be "Gliding meteorous," at the end of the poem, thus hiding from the reader, as it were, the presence of Satan. But the concept of a meteor that has descended to earth, particularly in this adjectival form, implies some incandescent light (and perhaps Milton knew that geologically the word points to water derived from the atmosphere, and thus there are the mist, the river, and the marish). A few lines later "The brandisht Sword" blazes "Fierce as a Comet" and desiccation envelops the land. The images all work together to emphasize again: *Satan*. For in book 2, lines 707–11, a much remarked simile asserts that,

> Incenst with indignation *Satan* stood
> Unterrifi'd, and like a Comet burn'd,
> That fires the length of *Ophiucus* huge

>   In th' Artick Sky, and from his horrid hair
>   Shakes Pestilence and Warr.[9]

The protecting Sword of God blazes to counter whatever aspect Satan or a disciple adopts, even when "fierce as a comet," to make certain that none but the worthy, the obedient, will enter the "happie seat" henceforth.

Paradise Lost is easy enough to read and understand its caution and advice for a general audience who know the well-known story only, even with Milton's amplifications. But for the "fit audience, though few" it says much more: it interrelates so much more about life, who we are, what may be our future, how we may influence our future, most emphatically demonstrating an amazing workmanship and artistry on the part of the blind man, Milton. It is not Milton's concept of Satan that has changed as we work our way through the poem: it is the reader's having fallen into his trap of finding in Satan a "heroic" figure that *should* have changed, for in life humankind does seem to find evil, immorality, and fairly exclusive selfness attractive. But for Milton such a concept is faithless of God and God's ways toward men. *Milton's* concept does not change (though over the years it has probably been honed to true and conscious recognition), but its presentation does allow for argument for an opposed concept, for development on the part of his fit reader of a "godly" concept, of a rejection of "mist" replaced by the sun of enlightenment.

4

Language takes on notable connotations, generally and also most specifically for an author, so much so that frequently when a word is used its connotations come to the fore, almost obliterating its denotation. Puns are, of course, built upon this kind of multiple meaning within a word. A well-known one is the adjective used in conjunction with the bridge that Sin and Death create from hell to earth: "Now had they brought the work by wondrous Art /

Pontifical, a ridge of pendent Rock / Over the vext Abyss, following the track / Of *Satan*" (10.312–15). The Latin *pons, pontis* is a bridge, but of course the form used here puns on "pontifical" as related to "papal," thus assigning art that produced the now-easy passage into hell to the Roman Catholic papacy and associating Satan with the pope. (This association had early been inscribed by the intolerant Milton of *In Quintum Novembris* in 1626.) It affords easy passage to hell and should be contrasted with Jacob's "Stairs" (3.510) leading from earth to heaven for the true servants of God. The bridge is referred to in 10.348 as "this new wondrous Pontifice" (at which point Satan meets his children), indicating its relationship with a "high priest of the Catholic church," "the Pope." (Forms of this basic word appear several times in the prose with similar sarcasm and bias. These examples do not show incertitude or change over the years or through any altered contexts as to Milton's attitude toward the papacy, and thus thereby the Roman Catholic religion.)

When the Lady defies Comus saying, "Thou hast nor Ear, nor Soul to apprehend / The sublime notion, and high mystery / That must be utter'd to unfold the sage / And serious doctrine of Virginity" (784–87), that word "mystery" indicates that she believes this doctrine to be beyond his comprehension, but she also refers to a religious article of faith known only to the initiated, a common enough practice of religiously oriented cults and ancient secret societies. For the Christian it implies a belief communicated to humankind through divine revelation and often one that human reason cannot validate or nature cannot exemplify. Here the concept of the awards of celibacy and virginity, and hinting at the virgin birth, is evoked, and thus a sexual context often hangs over the word as when "*Eve* the Rites / Mysterious of connubial Love" did not refuse (4.743) and when the narrator tells us that "those mysterious parts were [not] then conceald" (4.312). Not all uses, of course, will partake of the connotation—the "grievous Wolves, /

Who all the sacred mysteries of Heav'n / To thir own vile advantages shall turn" (12.508–10) or the minister who "sustains the person of Christ in his highest work of communicating to us the mysteries of our salvation" (*Reason of Church-Government*, 14; YP 1:767).

Pursuing such connotative language, though it may be subtle, even sly, will add seemingly hidden and thus often unacknowledged thought, characterization, satire, and ambiguity to a line or a passage. We may instance the word "dubious" in *Paradise Lost* 1.104: "His utmost power with adverse power oppos'd / In dubious Battel on the Plains of Heav'n." Satan uses the word to suggest that the revolt of the angels following his lead was not certain of outcome, but subtle Milton is pointing out that any battle against the omnipotent God is an action that in no way is "dubious" of outcome: God's "utmost" power cannot be matched by any "adverse" power, and such a battle is dubious because its outcome is certain. Satan's justification of his action in these lines has no substance (although Satan-as-hero critics have ignored these innuendoes). Or look at the lines in 4.295–96: "though both / Not equal, as thir sex not equal seemd," where the physicality of Adam and Eve's genital ("sexual") parts are not the same and thus, in Satan's viewing, "seemd," the narrative voice remarks, not equal in actions of "sex." Milton implies by that word "seemd" that their "sex" is, or could be, equal: that is, their sexual action and enjoyment could be equal, despite the obvious differences of gender and its attributes. The main point is that they are not equal *only* as their "sex" *seems* not to be equal. Adam and Eve are not equal only in physical ways: they are or may be equal in other ways. (The line, of course, sets up the following three lines, which have been so much debated in terms of masculine superiority over the feminine—without, unfortunately, attention to this preceding line.)

Or look at the word "gaze," which Milton in book 9 is careful to distinguish as not simply a look, an innocent steady seeing with one's eyes, but a libidinous staring with hopes of sexual gratification for the gazer. The first occurrence is in line 524.[10] The sensual reading of these lines as well as what will be discerned as a phallic reference later in the temptation scene has been frequently pointed out. That word "play" in line 528 is a dead giveaway of the sexual content. As Harold Fisch noted long ago, "Jewish commentators had glossed the word *play* (*saheq*) as a reference to sexual orgies," and "After tasting the forbidden fruit, Adam declares: 'But come, so well refresh't, now let us play, / As meet is after such delicious Fare' (IX, 1027–28)."[11] Satan employs the word soon after this first usage (line 535: "and gaze / Insatiate"); a few lines later we read: "Thee all things living gaze on, all things thine / By gift, and thy Celestial Beautie adore / With ravishment" (539–41), and he persists in lines 578–83.[12] Immediately afterward the "sly Snake" again praises in enticement

> thy Beauties...which compel'd
> Mee thus, though importune perhaps, to come
> And gaze, and worship thee of right declar'd
> Sovran of Creatures, universal Dame.   (613, 607–12)

Having taken the "yet sinless" Eve to the forbidden tree, which she looks upon but abstains to taste or touch, Satan "New part puts on, and as to passion mov'd, / Fluctuats disturb'd, yet comely, and in act / Rais'd," urging her "need of this fair Fruit" and as "Goddess humane, [to] reach then, and freely taste" (667–69, 731–32). (We observe the male sexual implications of "New part puts on," "Fluctuats," and "in act Rais'd.") His words too easy entrance into her heart won (733–34), and

> Fixt on the Fruit she gaz'd, which to behold
> Might tempt alone, and in her ears the sound
> Yet rung of his perswasive words, impregn'd
> With Reason, to her seeming, and with Truth,

which adds the sense of hearing to the scene, as she gazes on "that Fruit, which with desire, / Inclinable now grown to touch or taste, / Sollicited her longing eye" (735–38,

741–43). "Her rash hand" thus reaches "to the Fruit," which she plucks and eats (780–81). While Adam views the fair, enticing fruit Eve gives him, Adam's scrupling not to eat is not described in terms of sight—he does not "gaze" upon it—but as soon as he has partaken of it, "hee on *Eve* / Began to cast lascivious Eyes" (1014–15).

As we might expect, the proleptic dream recounted in book 5 has prepared us for this significant use of the word "gaze." Eve tells Adam of the voice who has said:

> Heav'n wakes with all his eyes,
> Whom to behold but thee, Natures desire,
> In whose sight all things joy, with ravishment
> Attracted by thy beauty still to gaze. (5.44–47)

Soon "One shap'd and wing'd like one of those from Heav'n / By us oft seen..., on that Tree he also gaz'd" (55–57), and now that little word "also" takes on a more forceful meaning. For, although Eve in her dream has not succumbed, transference of the word to her in her dream gives the reader a clue that she will succumb.[13]

"Gaze" is not always specifically imbued with this meaning, but it does raise questions, I would suggest, of a culpable excessiveness, a negativity that may not be without subtle errancy. In "Arcades," for instance, the Genius of the Wood leads the swains where they "may more neer behold" the countess, "Which I full oft amidst these shades alone / Have sate to wonder at, and gaze upon" (40–43). Many of my readers are probably remembering Samson's being "Made of my Enemies the scorn and gaze" (34) and his being "to visitants a gaze, / Or pitied object" (567–68). Even in *Paradise Lost* 5.272, we may be directed to a sly censure of those who would think Raphael a phoenix, a metaphoric likening that should be reserved for the Son alone:

> till within soar
> Of Towring Eagles, to all the Fowls he seems
> A *Phœnix*, gaz'd by all, as that sole Bird

> When to enshrine his reliques in the Sun's
> Bright Temple, to *Ægyptian Thebes* he flies.   (5:270–74)

Only the Son should be conceived of as enshrining his "reliques" (that is, remnants of his holy body and of belief and reverence) in the sun's bright temple. The "all" who gaze thus become idolaters who misconceive the true Christ. The last line here corroborates the wrongness of the gazing others in casting Raphael as a phoenix (indeed, it should be "the" phoenix since mythologically there was only one in existence at any given time—"a" immediately suggests a metaphoric blasphemy against the "only begotten Son") when he flies to "*Ægyptian Thebes*," for as Ovid had reported, the phoenix arose from its own ashes ("his reliques") in Heliopolis (that is, "the city of the sun") rather than in the neighboring city of Thebes (see *Metamorphoses*, 15.391–407). Modern scholarship has reported confusion in the Renaissance between Heliopolis and Thebes, but is Milton following that confusion unaware? or on purpose making a false identification?

As remarked in chapter 2, the word and the concept of "convey" and its substantive form, "conveyance," have not been studied in Milton's work. Although the questionable and fraudulent connotations that attach to those words do not seem to attach to Milton's contract for *Paradise Lost*, we cannot say this about Satan and his influence in *Paradise Lost*, the only poetic work of Milton's that uses the word "convey" in any of its forms. These negative connotations rear up in the use to which the word is used in the epic, implying Milton's awareness of this concept of "conveying" and a purposive use of it.

It is the creation of Pandaemonium "By strange conveyance" (*PL* 1.707) that is our first meeting with the word in the poem:

> A third [multitude of devils] as soon had form'd within the ground
> A various mould, and from the boyling cells

> By strange conveyance fill'd each hollow nook,
> As in an Organ from one blast of wind
> To many a row of Pipes the sound-board breaths.
>   (1.705–09)

It appears again through "dev'lish machination" in 6.515, when

>   Sulphurous and Nitrous Foam
> They found, they mingl'd, and with suttle Art,
> Concocted and adusted they reduc'd
> To blackest grain, and into store convey'd.   (6.512–15)

In book 10 Sin exhorts her son to help found a path to earth since something draws her on,

>   som connatural force
> Powerful at greatest distance to unite
> With secret amity things of like kind
> By secretest conveyance.   (10.246–49)

The final appearance of the word in the epic also has a reference to "ownership," for it is used by Adam in reacting to Nimrod and the tower of Babel:

>   to God his Tower intends
> Siege and defiance: Wretched man! what food
> Will he convey up thither to sustain
> Himself and his rash Armie.   (12.73–76)

There are two further uses of "convey" in *Paradise Lost*, both in book 8. The first is mixed: while it is not "negative," it is specifically put into a negative and doubtful context. Raphael, talking of suns and moons, those that shine on earth and those many others shining on places "unpossest / By living Soul," tells Adam that these latter

> Onely to shine, yet scarce to contribute
> Each Orb a glimps of Light, conveyd so farr
> Down to this habitable, which returns
> Light back to them, is obvious to dispute.   (8.155–58)

The other usage is negative in that it rejects the need for "conveyance" in angelic relationships: "nor restrain'd conveyance need" (8.628):

> if Spirits embrace,
> Total they mix, Union of Pure with Pure
> Desiring; nor restrain'd conveyance need
> As Flesh to mix with Flesh, or Soul with Soul. (8.626–29)

The prose shows 18 uses of "convey," some of which mean to convey information. On the other hand, *An Apology Against a Pamphlet* talks of Milton's acquittal "by the dexterity and conveiance of [the Remonstrant's] nonsense" (YP 1:911). *Of Education* shows unhappiness with certain military situations: "they would not suffer their empty & unrecrutible Colonells of twenty men in a company, to quaffe out, or convay into secret hoards, the wages of a delusive list, and a miserable remnant" (YP 2:412). The financial image that is raised is noteworthy. But a directly legalistic negative occurrence appears in the second edition of *Doctrine and Discipline of Divorce:* the "Statute of *Moses:* not repeald ever by him who only had the authority, but thrown aside with much inconsiderat neglect, under the rubbish of Canonicall ignorance: as once the whole law was by some such conveyance in *Josiahs* time" (YP 2:224).

The uses in the prose of "conveyance" with fraudulent intentions attest to the subtle meanings that Milton would have us acknowledge as we render interpretations of character and situation, and his conceptions connected with the clergy and discipline of the church that has come to dominate. For instance, *Animadversions* (1641) rebuts the Remonstrant's defense of "Our *Liturgie*" as "A pretty slipskin conveyance to sift Masse into no Masse and *Popish* into not *Popish*" (YP 1:687); in an argument against tithing, "Where did he [God] demand it, that we might certainly know, as in all claimes of temporal right is just and reasonable? or if demanded, where did he assigne it, or by what evident conveyance to ministers?" (*Hirelings*, YP 7:297); and in an argument against silent voting, "the foresaid remedies, cannot be troublesom and chargeable...[such as] only now and then to hold up a forrest of fingers, or to convey each man his bean or ballot into the box, without reason shewn or common deliberation" (*Readie and Easie Way*, YP 7:441 [2nd ed., 1660]).

Paying attention to Milton's language that is loaded with subtle meaning, recognizing when that meaning—particularly if it has negative or satiric qualities—is operative, as we see with "dubious," "seem," "gaze," and "convey," is most important in achieving a fuller reading of his work and in assessing a complete evaluation of his artistry. These meanings and usages may exist for him throughout his career, or they may intensify; they may accrue over time, but they clarify for his reader subtle meanings, ambiguous or destabilized meanings, if we prefer those words, and guide and conduce us to levels of conceptual thought that may otherwise lie hidden.

Eight

The Three Major Poems

The three major poems have entered our discussion often in the previous chapters. In relation to the subject of Milton's unchanging or changed mind the question of the dates of their composition must be considered. We can and should read a text as it is received, but we also should acknowledge that, as with *Comus*, the received text may be significantly different from an earlier version and in such a situation we cannot legitimately employ the received text to read that earlier version. There have been changes in the author's world between such dates that may have influence of various types upon that received version, and in any case the received text presents an accrual of whatever thought and changes of thought may have occurred over the course of its writing. But also, as with *Paradise Lost*, the received text, which is a culmination of writing from, apparently, 1640 through 1665, may retain earlier writing influenced by externals and by internalities of the mind present at those times. It has been argued that *Paradise Regain'd* and *Samson Agonistes* were both begun at earlier dates than 1670 (when their texts seem to have been completed and in the process of being printed, although the first edition of their single volume was 1671). Not everyone has accepted that such earlier compositional attempts and thus possible persisting elements are valid.

Arguments have postulated dramatic attempts for both works in the later 1640s when Milton was still considering a drama on *Paradise Lost*, which had been begun around 1640 and, it would seem, Milton worked on the epic in ensuing years until he was able to return to it more fully in 1661. Perhaps (and I feel probably) Milton returned to *Paradise Lost* periodically in later 1655 and again in 1658, at which times his composition had turned to epical writing. In 1660 too much was occurring (including his brief hiding from government authorities and then his brief imprisonment) to sustain the attention needed to develop and complete the text that appeared in August (?) 1667. Remarks by Thomas Ellwood, often cited in scholarship, suggest that the poem was complete by the time Milton was staying at Chalfont St. Giles in June (?) 1665 through February (?) 1666 to avoid the plague. It should be remarked that the text *may* have been complete prior to his stay at Chalfont St. Giles. Following the publication of *Paradise Lost*, he responded to Ellwood's question, "Thou hast said much here of *Paradise lost;* but what hast thou to say of *Paradise found?*" Milton gave no answer, "sate some time in a Muse: then brake of that Discourse, and fell upon another Subject." Later (how long we do not know), he showed Ellwood "his Second POEM, called PARADISE REGAINED; and in a pleasant Tone said to me, *This is owing to you: for you put it into my Head, by the Question you put to me at* Chalfont; *which before I had not thought of.*"[1]

The "Muse" in which Milton sat seems to have been given over to thinking about the question, and the fact that Ellwood—a typical, interested, religious, informed reader—did not fathom that paradise did not need to be "found," it needed to be "regained," and that indeed his epic had shown how it could be regained. (See Fletcher's enumeration of sections that make clear that "All this is carefully worked out in *Paradise Lost* which opens with the idea fully formed.")[2] The brief epic is presented in dramatic dialogue, not dissimilar to the "dramatic" (speech) sections of the long epic, which would seem to be retained (and altered) from some of its early attempts as recorded at least in the Trinity Manuscript. I am not suggesting that *Paradise Regain'd* was conceived as the poem it is during an earlier period; I suggest that, like *Paradise Lost*, sections had been written earlier that looked toward a drama on the temptation. Further, the brief epic has been analyzed as exhibiting prosody that would often place it after *Samson Agonistes* and before the completed *Paradise Lost* in some of its composition. (Most telling in such prosodic study, for one important criterion, are run-on lines as opposed to less "accomplished," end-stopped lines.[3]) Milton's thankful remark to Ellwood indicates nothing more than that he had not realized how ineffectual his epic was for his audience, who with this realization would now become even fewer than he might have thought.

The dramatic poem, it has been contended, was contemplated in the later 1640s (and even later) on various grounds such as content, both the interest in Samson in two topics suggested for dramas in the Trinity Manuscript and what was inferred as Milton's bleak view of the political and religious world of the times (with some reference as well to Psalms 80–85, which were written in April 1648), and prosody and orthography that emerge in the 1671 text. Those who have countered such early dating for the dramatic poem and accepted the traditional dating after the two epics (perhaps 1667 through 1670) seem to have misread the "early dating" arguments as placing full composition in an earlier period and as denying revision, expansion, and completion in the period of 1667?–70.

Whatever the fact of compositional date for any of these poems, it is clear that the diffuse epic was composed over a number of years—years that saw many changes in Milton's life, in the political world, in his own writing and thinking, in the religious establishment (particularly with its reversion after the Restoration to one excluding dissent and reverting to a state church similar to that of the past and to *The Book of Common Prayer*—a kind of return to the 1630s). The brief epic asserts the primacy of the inner light, as Michael Wilding cogently observes, pointing to its "individual conscience over the pressures of external authority, the stress on the accessibility to all men of 'the Spirit of god,'" and to the turn "to the private preparations of the soul for the paradise within."[4] While such belief may have existed well before the Restoration, it is present as *Paradise Lost* ends and is explicitly brought to the fore in *Paradise Regain'd*. Such clarification implies a development of recognition to the self at least, a recognition that certainly does not emerge in the attempts at writing a dramatic work on "Adams Banishment."

Behind the text of the dramatic poem has frequently been seen disillusionment with the Good Old Cause and the "palpable obscure," the "Palpable darkness" of the future's unenlightened world.[5] Again it is the individual Samson who, renovated, has effected freedom and salvation for himself—but through faith in God. There is no "paradise within" for him, but a prelude to such a development is shown in his going to the feast of Dagon "freely," accepting that "he may dispense with me or thee / Present in Temples at Idolatrous Rites / for some important cause" (1377–79). He finally understands why "I must not quarrel with the will / Of highest dispensation, which herein / Happ'ly had ends above my reach to know" (60–62). He had rather misthought that his strength (now his "bane," which has proved "the sourse of all [his] miseries" [64–65]) was all that was needed to be the great deliverer of his people. It is a rejection ultimately of the person alone (the

Samson of legend, the culture hero that Jackie Di Salvo delineates)[6]—that is, the externality of person, body as only needed—for the acceptance of the internality that God's presence will provide. As Adam learns ("the sum of wisdom"), "to obey is best,...ever to observe / His providence, and on him sole depend" (*PL* 12.575-76, 561-64), and he comes to this realization through the example of Jesus, which he has been allowed to foresee.

The Samson of the 1640s underwent diminution as emulative hero in the initial four decades of the seventeenth century, whom Joseph Wittreich has shown[7] was seen by Milton in 1644 as epitomizing England, "as a strong man after sleep, and shaking her invincible locks...an Eagle muing her mighty youth" (*Areopagitica,* YP 2:558). Milton thus joins the Puritan apologists in the 1640s that Wittreich finds exalting his heroic metaphor, through Samson's figure as a bearer "of the real strength, the true nobility, of the nation" (194). That England and that eagle both are and are not to be found in *Samson Agonistes* two decades later. Ironically it is Samson's strength that now effects a disastrous assertion over the Philistines. Inferentially it is not man alone but man *and* God who act. Jesus "stands" on the pinnacle obedient against temptation and with faith in God, and God's angels fly "nigh," receiving Jesus "From his uneasie station, and upbore" him to "a flowry valley" where he is "refresh'd" (*PR* 4.581-91).

1

There is much in all three poems to point to conceptual development from earlier times to whenever they were composed, and especially if they were composed over some period of time when Milton's life changed, his political world changed, and especially for these poems certain religious beliefs changed. We can look at a couple of examples. The characterization of Satan, and the generations of interpretations it has spawned, demonstrates the literary artist at work and the problems of reading. Rather than alteration of attitude toward Satan, what has often been the superficial reading by commentators that has made Satan a hero and has accused Milton of not playing fair by devolving Satan through depicting him in various animal images, Milton's opposition to "evil," and what proves to be incertitude of text as proffered the unfit audience though many has begun to develop different readings. As character, Satan becomes both positive and negative, although Milton's language, fully attended to, rejects that positive reading. (It is rather, as I quipped elsewhere, that Milton somehow knew that his readers would misread and make Satan the rebel with good cause.) Human acceptance of the tyranny of God, the injustice in the world, the position that authority, whether in the person of a king or an archbishop, spawns an acceptance and championing of one who opposes such oppressive authority. The Romantic advancement of Satan as hero is a good example of just such an inadequate reading of Milton's poem, but such a reading is the outgrowth of the monarchic world of the times, though little attention has been paid to its source when Satan is so viewed. Its source lies in the world of England that William Blake exposed in his poem "London" and in the madness of King George and the regency that "led" its people; in the oppression felt in the American colonies and their revolt against monarchic controls in the name of freedom; in the praise of Satan by the French literati—certainly the economic and political deprivations of the French by the monarchy and the clerics were patent, indubitable—until the Reign of Terror made clear what can ensue through disorder, as we see in the about-face of someone like Jean-Baptiste Mosneron-De Launay,[8] translator of and commentator on the epic in 1786 to whom Milton later becomes "seditious Milton" ("le factieux Milton"). No longer was "a blind fanaticism" (aveugle fanatisme) possible. The view of Satan as hero results in a rebellious antagonist against a tyrant or despot, and a liberator who will replace tyranny with republicanism for all constituents: yet it is finally to be read as diametrically opposite. However, for people like Mosneron, it is Milton who is at fault by portraying Satan as hero rather than recognizing that he is *not* a hero, and, of course, by not admitting that their reading has been tricked out through the genius of Milton's brilliant writing, which capitalizes on human failure to rise above demagoguery, to filter truth from fiction and egoism, to see through charismatic oratory.

Michael Bryson's *The Tyranny of Heaven* investigates the representation of God the Father and his kingly state for a pertinent exegesis of some of the issues involved here. Bryson concludes it is the Son in *Paradise Regain'd*, not God the Father and king, who offers the model of both theology and politics that Milton esteems as humankind's reformative path to earthly good and heavenly salvation. In his reading God the Father does take on certain attributes of the tyrant: he is "profoundly disturbing"; he represents what can go wrong in single-person rule; his is a rigid code of justice; and he has thus been portrayed by people as "*wickedly imagined.*" "The Son takes the 'regal Scepter' from the Father, but he does not return it to the Father, now or ever," with reference to book 3 and the future foretold. This is a corrective resolution of the misreading of Satan as hero. "The Son prefers the internal, private (in the sense both of individual and non-hierarchical, non-magistratical) government of truth": it is a government of inner man, worshipping God, and establishing the paradise within.[9]

James Driscoll's analysis of "the Son-Satan polarity with the warring opposites of thought and feeling" is reflective of these remarks on what is at play in readings of the hero, the tyranny of God, and the love of the Son. "The opposing ethics of obedience to authority and of defiant rebellion characterize the hostile brothers [sic] stage of individuation with its war of ego and shadow, thought and feeling."[10] What occurs with the paradise within, if and when it is established, is what Driscoll tells us the self can finally achieve to transcend the ethics born of ego and shadow. The contrast of the Son and Satan is evident and has been frequently substantiated in criticism, even to Joseph Addison's countering of John Dryden's assignment of the hero of the poem as Satan. In the *Spectator* Addison states that, if there has to be a hero of the poem, he posits the Son.[11] The unchanging faith of Milton emerges in both epics in such readings as Bryson's and Driscoll's, but these poems likewise reveal a change in philosophic beliefs, in mundane political theories, and in a revision of hope that realistically knows the believers are few and any external correction must be through an individual's internal change.

Perhaps my reader is remembering that in *Paradise Regain'd* Belial advises setting women in Jesus' eye and Satan's rejoinder that this is a different man, one "wiser far," "of more exalted mind" (*PR* 2.153, 205–06). Is this not a very subtle contrast between Jesus, Son of God, and Satan? Certainly the sexual demonstration of the tempter pursuing Eve to sin contrasts strongly with the human Son of Man, if we decipher "more exalted mind" when casual sexual enticement is raised (particularly when multiple enticers are implied). The point is clear, although not seen by most commentators on the pertinent passages in book 2: far be it for Satan to let Belial suggest anything to *him*. He rejects Belial, not the temptational suggestion. And so in the banquet scene Satan provides supposedly enticing "Tall stripling youths," alluding to the rumor of Jesus' homosexualism, which critics do not want to have even suggested or recalled for the Son of God, although it was a common enough issue. (This is part of the second temptation, *concupiscentia oculorum*, with its emphasis on "the world" and covetousness, with the "acclaim" given those who have accumulated "objects" and "positions." These are *youths*, not *a* youth.) Yet what commentators on the homosexual interpretation of the lines ignore is that Satan takes Belial's advice and has "Nymphs of *Diana*'s train, and *Naiades*...And Ladies of th' *Hesperides*, that seem'd / Fairer then feign'd of old, or fabl'd since / Of Fairy Damsels" (*PR* 2.355–59) waiting to step in if the "youths" do not have the desired effect.

Perhaps the greatest contrast here between Jesus, Son of God and Son of Man, and Satan is the evocation of the mystery that the Lady accuses Comus of being incapable of understanding: we are perceiving an unchanged mind about Milton's morality and his God. But are we not, also, witnessing a comprehension of one of the great lures of humankind, sex? Such extrapolation into Luke 4 and Matthew 4 (we know the strategy by way of some recent novels and movies) humanizes Jesus and yet removes him from carnality, for he too can "Command a Table in this Wilderness" *and* "swift flights of Angels ministrant / Array'd in Glory on my cup t' attend" (1.384–86). Satan offers "specious gifts" that are "no gifts but guiles" (391). In 1626 Milton escaped from the guiles of "bands of maidens, stars emitting seductive flames, [who] go dancing by," and "from afar the infamous halls of faithless Circe" (*Elegia prima*, 51, 87). The "help of divine moly" is needed by him, a mere mortal; not so, Jesus, Son of God.

Or, contrasting the table of "cates" offered Jesus, note the seeds for the "Intemperance more / In meats and Drinks" (*PL* 11.472–73), the "ungovern'd appetite" and "gluttonous delight" (11.533), "The Men...in the amorous Net / Fast caught...[by] A Beavie of fair Women" (11.585–87, 582), which hark back to Belial, the "Spirit more lewd...more gross to love Vice for it self" (1.490–92), and his "Sons...flown with insolence and wine" who execute gang-rape (1.501–05). We do not have a question of ambiguity here because the reader should understand the proleptic trope being used. The certitude is the belief in the nature and prosecution of intemperance, especially here in its sexual orientation. Casting doubtfulness on Milton's part on any of these passages in either epic is erroneous, despite what is multiple of interpretation in the language, images, and presentation. Though seemingly very disparate, the two epics do echo sameness in circumstances and images, as Fletcher's tallying of other likenesses concerning the Son has enumerated.

Paradise Regain'd, enunciating belief, submits the heart of Milton's unchanging mind, and the problems of interpretation of the companion poem in the 1671 volume, *Samson Agonistes*, herald why the Incarnation was necessary to moralists like Milton. The Israelites (Danites) have not been delivered from the hands of the Philistines no matter how we want to read Samson's final action. *Paradise Regain'd* propounds an unchanging theological belief in God and God's "ways" to humankind. *Samson Agonistes* ventures to assert through the Chorus and their reading of Samson's action and fate a long-held belief in God's omnipresence and omniscience, in spite of the interpretive questions of the dramatic poem and its final action. The brief epic is conscious of the intractable minds of its readers who misunderstand, for instance, the theological affirmation of the so-called rejection of learning in book 4. The dramatic poem as I have posited elsewhere "has much of uncertainty about it, which will not be and need not be removed, but...it depicts yet once more Milton's consistency of belief."[12] The Chorus's reliance in their final words on God's unexpected return to save "his faithful Champion" would seem to echo Milton's position in his paraphrase of Psalm 114, a consistency of belief in God and God's way surely. But are not we the readers expected to interrogate such a facile attitude and come to realize that for Milton humans must act as well as depend only on God to take care of them? As Michael counsels Adam, "onely add / Deeds to thy knowledge answerable, add Faith, / Add Vertue, Patience, Temperance, add Love," such as Jesus, whose "suffering for Truths sake / Is fortitude to highest victorie" (*PL* 12.581–83, 569–70). Herein we have Milton's belief sustained but his awareness—developed perhaps, emergent as time went on—that humankind must also act, and it is the individual who, "amending" himself or herself "light after light," will "safe arrive."

The uncertainties of *Samson Agonistes* are manifest, yet a consistency of belief emerges in a kind of reprise of the thesis of *Paradise Regain'd* and in the renovation of Samson. As I have written earlier, "Against all these types of slippage or possible slippage from being one of God's true servants Milton has presented the Jesus of *Paradise Regain'd*. That poem's precedence of *Samson Agonistes* in the 1671 volume underscored Milton's consistent belief in faith and covenant and the keeping of the Law, particularly as contrasted in their revocation by the Samson that existed before the beginning of his poem, and their reassertion through a renovated Samson as the poem ends for God's 'servants' who have now been offered 'new acquist / Of true experience.'" The import of those final words is a belief that *renovation* can occur through God's ways, that Samson is finally presented as renovated through the "changes" experienced in his rebuffing of Manoa, Dalila, Harapha, and initially the Philistines, over the course of the poem.[13] Whether Samson's final action is productive and what he might have called a "delivery," or is meaningful at all, or is in effect only suicide, as some readers of the Bible and of Milton's poem have argued, Samson says he goes to the feast of Dagon "For some important cause": "This day will be remarkable in my life / By some great act, or of my days the last" (1388–89). That very important word "or" subsumes my three possibilities and the "ors" separating them.

The irony of hope in this poem, deals with external occurrences in the future that do not come to pass. Real hope for Milton lies in the individual, in the internal, here in Samson (not unlike the Son during the third temptation), who goes with faith in his God and in God's covenant with him—a situation in which any person (who is a believer in God) might find himself or herself. In the battle of words the thought that they subtend, we all know, may (indeed, finally will) be rethought.

It has also long been clear that governmentally and politically Milton underwent reexaminations, awakenings—often in what seems like delayed reactions that we would like to believe someone like him would have been more immediately attuned to. Indeed, one may wonder whether reaction such as that in political thinking has truly been full and complete or only partial and aborted. At least in class stratifications there is conflict with governmental postulates. And while a superficial look at Milton's concepts of legal matters and moneylending (fraud and usury) tends to see no essential change, for he does continue throughout his life—even, evidence shows, up to a time just before his death—to be a moneylender, and while he writes in approval and justification of such activity, there is an awareness of the potential of fraud that lurks in his remarks, of the possibility of not being the exemplary God-fearing and abiding servant he would constantly wish to be. Beneath this phase of his life lie hints of hypocrisy and conceptual adjustments to excuse both the act and the hypocrisy. A not very dissimilar hypocrisy—one unadmitted to the self—emerges in concepts of the separation of church and state, and the theocratic state that he contributed to and apparently approved in the outlawing of Roman Catholicism and Episcopacy. His toleration does know bounds, as well as his republican stance.

Of importance to us as students of Milton's creative work are the examples of belief that works like the Nativity ode or *Lycidas* or the three major poems adumbrate. There is a steady belief in God, a faith in God and his works, in God's looking out for his children, his help in time of need, his righteousness and love—through his Spirit and through his Son—and the Truth of his Holy Scripture (the Godhead's and at the same time God the Father's, which is by no means unusual for many [most?] believers). Therein is "Milton's unchanging mind." Yet one wonders: would the trajectory resultant from reexamination ever ultimately lead to a questioning of the virgin birth or of the irrational acceptance of the Latin reading of Isaiah when the Hebraic reference is to Istar, a minor god worshipped as the morning star (or to Helel, the morning star, and Shahar, the Son of the Dawn)? Accommodation and typology may go only so far for a thinking and realistic person. Of great importance in this same way is the text of Psalm 2, which appears often in *Paradise Lost* and is the focal point in Satan's rebellion:[1] reference is not to a Christian Son, of course, but apparently to a Hebrew merchant providing for his mortal son or, as the translation construes it, to a Hebrew member of a royal line announcing his enthronement. The psalm is *not* part of the original David psalms, and it may have been employed only once for a specific ruler. The Christian interpretation (here, identification) and typological seeking of "proof" of New Testament texts raise the question of faith and reason. Over the years, Milton maintained faith in some things and allowed reason to alter other frequent beliefs and "answers" to life's existence. But there has been a stopping point in the rational view of things, and one might wonder whether time would continue to chip away at further items of belief.

1

Yes, there has been conceptual development and, yes, there have been aspects of life and thought that seem not to have even been questioned, let alone altered. Are we observing a person who is some superobjective, always right and always in command of his thought and mind, human being? Is he not, like all of us, one who is not always certain, who does change his mind about some things, who may fall short of complete analysis of all the mysteries of life, who may simply not allow himself to entertain reconsideration of some fundamental beliefs even though hints of the possibilities may be discerned by readers? A significant philosophical movement of his age looms up here, dating from college days at least to a time not far from his last existence on earth. That is, the concepts of "revelation" on which so much theology has been and is based, and its questioning as deism gained ground in the seventeenth century, and of manifestation, one not depending upon revelation, and which came to dominate. These emerge in a study of Milton and his works and suggest that Milton did not fully understand the changes that were occurring in philosophical (including religious) thinking during his lifetime. There seems to be an aversion to accepting that God's revelation as a strong factor in belief was beginning not to exist for some people in the seventeenth century and was not adequate as an explanation for the science of life, and to accepting that the need for a different kind of manifestation to evidence God's existence obliterated even a subtle revision of belief in God's omnipresence, omnipotence, and omniscience.

The meanings of the words "revelation" and "manifestation" are important because they take on different concepts as the century (and the next) proceeded. An underlying thought in the paragraph above is that God was manifested as being God through his revelation of himself and his acts, an explanation of life that continues for some believers in God. For some, the intricacies of the human body and generation, for example, can exist only through his "intelligent design"; thus, God has revealed himself through the object and the object thus manifests God's existence. Revelation was seen in signs or in "visitations, in unexplained events or through a text of the Bible: the usual acceptance of God's revelation of himself to humankind came through such manifestation as these media provided. Clearly a manifestation appeared through the interpretation of the sign, the visitation (as well as belief in its occurrence—a phenomenon that even today, every once in a while, finds believers, such as sightings of the Virgin Mary), visions and dreams, an event, inner feelings, and especially the biblical text. For Milton it is the Holy Scripture that presents God's revelation: what it says and what it does not say, and of course that demands interpretation, which may vary a little or greatly among those who rely upon their readings. The Enlightenment brought with it an emphasis on reason, a rationality of what is interpreted, and an individualism that did not merely accept tradition without examination. Milton arises here—in this kind of philosophizing, in the aspects of individuation that attach to him, as they do in literary development and achievement—between the past and the coming age. Last of the Olympians, he has been called, but first of the moderns. Gordon Teskey's accurate statement "Milton represents a watershed in the seventeenth century" is explained thus: "Milton is the last major poet in the European literary tradition for whom the act of creation is centered in God and the first in whom the act of creation resonates with the world as a whole, communicating spirit from afar."[2] It is not only in the arena of literary things that this view of Milton as a "watershed" can be seen. "In terms of intellectual history, Milton has...been seen to occupy a position almost precisely at the point of cleavage between cultures devoted, respectively, to religious and scientific pursuits," John Rumrich shows in contrasts between the medieval mind and the modern mind. *Paradise Lost*, "written during a period of shifting epistemological assumptions," is thus seen as transitional,—Milton's reflection of "the increasingly scientific bias of his times," his interest in nature and the natural world, in nutrition, and yet the medieval cast of the moral significance of all knowledge attest to this watershed position.[3]

Michael Lieb examines these two concepts of God's being in Milton's theology, revelation and manifestation: "Milton views both conscience and right reason as the product of grace. This characteristic aligns them with the experience of revelation as the result of what it means to be receptive to the presence of God.... Thus, Milton argues that as noble and as powerful as conscience and right reason might prove themselves to be, their true significance must be understood in the context of the revealed word of God."[4] The revealed word of God is the Holy Scripture, and Lieb refers to *De doctrina Christiana* in the Columbia Milton (14:60) for some "representative moments in which the divine glory reveals itself. These moments, Milton implies, are accessible most immediately and almost exclusively through an encounter with the Old Testament."[5] It is in God's revelations—in his revealing of himself—that he is manifested. The problem of these words as they come to indicate differing philosophic approaches to God's existence for an ordinary human lies in the interpretation that the biblical text manifests God's presence in human terms: "God makes his presence known in the human heart. He is revealed in every time and every place through the behavior of tested men to attest to him. By means of his free agent Samson, God manifests the renewal of freedom to all individuals."[6] To Thomas Chubb, "Revelation is the act of God in disclosing or communicating truth to the human soul"; "Theology presumes to find in revelation the cause of religion.... R. A. Lipsius pronounces mystical experience to be the vital center in religion and the essential in revelation."[7] The problem for the rational mind is that such revelation accepts the existence of God to begin with, then proceeds to accept what is reported or interpreted as truth (miracles like the dividing of the Red Sea or Jesus' curing of the blind man come immediately to mind), and these then exemplify God's existence and presence. This, however, confounds the two words as coincident. If something is manifested, God has revealed himself; if God has revealed himself in Holy Scripture, then we have a manifestation of him in what is written or reported. (Throughout history has been the belief that God directed the writing of the Bible—not only through inspiration of the Gospels and Paul, but the recorders of all the stories of the Old Testament. The Bible is the Word of God.)

To cite Lieb again, the concept of the *deus absconditus* has led to a reading "through which the 'total otherness of deity' is manifested." The first form of that manifestation is "in the experience of God hidden '*in* his revelation,' the second form in the experience of God hidden '*outside* his revelation.'" At the same time, "Such an encounter encompasses what might be called the essential theophanic basis of God's self-manifestation. At issue are revelations of the glory of God ranging from the Sinai theophany and visions of God in the minor and major prophets to the apocalyptic renderings both in the Old Testament and the New Testament."[8]

I have previously cited, in *Rethinking Milton Studies*, the important study of Richard Elliott Friedman, *The Disappearance of God*. He speaks of three mysteries: "the disappearance of God in the Bible as his face increasingly becomes hidden and as his retraction from interrelationship with man shifts from 'divine' to 'human'; the death of God as Nietzsche's Dionysianism triumphs over Apollonianism, and insecurity and moral tumult ascend; and the fusing of religion and science in theories of universal origin... alongside the visions of the Kabbalah. The elucidation of all three mysteries is faith."[9] This shift in belief was occurring during Milton's lifetime, as I pointed out even earlier in '*Arms of the Family*':[10] "With the Diggers, we have clear indication of the change from Revelation to Manifestation of God as guiding principle," for emphasis was changing from biblical manifestation to the manifestation within nature, the land itself, as reflective of a Godhead. Engaging what was happening during the Interregnum decade but not with the application that I suggest, John Rogers tells us that "the country's standing groves of trees had begun to acquire an unmistakable set of nationalistic associations," and records John Evelyn's identification of the kingdom's forest and its military strength as well as Andrew Marvell's use of the "image of a tree to represent the vitalist hope in a naturally determined revolution." For Milton, "The animism of the poem's universe thus allows matter to proceed up to the maker 'If not deprav'd from good' (5.471)," in reference to *Paradise Lost*.[11]

Joseph Glanvill in *The Agreement of Reason and Religion* (1676) epitomizes what had occurred philosophically: he argues that "the Being of a God, the Foundation of all, is proved by Reason," not by revelation, for "*Revelation supposeth* the Being of a God, and cannot prove it.... The *Knowledge* of his Being must *precede* our Faith in revelation; and so cannot be deduced from it." He maintains that "Reason proves the Divine Authority of Scripture," and "*The denial of Reason in Religion hath been the principal Engine that Hereticks and Enthusiasts have used against the Faith*"; such denial leads to the "follies and impostures" of Arianism (including Socinianism). Important as a foundation for reason is the world as it is, nature, the changes of day and night, the seasons, the experience of living.[12]

The intricacies of the world of humankind were well explored by Isaac Newton, as we are all aware, but I am not sure that everyone recognizes that, hard put not to appear atheistic, a mere mechanic, Newton used those intricacies in the formulation of belief I have described above. The first edition of *Philosophiæ naturalis principia mathematica* (1687) brought forth rebuttals and atheistic charges from people like George Berkeley and Gottfried Leibniz. Accordingly, in its second edition of 1713 was added in book 3 a "General Scholium" at the end of the *Mathematical Principles* governing his analysis of "The System of the World." Here Newton summarizes that

> The six primary planets are revolved about the sun in circles concentric with the sun, and with motions directed towards the same parts, and almost in the same plane. Ten moons are revolved about the earth, Jupiter, and Saturn, in circles concentric with them, with the same direction of motion, and nearly in the planes of the orbits of those planets; but it is not to be conceived that mere mechanical causes could give birth to so many regular motions,

since the comets range over all parts of the heavens in very eccentric orbits; for by that kind of motion they pass easily through the orbs of the planets, and with great rapidity; and in their aphelions, where they move the slowest, and are detained the longest, they recede to the greatest distances from each other, and hence suffer the least disturbance from their mutual attractions. This most beautiful system of the sun, planets, and comets, could only proceed from the counsel and dominion of an intelligent and powerful Being. And if the fixed stars are the centres of other like systems, these, being formed by the like wise counsel, must be all subject to the dominion of One; especially since the light of the fixed stars is of the same nature with the light of the sun, and from every system light passes into all the other systems: and lest the systems of the fixed stars should, by their gravity, fall on each other, he hath placed those systems at immense distance from one another.

This Being governs all things, not as the soul of the world, but as Lord over all; and on account of his dominion he is wont to be called *Lord God παντοκρατωρ,* or *Universal Ruler;* for *God* is a relative word, and has a respect to servants; and *Deity* is the dominion of God not over his own body, as those imagine who fancy God to be the soul of the world, but over servants. The Supreme God is a Being eternal, infinite, absolutely perfect.... All the diversity of natural things which we find suited to different times and places could arise from nothing but the ideas and will of a Being necessarily existing.[13]

The "Knowledge of his Being" for Newton (and so many others then as well as now) lay in the world, in nature. It is a reasoning that does not assume the Bible as all truth, "written" by God through his messengers, or through visitations to human beings: that is, it rejects revelation as defined above and as the result of biblical manifestation as defined above. (Today many who espouse something like "intelligent design" would probably not admit to the rejection of knowledge and truth from the Bible, yet that *is* the inference to which it points.) "Knowledge of his

Being" for Newton, as for Glanvil, as for the coming age, demanded a different kind of manifestation, a tangible one. Milton does not step this far; he does not reject the Holy Scriptures as truth and thus as a compendium of manifestations through which God has revealed himself. But *Paradise Lost* greatly advances the movement that will bring about such thinking and such ultimately transcendental philosophy as the future held. Current Milton scholarship has often stressed the ecological world and its importance that the epic provides: such studies lay a strong foundation for what I am suggesting, emphasizing Milton's watershed position.[14]

Milton's description of Eden and its "nature" are frequently discussed in exemplary terms in the eighteenth century. In *An Essay on Design in Gardening*, George Mason repeatedly examines, alludes to, and quotes from *Paradise Lost* and the companion poems, attesting that Milton's model of Eden is "unimpeachable." Milton's landscape is often the source for advising readers "On Modern Gardening," as in Thomas Tyers's *An Historical Rhapsody on Mr. Pope* and Horace Walpole's essay of that title. Daniel Malthus, in the preface to his translation of René Louis, Marquis de Girardin's *An Essay on Landscape*, offers the significance of gardening in Milton, employing, as others do, the companion poems and the diffuse epic.[15] The philosophic import in regard to Godhead is the unstated foundation of these paeans to the land, to nature, with human beings joining the Creator. For Milton earlier there is God in nature as the morning hymn of Adam and Eve praises him: "These are thy glorious works, Parent of good"; "On Earth joyn all ye Creatures to extoll / Him first, him last, him midst, and without end"; "Thou Sun, of this great World both Eye and Soul, / Acknowledge him thy Greater, sound his praise / In thy eternal course" (*PL* 5.153–73). And it is in the wilderness, a "Desert wild," "A pathless Desert," with nonetheless "ancient Oak, / or Cedar," "Among wild Beasts" who "at his sight grew mild," that

Jesus is led to some intent unknown, "For what concerns my knowledge God reveals" (*PR* 1.293, 193, 296, 305–06, 310). (I do not mean to be flippant, but Jesus is certainly *not* reading the Holy Scripture.)

The Reason of Church-Government in 1641/42 declares that "God...ordain'd his Gospell to be the revelation of his power and wisdome in Christ Jesus" (YP 1:750), and *De doctrina Christiana* maintains that "the only authority...was God's self-revelation" in "the Holy Scriptures" (YP 6:118). In *A Treatise of Civil Power* (1659) Milton stresses reason and God's "Holy Spirit within us" (YP 7:242): things belonging to knowledge and service to God "are either above the reach and light of nature without revelation from above...or such things are enjoind or forbidden by divine precept, which els by the light of reason would seem indifferent to be don or not don." Persisting to the end is the belief that "True Religion is the true Worship and Service of God, learnt and believed from the Word of God only. No Man or Angel can know how God would be worshipt and serv'd unless God reveal it. He hath Reveal'd and taught it us in the holy Scriptures by inspir'd Ministers, and in the Gospel by his own Son and his Apostles" (*Of True Religion,* YP 8:419). William B. Hunter affirms that

> His emphasis upon the sole authority of scripture as interpreted by the 'Holy Spirit within us' dominates his mature thinking. Such emphasis upon the guidance of the Spirit opposes him to all traditions supporting external authority (*i.e.*, the authority of the historical church as exemplified by the Church of Rome and the Church of England) and leads to concurrence with such divers groups as the Quakers, the Baptists, and the radical Arminians. (*Civil Power*, YP 7:242n10)

Yet the significance of what God had created—from his hand, and seen and capable of experience by all—is also beneath the picture of nature we find in the epics.

Perhaps the most obvious clue to Milton's position is his emphasis on Providence, which begins *Paradise Lost* as he states his higher argument to be to "Assert Eternal Providence / And [thereby] justify the ways of God to men," and which ends the poem as Adam and Eve leave Eden with Providence their guide. God has *provided* nature in all its aspects, all its forms, all its happenings to humankind. We see that Providence, he would seem to be arguing, in such manifestations of God, although he still accepts God's revelation of those manifestations. The significance of Providence to the eighteenth century, which involves the increasing "hiddenness" of God, is exemplified in the writing of Henry Fielding: "Providence in his hands is presented as little more than ethical and sociological determination."[16]

In *Milton's Wisdom*, John Reichardt balances Milton's view of the book of Nature and the Holy Scripture, examining the ways in which God would be encountered by man: through manifestation and through revelation. For Milton, hearing the Word eclipses the "creatures," surely, yet the crossroad or turning point is foreshadowed in books 11 and 12, I suggest, in the attention both to the effects of the Fall on human beings, on animals, on the land, *and* to these "creatures/created things" themselves (see *PL* 11.141–225). Reichardt reminds us that "The pairing of Scripture and the works of nature as the prime books in whose pages we may read God's ways was, by the end of the sixteenth century, altogether commonplace, and not among the theologians only." He likewise challenges remarks by some others that would seem to counter this point.[17] As I read Michael's response to Adam's lament about his "departing hence" from paradise, he is correcting Adam's avoidance of the obvious "truth" (11.315–29) about God's presence—indeed, he is always correcting Adam in these two last books! Adam, after recalling God's "Presence Divine," his standing "Visible...under this Tree," says,

> So many grateful Altars I would rear
> Of grassie Terf, and pile up every Stone
> Of lustre from the brook, in memorie,
> Or monument to Ages, and thereon
> Offer sweet smelling Gumms and Fruits and Flowrs.[18]
> (*PL* 11.323–27)

Michael subtly but also directly admonishes:

> *Adam*, thou know'st Heav'n his, and all the Earth,
> Not this Rock onely; his Omnipresence fills
> Land, Sea, and Air, and every kind that lives,
> Fomented by his virtual power and warmd
> ....
> surmise not then
> His presence to these narrow bounds confin'd
> Of Paradise or *Eden:*
> ....
> Yet doubt not but in Vallie and in Plain
> God is as here, and will be found alike
> Present, and of his presence many a signe
> Still following thee, still compassing thee round.
> (11.335–52)

To see God, to know of God's presence, one must observe nature, an axiom that the ensuing years after 1667 will proclaim in many ways.[19]

At an early age Milton, the student, did not distrust nature, but saw it as relief from scholastic philosophy and as access to the Creator's wisdom as well, as Reichardt maintains. The early poem *Naturam non pati senium* (dating variously from 1628 to July 1631) engages the controversy of whether nature decays or not, a philosophic arena that underlies the advancement of deism, as well as the opposition of the ancients and the moderns in literature. This developing attitude (in a way, a better word than "philosophy" in these early stages from the late sixteenth century onward) saw the existence of God in natural phenomena and their "established" laws, not in miracles, and through reason's observation of the benevolent design of the universe. The growing world of scientific knowledge strongly, though not usually directly, opposed the traditional myths and illusions in humankind's attempt to fathom what the world and its people are. One's reason and understanding of nature led to a frequent individual determination of religious doctrine—a factor still operative in the decline of some churches. (The removal of God as all through the advancement of scientific research and reason has, of course, led to an exodus from traditional churches and religion to the varied and widely inclusive "Christian" world that takes the Bible as the literal Word of God, thereby making one's religion basically individual, private, not in need of traditional discipline.)

Provoking the argument of Milton's poem was the rebuttal of the concepts one would encounter in Godfrey Goodman's *The Fall of Man; or, The Corruption of Nature, proved by the Light of Our Naturall Reason* (1616), which George Hakewill in 1627 denied in *An Apologie of Declaration of the Power and Providence of God in the Government of the World*. The poem argues that "nature does not suffer decay": it is optimistic about the Providence of God and the undiminished nature of human life and of nature itself. Did Milton, however, exhibit some acceptance of such change around 1642 as Zera Fink posited, or is there maintenance of an absolute acceptance of the omnipotent Father's transfixing "in balance the scales of the fates and even / commanded each individual thing in the great order to preserve / its uninterrupted course perpetually"?[20] Regardless, by the time he wrote *Paradise Lost* he had accepted that the earth does decay: "higher Argument / Remains, sufficient of it self to raise / That name, *unless an age too late,* or cold / Climat, or Years damp my intended wing" (*PL* 9.42–45; my emphasis). The phrase surely alludes to the change from one age to a later one, when the world itself may have altered; it is not a reference to his own increasing "Years." A view of nature as decaying led to a different kind of God from that in traditional, organized, Western religions. In deistic thought God has created nature, but he does not interfere with what happens in nature: "study" nature becomes the byword, for in the life and growth of the flower and its decline and death is humankind's being. (Ralph Waldo Emerson's poem "The Rhodora: On Being Asked, Whence Is the Flower?" [1834] offers an example, as "The purple petals" fall into the pool making it black "with their beauty gay." "Why thou wert there.... The self-same Power that brought me there brought you.")

The question remained throughout the century and, as is well evidenced, tilted in favor of a deistic and transcendental view as the years leading to the nineteenth century approached. There were many who no longer regarded God's omnipresence in directing the world that he had created—the wound-up clock that is now slowing down and heading toward stoppage. In 1681 Thomas Burnet published his *Telluria theoria sacra*, translated in 1684 as *The Theory of the Earth* and in 1691 as *The Sacred Theory of the Earth*—the variously influential thesis that is basic to the world analyzed so brilliantly by Marjorie Hope Nicolson in *Mountain Gloom and Mountain Glory*.[21] Burnet's is not a world of miracles: its foundations in scientific inquiry, though he was a cleric and master of the Charterhouse, place him closer to people like Matthew Tindal, also a cleric. Among the letters he exchanged with Gottfried Wilhelm Leibniz are discussions of *Paradise Lost* and theories of the earth.[22] While Milton remained true to his conviction of the Word of God and God's Holy Scripture—the unchanging mind—he, like the Deists, came, through reason, to question things like the Trinity and proceed into his own "Church of One," as it so frequently has been labeled, and to see in manifest nature God revealed.

The problem with the Trinity, but not with something like the virgin birth, was its absence from the Word of God found in the Bible, but it does exemplify a development of thought and belief—of reason since biblical "truth" was missing—and, despite the "orthodoxy" of nature in *Paradise Lost*, he is on the verge of so exalting nature that an inroad into manifestation as revelation is not far behind. There has been development—perhaps unadmittably psychological. We would do well to remind ourselves of John Knott's provocative discussion of the way in which Milton's earlier confidence in the power of Scripture passed into the elusiveness of its truth as the "struggle of truth and error proved to be more complex."[23]

2

The doctrine of *scriptura sola* as Ken Simpson examines it[24] and which I have implied frequently already sets up another example of a kind of conflict between Milton's thought and his performance, but thus it demands consideration of change over time. Chapter 4 remarks upon the opposition of many ministers to the *Book of Common Prayer* and its mandate.[25] Simpson points out that "Because the preacher must channel the Spirit into the hearts of his congregation by the force of his own words, the liturgy of the Book of Common Prayer... is denounced as formal, external, a violation of the Spirit" and cites *Animadversions* (YP 1:682, 687) to define Milton's attitude toward the liturgy as a "rote lesson" and a "heathenish Battologie of multiplying words." Yet as Donald Roberts pointed out (see chapter 1, note 34), Milton seriously paraphrased a Collect from the *Book of Common Prayer* in the *Second Defense*, and as John King demonstrates, Milton employed the liturgy for satiric intent—irony, inversion, and burlesque. On the positive side, the Word, as Simpson tells us, "was regarded as a purer means of God's communication to believers" than even the Lord's Supper and baptism.[26] On the negative side, the use of the *Book of Common Prayer* in its rites and ceremonies such as marriage and communion subtly points to Milton's satiric intent in *Paradise Lost*.

The earlier Milton, it has been argued, and I think demonstrated, employed the liturgy as the *Book of Common Prayer* had calendared it for significant religious and life events. A. B. Chambers, in discussing the Nativity ode, writes, "it is a poem not about the birth itself but about the meanings and implications of Christmas day," and goes on to show "how heavily Milton depended on liturgical materials." The pericopes that Milton cites "are more than sufficient...to put beyond doubt the liturgical nature of Milton's language and imagery." According to William B. Hunter, "The application of the Calendar [prefixed to the prayer book] to explain biblical references in certain poems in English literature of the period can thus produce interesting insights as their authors participated in the daily readings." Milton "would have expected his readers to recognize the relationship between his poem and the reading of the day" (that is, here, in *Arcades*).[27] Liturgy has long been an important source of religious life, and Lieb has much to comment about it in *Poetics of the Holy* but without any reference to the *Book of Common Prayer*, since he is not dealing with contemporary pertinency. He notes significantly, among others, Saint Augustine in *The City of God* and the Divine Liturgy of James.[28]

Again it is meaning and usage of language that can wind us up into confusion. "Liturgy" denotes public religious service and implies a formulary. Milton's employment of biblical texts will pull into awareness the context, the spillover into other worlds and times, the lesson to be learned and applied and in that a description or analysis of the person or event involved. But this "private" (*scriptura sola*) use should not be called liturgy. Early on, as Chambers and Hunter argue, the occasion for recitation of a biblical text as laid out in the *Book of Common Prayer* evokes that occasion meaningfully for Milton's text. He has used the liturgy. But with his rejection of church discipline after 1637–40 would seem to come a rejection of the prayer book, and it has been suggested that by 1641–42 Milton had rejected its liturgy as well. The ordinances of

September 1644 and August 1645 officially removed the use of the *Book of Common Prayer*, and Milton's discussion a few years later in *Eikonoklastes*, "Chapter XVI. Upon the Ordinance against the Common-Prayer Book," makes clear his agreement. To him, "an Englisht Mass-Book, compos'd for ought we know, by men neither *lerned*, nor *godly*" is not lawful, for it will "at any time *deprive* us the exercise of that Heav'nly gift, which God by special promise powrs out daily upon his Church, that is to say, the spirit of Prayer" (YP 3:507). In the second book of *De doctrina Christiana*, chapter 4, "Of External Worship," his position is most clear: "Even the Lord's Prayer is a pattern or model, rather than a formula to be repeated verbatim either by the apostles or by the churches today. So it is clear that the church has no need of a liturgy" (YP 6:670). (We cannot be certain when these words in *De doctrina Christiana* were originally written, although their dating makes no difference to the important point here, but they are in close agreement with his position in the forties, a time when he was clearly beginning to work on what became that doctrinal treatise.)

Naturally Hannibal Hamlin frequently attends to biblical texts in *Psalm Culture and Early Modern English Literature* as well as the *Book of Common Prayer*. Hamlin calls attention to the fact that Adam's words prefacing his and Eve's prayer that ends book 10 of *Paradise Lost* are repeated in the description of their praying. He observes,

> This type of precise and immediate repetition occurs nowhere else in the poem and certainly underlines the importance of the passage. It somewhat resembles the pattern of the Book of Common Prayer in which one reads first the rubric describing what should be said, and then the text itself, though its more obvious source is in the formulaic use of repetition in Homeric epic.... Whether or not this repetition is intended to invoke the ritual repetition of the church liturgy, there are other clear signs that this scene is depicting the first "service" of penitential worship.

This "original" scene of penitence and contrition in the heart carries forward into the next book, with Psalm 51 being central to it (see *PL* 11.22–33). "Given the hostility of Milton and seventeenth-century Puritans to the high-church, 'popish' ceremonialism reinstituted in the English Church by Archbishop Laud, it is surprising to find just such a service celebrated in heaven, complete with incense swung from a 'Golden Censer.' It may be, however, that ceremonies that were idolatrous on earth were acceptable and pleasing in heaven."[29] This, of course, is the point I advanced before concerning bowing and kneeling; here the Son requests the Father to "bend thine ear / To supplication." Is it a coincidence that Psalm 51 is the prescribed reading for Ash Wednesday (as Hamlin observes)? Diane McColley elaborates the structural interfacing of "Te Deum laudamus," the anthem to be sung daily at morning prayer throughout the year, in the hymning of the angelic host in book 3 after the Son's offer to be incarnated as Savior for humankind. The anthem is the *only* nonscriptural canticle in the daily office of the *Book of Common Prayer*, as McColley tells us.[30]

The "truth" of liturgical readings and their relationships continues for Milton: employment of scriptural texts in his work has much to do with their existence in divine circumstances, their appropriateness to occasion and *not* to their appearance in the *Book of Common Prayer*'s calendar of readings. The allusiveness of meaning that a reading for a specific occasion or holy day as the church's prayer book prescribes seems to persist up to the turn of external discipline in the late 1630s.[31] Thereafter there would seem to be bifurcation into the "truth" of Scripture that the private person may employ and a liturgy of misuse by the church, in its assumptions and in what amounts to its removal of *scriptura sola*. This liturgy produces a mere repetition, always the same, always susceptible to the nonpersonal, the nonheartfelt. King explores the formulaic liturgy of ritual and the demands of the church and how they become fair game for satiric purposes. The biblical text, however, is not being satirized; it is formulaic, ritualistic, and thus meaningless as heartfelt truth, as the church practice iterates. But this is not really different for Milton from the parody against the Roman Catholic Church's dogma as in Eve's words at the Fall or the "transubstantiation" of the meal prepared for Raphael in book 5, lines 433–43.[32]

The public, standardized prayer that the *Book of Common Prayer* created opposes the private and heartfelt prayer that a specific occasion or specific point in time for the individual creates.[33] The abuse of Scripture which Puritans—and Milton—found in what had become the church's regulations (the "Prelate Lord's" regulations, thus linking it to Roman Catholicism), and what to Milton, in its public rote repetitions, felt was insincere for the individual, is denounced vehemently in *On the Forcers of Conscience* (dated around early 1647). The formulary thinking of the English church becomes another example of the incomplete Reformation from Catholicism that the Puritans protested. Referring to the Presbyterian-controlled House of Commons and their abolishment of public and private use of the *Book of Common Prayer* in August 1645, Milton castigates the actions of the Westminster Assembly as being only a part of the renaming of Catholic priest as "presbyter":

> Because you have thrown off your Prelate Lord
> And with stiff vows renounc'd his Liturgie
> To seise the widow'd whore Plurality
> From them whose sin ye envi'd, not abhorr'd.

The crux of the matter is the external/internal world of belief and faith, and their expression.[34] As he wrote in 1641, "to satisfie us fully in that, the Scripture onely is able, it being the onely book left us of *Divine* authority" (*Of Prelatical Episcopacy*, YP 1:624–25). Noting the prelates of the state church he laments as reason for his defection: "your lawlesse government, your ceremonies, your

Liturgy, an extract of the Masse book translated" (referring to the Roman missal; *Reason of Church-Government*, YP 1:787). Milton's position and its deductive source is clear: "Another reason which he [the Confuter] brings for liturgie, is *the preserving of order, unity, and piety*, and the same shall be my reason against Liturgy. For I Readers, shall alwayes be of this opinion, that obedience to the Spirit of God, rather then to the faire seeming pretences of men, is the best and most dutifull order that a Christian can observe" (*Apology*, YP 1:937). In an argument pointing out externality, he exclaims, "a Liturgy farre more like to the Masse-book then to any Protesant set forme, by his own words must have more communion with the *Romish Church*, then with any of the reformed" (*Apology*, YP 1:940).[35]

The intentionalities in Milton's "career" that he outlines in *Reason of Church-Government* cannot be ordered by such an external world as he has found the church creating. We have again a clear case of a changed mind as a result of externals, but at the same time the internal mind has rejected ideas and attitudes, not previously recognized as having their genesis in that external world. It is another case of "Yet Once More": what remains after all is shaken is faith, personal and not controlled by "things that are made"—human structures, human actions, human conceptions. The rejection of the church's liturgy is *not* a rejection of the biblical text or its efficacy. Important is any biblical text's context, and that context is implied in its usage by Milton, as for obvious example, the text of 1 Corinthians 15:28. Milton's presenting an Eve who alludes to the protevangelism in the last "speech" of *Paradise Lost* and connects it with the "all" of that frequent biblical text is, of course, reminding his readers that Jesus, the Incarnated Son of God, who has become the Christ in his resurrection from the dead ("The last enemy that shall be destroyed is death"), has reversed Adam's act and "all" "In Christ" "shall be made alive" (15:26, 22). The occasion of the biblical text—that is, the resurrection of Christ and belief of the faithful like Milton—reverses the history that the poem has regrettably had to recount in books 11 and 12 and proclaims that when "cometh the end," *all* shall join God once the Son has himself "put down all rule, and all authority and power" (15:24). It is the completion of the metaphoric return that Milton had envisioned when Michael "reduc'd / His Armie.../ Under thir Head imbodied *all* in one" (emphasis added).[36]

3

An epitome of what occurred during the seventeenth century, including the change in thinking and attitudes of Milton, with results seen in his two epics, is Debora Shuger's statement: "And it is this shift from social radicalism to interiority that subsequently becomes the governing narrative of the modern epic. *Paradise Lost* and *Paradise Regained* thus both reject Milton's earlier revolutionary idealism and subsequent discovery of the saving imagination."[37] What Michael Wilding has seen as Milton's development in *Paradise Regain'd* that we have observed in chapter 8 is related to this epitome. The development that the mind has undergone is clear from this view: it is a development in political (governmental) thought but also in religious thought. The external world, and its changes or its more incisive understanding, has determined the internal world, leaving faith and leaving imagination with its ultimate pre-view of hope. But that hope is realistically recognized to be a potential failure for the external world, and can be realized only in the individual. *Paradise Lost* ends with the human couple now embarking on their life's journey, "with wandering steps and slow." The reader—with Milton—should ponder whether the Providence of God that accompanies them will prevail or whether the implication of Satan's presence will frequently dominate. We know from books 11 and 12, at least, that both will occur. In looking over the history of the world as depicted in the Bible—and Milton's full subject in his epic makes books 11 and 12 necessary and basic, certainly no "untransmuted lump of futurity"—Milton had to be discouraged by the Nimrods that will emerge: hope can lie only with the Abrahams or Joshuas. The hope that humankind will follow the example of Jesus, reacting to all the temptations of the world, needs more than imitation: it needs an inculcation of the virtues that are Jesus, Son of God and Son of Man; it needs "deeds / Above heroic," even "though in secret done" (*PR* 1.14–15). It is not simply obedience that is counseled: it is the achievement of independence of personal worth, an essentiality in one's being. The irony of hope, as *Samson Agonistes* exemplifies, is that people wait for the *deus absconditus* to appear and act for them or at least to show them the way (as Samson is interpreted as being shown and doing when he proceeds to the feast of Dagon, "For some important cause"). Yet his act brings no change, and the people continue to await God's not hiding his face and unexpectedly to return. But the renovated Samson has joined the saints: he has done nothing external of true consequence; he has grown internally and essentially. His external act of collapsing the Philistine temple has set up the possible fulfillment of what could be a hope of the people of Dan: escape from Philistine yoke. But to no avail. Has any hope of escape passed their minds? In her interrogation of hope Mary C. Fenton confirms that "hope is bound to both the internal and external, the spiritual and the material. Milton's attention to interiority centers on the individual's hope for the renovating promise of Christian salvation, and yet Milton insists that this hope guides individuals toward exteriority, toward the life lived, toward the actively disciplined and virtuous life."[38] Ironically the Chorus merely waits for the *deus absconditus* to appear.

I have reviewed some religious problems in chapters 4, 5, and 6 in terms of internalities and externalities and developments in the concepts they induce. The externalities of chapters 2 and 3 have differing effects, for a kind of hypocritical overlay persists in matters of financial concern, in social and economic class stratification, and in meritocracy in government with even a theocratic dimension. While the religious world of belief seems to have changed in a rather full examination, one wonders whether a future would have led to further, similar refractions of doctrine. And what of the sphere of gender and marriage—male/female, husband/wife? A comparison with most seventeenth century writers puts Milton well ahead in the concern for the status of woman domestically, economically. Yet we have no attention to franchise for women, to empowerment of women in church discipline. In home and personal relationships the alleged misogyny of Milton (seen in Pauline influences as well as in Raphael's inexperienced and thus irrelevant comments) continues to receive critical attention.[39] Perhaps in this arena the positive statement for Milton is that his thinking did not proceed so far as it might have (not so far as some males—but not all males or even females—thinking today).

We have a Milton of frequently changed mind, as I trust this study has verified, and a Milton of unchanged mind where faith and God supervene. But I trust it has also been shown to be cogent that he did not pursue many obscure dilemmas that others have, partially because of his blinding faith, and that he, like all of us, could be (and was) delimited by his personal being and world, by life situations, and by faith. I have previously submitted as Milton's contribution to political theory (and I would add, his contribution to religious and social theory, despite what comes to be his own incomplete traversing of that road) the realization that it is the re-formation of the citizen, not the institution, that will achieve the most desirable world for humankind.⁴⁰ We do perceive one of the early moderns, but we also confront one from the past whose "radicalism" has been tempered by the conservatism of religion and the inflexibility of the social status quo: Milton's changed mind, and yet Milton's unchanged mind.

NOTES

Notes to Chapter 1, "Milton and Constancy of Thought"

1. Milton's poems are cited from my edition of *The Complete Poetry of John Milton* (Garden City, N.Y.: Doubleday Anchor, 1971); prose works are from *Complete Prose Works of John Milton,* 8 vols., ed. Don M. Wolfe et al. (New Haven: Yale University Press, 1953–82), hereafter cited as YP; foreign language prose texts, including the *Commonplace Book,* vol. 18 (1938), are from *The Works of John Milton,* 18 vols. in 21, ed. Frank Allen Patterson et al. (New York: Columbia University Press, 1931–38), hereafter cited as CM; the Trinity Manuscript is from *John Milton Poems Reproduced in Facsimile from the Manuscript in Trinity College, Cambridge* (Menston: Scolar Press, 1970).

2. Edward Le Comte, *Milton's Unchanging Mind* (Port Washington, N.Y.: Kennikat Press, 1973). He actually uses this citation of Satan's "boast" as an epigraph to epitomize Milton's "unchanging" mind!

3. As in the examples compiled in Edward Le Comte, *Yet Once More: Verbal and Psychological Pattern in Milton* (New York: Liberal Arts Press, 1954). The phrase "Yet once more" is, of course, part of the first line of *Lycidas,* and expresses there a return to a subject (or thought) or poem (or kind of poem) that has appeared before. Its use as this book's title, however, depreciates its significance. Its source in Hebrews 12:26–27 indicates not only what occurs within this poem but also what is the main thesis of the current book. God speaking from heaven says, "Yet once more I shake not the earth only, but also heaven. / And this *word,* Yet once more, signifieth the removing of those

things that are shaken, as of things that are made, that those things which cannot be shaken may remain." Within the poem the question "What boots it with incessant care / To tend the homely shepherd's trade / And strictly meditate the thankless muse?" is shaken, and what remains is faith in God, in him who "walkt the waves." I argue here that many concepts will be shaken in life, including Milton's concepts, to be altered or to be removed, but that which cannot be shaken—Milton's faith—will remain.

Le Comte's second and third essays appear also as: "*Areopagitica* as a Scenario for *Paradise Lost*," in *Achievements of the Left Hand: Essays on the Prose of John Milton*, ed. Michael Lieb and John T. Shawcross, 121–41 (Amherst: University of Massachusetts Press, 1974), for which it was initially written, and "Milton as Satirist and Wit," in *Th' Upright Heart and Pure*, ed. Amadeus P. Fiore, 45–59 (Pittsburgh: Duquesne University Press, 1967).

4. "It was from out the rinde of one apple tasted, that the knowledge of good and evil as two twins cleaving together leapt forth into the World. And perhaps this is that doom which *Adam* fell into of knowing good and evill, that is to say of knowing good by evill.... Assuredly we bring not innocence into the world, we bring impurity much rather: that which purifies us is triall, and triall is by what is contrary" (YP 2:514–15). For the early remnants of the morality play on *Paradise Lost*, see the Trinity Manuscript.

5. An infelicitous relationship with all his daughters has not yet been fully obliterated, as a couple of recent e-mails on the Internet continue to pontificate. I remind my reader that in 1665 when *Paradise Lost* was apparently complete (its manuscript is in the hand of an amanuensis, designated Amanuensis D), his eldest daughter, Anne, was 19, the middle daughter, Mary, was 17, and the youngest daughter, Deborah, was 13. And significantly, Anne was mentally challenged (even unable to sign her name), and the poem had been developed over numerous years. Much of what was the 1665 version would have been worked up, using whatever episodes written earlier were pertinent, beginning in 1661 when Mary was 13 and Deborah was 9. Does anyone really believe that these children were the amanuenses for *Paradise Lost*?

6. But I hasten to commend the discussions of some very sticky points of interpretation and of pertinent backgrounds to Milton's work and thought that are illuminated by numerous correspondents on the Web. There is so much that one can learn from one's colleagues!

7. I refer to such discussions as Charles Leslie, *The History of Sin and Heresy Attempted* (London: H. Hindmarsh, 1698); Samuel Johnson, "The Life of John Milton," *Prefaces, Biographical and Critical to the Works of the English Poets* (London: J. Nichols, 1779); F. R. Leavis, "Milton's Verse," *Sewanee Review* 2 (1933): 123–36; T. S. Eliot, "A Note on the Verse of John Milton," *Essays and Studies by Members of the English Association* 21 (1936): 156–64. Even theorizing about Milton, though not so egregious as S. B. Liljegren's in *Studies in Milton* (Lund: Gleerup, 1918), or Heinrich Mutschmann's in *Der andere Milton* (Bonn: K. Schrœder, 1920), emerges to explain a reading or dispel a question.

8. See, for examples, Elizabeth Sauer, "Toleration, the Irish Crisis, and Milton's *On the Late Massacre in Piemont*," 40–61, and Mary C. Fenton, "Milton's View of Ireland: Reform, Reduction, and National Polity," 203–29, both in *Milton Studies*, vol. 44, ed. Albert C. Labriola (Pittsburgh: University of Pittsburgh Press, 2005); John T. Shawcross, *"The Arms of the Family: The Significance of John Milton's Relatives and Associates* (Lexington: University Press of Kentucky, 2004), esp. 140–41, 158–60, 165–66; Michael Bryson, *The Tyranny of Heaven: Milton's Rejection of God as King* (Newark: University of Delaware Press, 2004); John Leonard, "'Thus They Relate Erring': Milton's Inaccurate Allusions," in *Milton Studies*, vol. 38, *The Writer in His Works*, ed. Albert C. Labriola and Michael Lieb (Pittsburgh: University of Pittsburgh Press, 2000), 96–121; Lawrence F. Rhu, "*Paradise Lost* and Traditional Exegesis," in *The Idea of Biblical Interpretation: Essays in Honor of James L. Kugel*, edited by Hindy Najman and Judith H. Newman, 485–512 (Leiden: Brill, 2004), 491.

9. William R. Parker, *Milton's Contemporary Reputation* (Columbus: Ohio State University Press, 1940), 60–61n4.

10. Robert Ellrodt, "Milton's Unchanging Mind and the Early Poems," *Milton Quarterly* 22 (1988): 59–62; quotation at 59; Cleanth Brooks and John Edward Hardy, *Poems of Mr. John Milton: The 1645 Edition with Essays in Analysis* (New York: Harcourt, Brace, 1951), 256; Le Comte, *Yet Once More*, 5.

11. Jonathan Goldberg, "Dating Milton," in *Soliciting Interpretation: Literary Theory and Seventeenth-Century English Poetry*, ed. Elizabeth D. Harvey and Katharine Eisaman Maus, 199–220 (Chicago: University of Chicago Press, 1990), 200.

12. One example of this reading of Milton and his work is Mary Ann Radzinowicz's *Toward* Samson Agonistes: *The Growth of Milton's Mind* (Princeton: Princeton University Press, 1978).

13. Goldberg, "Dating Milton," 201.
14. See Shawcross, "*The Arms of the Family.*" 146–61.
15. A study by Louis Schwartz entitled *Conscious Terrors: Milton and Maternal Mortality* (Burlington, Vt.: Ashgate, forthcoming), demonstrates so well what I mean by development in Milton's thinking and attitudes. He presents extensive evidence of what I call "change" ("development") in examining "the implications that ... trends in religious thought and social change had for Milton as he set about trying to fit his sense of the seeming injustice of childbed suffering with his vision of a just and good divinity." In the course of this study the vexing problem of Milton's attitudes toward women is reviewed and altering concepts, growing out of life experience as well as religious belief, are clearly established. Another forthcoming study in *Milton Quarterly* by John Creaser, "'Fear of Change': Closed Minds and Open Forms in Milton," explores Satan as an archconservative (as Le Comte's epigraph also should have registered for him) and Milton as open to change and unlimited possibilities.
16. John P. Rumrich, *Milton Unbound. Controversy and Reinterpretation* (Cambridge: Cambridge University Press, 1996), 24.
17. Peter C. Herman, *Destabilizing Milton:* Paradise Lost *and the Poetics of Incertitude* (New York: Palgrave Macmillan, 2005). This study relates in various ways to the subject of the present book and I am gratified to find our overall positions in agreement. However, I must protest a number of specific statements in it that raise questions of interpretation and careful reading as well as what become unqualified statements often resting upon the equivocal statements of others. An important examination of the problem of interpretation of Milton's texts—its destabilization—is Joseph Wittreich, *Why Milton Matters: A New Preface to His Writings* (New York: Palgrave Macmillan, 2006); see specifically xiv–xxiv of the preface for critical cruxes that have been raised.
18. Another example of potential incertitude early on lies in prophecy and hopefulness such as that expressed in *Of Reformation* (YP 1:600–601): "The Magistrate whose Charge is to see to our Persons, and Estates, is to bee honour'd with a more elaborate and personall Courtship, with large Salaries and Stipends, that hee himselfe may abound in those things whereof his legall justice and watchfull care gives us the quiet enjoyment. And this distinction of Honour will bring forth a seemly and gracefull Uniformity over all the Kingdome." Hope always implies the threat of failure—it is always uncertain. Likewise, it may

represent the unchanged mind as it persists in time, but it may also relate to the changed mind when it fails and is replaced by a different future from that formerly envisioned and, accordingly, by a different hope.

19. Line 70 in *Lycidas* ("Fame is the spur that the clear spirit doth raise") has not been seen as including a reference to either the Holy Spirit or the Spirit of God; the first it certainly is not. Compare the annotation in *A Variorum Commentary on The Poems of John Milton*, ed. A. S. P. Woodhouse and Douglas Bush (New York: Columbia University Press, 1972), vol. 2, part 2, p. 663. As noted, "clear" means "noble," and Milton used "cleare spirit" in *Animadversions* (YP 1:719) "apparently in the sense of noble, generous or exalted in mind": "Certainly never any cleare spirit nurst up from brighter influences with a soule inlarg'd to the dimensions of spacious art and high knowledge." The admixture of pagan deities that are identified with Christian deities and the Christian God-Man is a major reason for Samuel Johnson's disapproval of the poem: "The poem has yet a grosser fault. With these trifling fictions [Jove and Phœbus, Neptune and Æolus, etc.] are mingled the most awful and sacred truths, such as ought never to be polluted with such irreverend combinations"; see Johnson, "Life of Milton," in *Milton 1732–1801: The Critical Heritage*, ed. John T. Shawcross (London: Routledge & Kegan Paul, 1972), 293–94.

20. See later as well as note 32 below. In *Of Reformation* (1641), however, Milton calls upon God not to leave the church "prey to these importunate *Wolves*," with a specific apostrophe to the triunal being: "Thou therefore that sits't in light & glory unapprochable, *Parent* of *Angels* and *Men!* next thee I implore Omnipotent King, Redeemer of that lost remnant whose nature thou didst assume, ineffable and everlasting *Love!* And thou the third subsistence of Divine Infinitude, *illumining Spirit*, the joy and solace of created *Things!* one *Tri-personall* GODHEAD!" (YP 1:613–14). This address seems to indicate firm and continued belief in the Trinity, but it is a tract devoted, perhaps influentially, to the church and directed to "a FREIND."

21. This Pauline dictum underlies a much debated and much condemned line of *Paradise Lost:* "Hee for God only, shee for God in him" (4.299). The passage is said by the narrative voice and has been assigned to Milton as an unshakeable attitude about gender. (Herman seems to accept others' gendered readings of the divorce tracts as "certitude," ignoring all of Milton's remarks here.) Yet *Tetrachordon*—and we should remember the audience and intentionality involved—has that element

of "incertitude," as noted by his reference to the Hebrew text, which is the basic source of the story of Adam and Eve. It is only when Milton inserts the Pauline view of the relationship of husband and wife into this divorce tract that "superiority" and "inferiority" enter—and even not absolutely then as the continuing comment makes clear. However, having said that, I remind my reader not only that the Bible arose from a Hebrew culture but that the female has been (and in the Orthodox branch of modern Judaism still is) very often treated in an inferior way; we need only to remember the differences among Orthodox, Conservative, and Reformed Judaism as to synagogue services and seating, and the recent celebration of bat mitzvah. We can also note the fairly recent (American) Southern Baptist ruling of the wife's being subject to the husband, which has led to a sharp division in that church's ranks. Still, the subordinational relationship between Adam and Eve up to the end of book 10 in *Paradise Lost* is analogous to the relationship between God the Father and God the Son.

Students of Milton apparently need to be reminded of the Hebraic sources of the Old Testament, the Hebraic and Miltonic *deus absconditus* that Michael Lieb, *Theological Milton: Deity, Discourse, and Heresy in the Miltonic Canon* (Pittsburgh: Duquesne University Press, 2006), has exposed in *De doctrina Christiana*, as well as the "theopathetic deity" of all of Milton's works, and "the essentially Hebraic notion that *adonai 'echad*, God is one (Deut. 6:4)" (100). Indeed, the importance of Hebraic studies and culture as laid forth in the Old Testament for a full understanding of Milton's thought has recently been reaffirmed and extended significantly by Matthew Biberman, *Masculinity, Anti-Semitism, and Early Modern English Literature: From the Satanic to the Effeminate Jew* (Burlington, Vt.: Ashgate, 2004); Jason P. Rosenblatt, *Torah and Law in* Paradise Lost (Princeton: Princeton University Press, 1994), and *Renaissance England's Chief Rabbi: John Selden* (Oxford: Oxford University Press, 2006); and Jeffrey S. Shoulson, *Milton and the Rabbis: Hebraism, Hellenism, and Christianity* (New York: Columbia University Press, 2001).

22. When dealing with the prose works, we must remember that Milton is offering a text that involves argument, and as a student who is part of a debating team knows, one may argue a question in the affirmative one day and in the negative the next. This is the heritage of the kind of oratorical education that Milton underwent: one marshaled all kinds of arguments for and tried to refute any arguments against the position one was pre-

senting. The orator, indeed, might even leave out adverse material, deceitful and dishonest as that may seem. The orator's own beliefs are (or were supposed to be) immaterial, although one might be more driven by personal opinion. (We assume, probably correctly, that Milton believed that "Learning brings more Blessings to men than Ignorance" [*Prolusion VII*], but are we sure that he found Pythagoras's theory of the Harmony of the Spheres [*Prolusion II*] valid of truth or only valid for metaphoric language?) Yet, it seems, Miltonists take everything that appears in Milton's prose arguments at face value and as one of his absolute beliefs.

23. Herman, *Destabilizing Milton*, 136–37.

24. To cite one example of this kind of received belief, a "Christian" as a younger person almost surely believed in a virgin birth, and on faith may continue into adulthood to believe this, but as an older person he or she will probably wonder about such a "miracle," which will be rejected by many. Some will remain Christian and believe; some may cast this concept out and yet retain other Christian beliefs; some may find themselves rejecting the term "Christian" entirely, in large part because of such a nonhuman, unrealistic story. Here the idea of "virgin" would seem to mean an absence of sexual intercourse, both before the birth (with her husband Joseph) and as source of the conception of Jesus. It is only on faith that belief in a virgin birth will persist—whether it is faith in Gospel readings or faith in one's religious superiors or the repeated concept of the virgin birth that one hears from childhood on, which, if questioned, becomes an "Idol" (in this case an example of all four idols) such as Francis Bacon wrote of. There are few—both believers and nonbelievers—who will pursue the basic question of sexual circumstance. Since the subject is Jesus, the Son of God, who will become the Christ, the "lewdness" of sexuality cannot be allowed to enter the explanation of Jesus' existence (and allowing Joseph to be the father of Jesus denies the patrimony of God). All of this is answered by faith in God and God's miracle, and Milton accepts virgin birth without any question (see chapter 5).

Confounding the popular meaning of Mary as virgin, however, is Catholic dogma, which in the nineteenth century added to its understanding of the virgin birth by alleging an Immaculate Conception, but this relates to something quite different, and sexual overtones of the term are ignored. Any human parallel is dismissed (in this denial of physical relationship): this is a miracle of God and the point is not the conception itself, but the nature of the embryo in the conception. The Immaculate

Conception is derived from the New Testament apocryphal Book of James, known as "Protoevangelium Jacobi," written in Greek and surmised to have been written around AD 170–80, not completed apparently until the fifth century. (The oldest known manuscript in Greek is Bodmer Papyrus V in the Bibliotheca Bodmeriana in Geneva.) In the Book of James it is Anne, mother of Mary, who is recipient of God's preparation for the Incarnation by bearing a child who does not have the taint of original sin. The conception of Mary which Anne undergoes is thus "immaculate," and Mary is thereby born without spot of the "sin" that besets all other humans. She maintains her virginity in childbearing, though otherwise the result of sex, and indeed, there has even been belief that Mary and Joseph never engaged in intercourse, certainly not before the virgin birth but also not afterward. The matter of belief and faith in God, including faith in God's miracles, nullifies these questions and makes them blasphemous. It also obviates the moral and rational question that early Christianity argued.

25. An important way of reading any piece of literature, as influenced by the so-called New Criticism of the 1930s, is to read it without attention to its specific author or its specific moment in time or influences which may be discerned within it. Milton's work seems to defy such reading, however, for he often inserts (or seems to insert) himself into his writing, and *Sonnet VII* or *The Reason of Church-Government* are clear examples. Even dramatic works like *Comus* or *Samson Agonistes* have been seen as reflecting Milton the person and the Milton of a specific moment in time, though drama usually eschews direct authorial interference regardless of the personal background out of which the dramatic work (play or poem) may have arisen.

26. There are various other late changes and additions in the "final" text of *Comus*, which provide the subject of most criticism on the poem. Called *A Maske Presented at Ludlow Castle*, but generally known by its renamed adaptation *Comus*, a theatrical version by John Dalton and Thomas Arne in 1738, was written to celebrate the appointment by Charles I of John Egerton, Earl of Bridgewater, as Lord President of Wales, when in September 1634 his family joined him at Ludlow Castle, Shropshire. The manuscript version in the Trinity Manuscript is variously dated from 1634 through 1637 or from 1637 only. Sections, like the revised epilogue that was worked out in the manuscript, were added or revised (sometimes by repositioning passages from the initial writing in the manuscript) in 1637. The poem was published with the date 1637 but it may have actually

appeared in the first months of 1638, the title page date in that case being Old Style. (Although there are exceptions, printers used Old Style dating, such as may be given here, until around March 15, after which the printed date would record the next year. The accurate date for publication, if between January 1 and the middle of March, according to modern dating would be 1638.) In any case, the text of the first printed version is *not* the text that was presented in performance in 1634.

27. That Milton provided something like an "Academical Institution" may be an overstatement in our understanding of those words. Edward Phillips in his life of his uncle tells us that "the accession of Scholars was not great," that "several Gentlemen of his acquaintance" made application "for the Education of their Sons," and that Milton "laid out for a larger House, and soon found it out." (This is the house in the Barbican, the move apparently occurring from Aldersgate Street in September 1645, where his father and his in-laws later joined his family.) Aside from his nephews, there were some pupils before this date, and there were a few individual students after he moved from the Barbican. The total number of students is uncertain, but it seems to be no more than 12 and possibly fewer; the time period stretches from 1639 through 1672; thus, only a few students would have been together during any specific time. See William Riley Parker, *Milton: A Biography*. 2nd ed., ed. Gordon Campbell (Oxford: Clarendon Press, 1996), 924–25n19. For Phillips, see Helen Darbishire, ed., *The Early Lives of Milton* (London: Constable, 1932), 67, 66. For the Phillips boys and their probably being orphans in 1639, see *"Arms of the Family,"* 89–94.

28. John Spencer Hill, *John Milton: Poet, Priest and Prophet: A Study of Divine Vocation in Milton's Poetry and Prose* (Totowa, N.J.: Rowman and Littlefield, 1979).

29. Jameela Lares, *Milton and the Preaching Arts* (Pittsburgh: Duquesne University Press, 2001), 29. On the influence of the ministry on Milton's work specifically, see 17–29 and passim.

30. See ibid., chap. 4, *"Paradise Lost* and the Sermon Types," 141–68.

31. Peter C. Herman, *Squitter-wits and Muse-haters: Sidney, Spenser, Milton, and Renaissance Antipoetic Sentiment* (Detroit: Wayne State University Press, 1996), 177.

32. I employ the term "God" to mean the deity as unified being without reference to the question of persons, as it is usually meant and interpreted. The term "Godhead" likewise means "God" and has sometimes been employed to equate "divine nature"; it does *not* mean just God the Father. Yet Milton

frequently employs "God" to mean only "God the Father." His position on God the Son as being included in "Godhead" seems inconsistent and at times confused. God the Father, God the Son, and the Holy Spirit are specifically named here if meant. I must also point out that it is God the Son who represents Mercy (love, charity, the feminine), not God the Father. And God the Son *is* God although Milton (and many people) interchange God and God the Father. It is Adam who speaks the only occurrence of "mercifull" in the poem (*PL* 12.565), talking of "the onely God," observing "His providence," depending solely on him. In book 3 God the Father states:

> Man therefore shall find grace,
> The other none: in Mercy and Justice both,
> Through Heav'n and Earth, so shall my glorie excel,
> But Mercy first and last shall brightest shine.
>
> (*PL* 3.131–34)

God the Father is Truth, God the Son is Mercy, the Holy Spirit is Justice (compare Psalm 85). The "mercifulness" (love, charity) of God the Son is constant for Milton, and thus for God; Mercy and Justice are "discerned" in the Father's face (3.407). However, the Truth and the Justice that are also God may on occasion obliterate Mercy (3.202). In the Fall, Justice will see "the mortal Sentence" denounced, and Mercy in colleague with Justice will judge humanity. The Son "shall temper so / Justice with Mercie, as may illustrate most / Them full satisfied, and thee appease" (10.48–60, 77–79). (Compare Herman's questionable understanding of "God's mercifulness" in *Destabilizing Milton*, 114.)

33. See his letter to Charles Diodati, dated "23 IX 1637" (that is, November 23, 1637): "I will now tell you seriously what I am thinking of: to migrate into some inn of the lawyers where there is a pleasant and shady walk, because there there is a more convenient habitation among a number of companions, if I wish to remain at home, and a more suitable headquarters if I choose to make excursions to any place" (my translation; see *The Prose of John Milton*, ed. J. Max Patrick et al. [Garden City: Doubleday Anchor, 1967], 611). The Latin (and Greek) of this letter, number 7 in *Epistolarum Familiarium* (1674), is: "Dicam jam nunc serio quid cogitem, in hospitium Juridicorum aliquod immigrare, sicubi amœna & umbrosa ambulatio est, quod & inter aliquot sodales, commodior illic habitatio, si domi manere, & ορμητηριον ευπρεπεστερον quocunque libitum erit excurrere."

34. Pointedly, as Donald Roberts notes (YP 4:1.620n299, and referring to 587n173), Milton paraphrases a Collect of *The Book*

of Common Prayer for "The order for the administration of the Lords Supper, or holy Communion": "Almighty God, vnto whom all hearts bee open, all desires known, and from whom no secrets are hidde" (here cited from the 1621 edition by Bonham Norton and John Bill, B₁r, second gathering; in black letter). For discussion and English text of these quotations from the *Second Defense*, see YP 4:1.614–20.

35. John N. King, "Milton and the Bishops: Ecclesiastical Controversy and the Early Poems," in *Centered on the Word: Literature, Scripture, and the Tudor-Stuart Middle Way*, ed. Daniel W. Doerksen and Christopher Hodgkins, 277–97 (Cranbury, N.J.: Associated University Press, 2004). Christopher R. Hair, "Seventeenth Century Discord and the Paradise Within: Genesis in the Works of Winstanley, Milton, Hutchinson, and Cavendish" (Ph.D. diss., Department of English, University of Kentucky, 2005). See also the most pertinent remarks by Barbara K. Lewalski, in "Milton on Liberty, Servility, and the Paradise Within," in *Milton, Rights, and Liberties*, ed. Christophe Tournu and Neil Forsyth, 31–53 (Bern, Switzerland: Peter Lang, 2007).

36. Hair, "Seventeenth Century Discord," 69.

Notes to Chapter 2, "Milton and Legal Matters"

1. Charles Ross, *Elizabethan Literature and the Law of Fraudulent Conveyance: Sidney, Spenser, and Shakespeare* (Burlington, Vt.: Ashgate, 2003), 22, 133.

2. From J. Kersey's seventh edition of Edward Phillips, *The New World of English Words; or, A General Dictionary*, revised, corrected, and improved (1710).

3. A. B. Simpson, *An Introduction to the History of Land Law*, 2nd ed. (Oxford: Clarendon Press, 1986), 186.

4. See Parker, *Biography*; J. Milton French, *The Life Records of John Milton*, 5 vols. (New Brunswick: Rutgers University Press, 1949–58), and his *Milton in Chancery: New Chapters in the Lives of the Poet and His Father* (New York: Modern Language Association, 1939); and Gordon Campbell, *A Milton Chronology* (London: Macmillan Press, 1997).

5. Stephen Fallon, "'Elect above the rest': Theology as Self-Representation in Milton," in *Milton and Heresy*, ed. Stephen B. Dobranski and John P. Rumrich, 93–116 (Cambridge: Cambridge University Press, 1998), 99; and David Hawkes, "The Concept of the 'Hireling' in Milton's Theology," in *Milton Studies*, vol. 43, ed. Albert C. Labriola, 64–85 (Pittsburgh: University

of Pittsburgh Press, 2004), 67. Both are cited by Nicholas von Maltzahn in a forthcoming article entitled "Making Use of the Jews: Milton and Philosemitism."

6. The tract was apparently written in 1652 or 1653 when the matter of hirelings in the church had become an important divisive issue, and was revised slightly in 1659 when it was published. See John T. Shawcross, *Rethinking Milton Studies: Time Present and Time Past* (Newark: University of Delaware Press, 2005), 69–74.

7. Hawkes, "The Concept of the 'Hireling,'" 67, 69; Blair Hoxby, *Mammon's Music: Literature and Economics in the Age of Milton* (New Haven: Yale University Press, 2002).

8. David Hawkes, ed., *Paradise Lost: John Milton* (New York: Barnes & Noble Classics, 2004), xix, xxv. The sexual comparison of usury and sodomy saw usury as perverting "the properly barren nature of money, artificially making it 'breed', just as sodomy perverts the properly generative nature of sex, making it sterile" (xxv). Compare my comments about Milton's marriage to Mary Powell in "Arms of the Family," 8, 10 12, where I also imply the misreading of Milton's financial condition (see 39–41, 214–15n91, and passim).

9. Reference is to John Pell's letter to Theodore Haak (January 27, 1666) that "Mr Milton...is one of those who have lent M. Gr. money upon his land." See Nicholas von Maltzahn, "Naming the Author: Some Seventeenth-Century Milton Allusions," *Milton Quarterly* 27 (1993): 10, 6. The letter is a transcription by John Aubrey in Bodleian MS Aubrey 13, f. 92. Note also that Milton provided a bond for Richard Hayley (or Haley) of Elstree, Hertford, on July 27, 1674, for £40 (document in the New York Public Library), yielding further evidence of Milton's continued moneylending, even within a few months of his death.

10. Von Maltzahn, "Naming the Author," employs the term "usury." He particularly cites the protracted "generosity to his in-laws the Powells," who seem not at all to have evoked highly charitable feelings. "First was his own situation as a usurious Citt, brought up in a usurer's household and himself a usurer," von Maltzahn comments in relation to the possibility of Milton's being "mistaken for one of the 'scribes and Pharisees' he so often attacks." Parker, *Biography,* 397–400, explores the problems that Milton encountered as a result of all the financial business with the Powells (and others) after Parliament passed a law on August 1, 1650, "designed to end a very common means of defrauding the Government—the conveyance, by defeated Royalists, of part or all of their property into friendly, republican

hands in order to avoid seizure or penalties." Milton's incomplete petitions to the Committee on Compounding resulted in fines (which he paid), the canceling of payment of rents from his tenants, and rescinding the allowance of Anne Powell's thirds.

11. John Lilburne, *An Outcry of the Yougmen and Apprentices of London* [London, 1649]; and Hoxby, *Mammon's Music*.

12. J. Kersey, *The New World of English Words*, defines "to convey" as "to carry, to send into another Place, or Country, to make over an Estate, &c.," and "conveyance" as "In a Law-sense, an Instrument or Deed, by which Lands or Tenements are convey'd or made over from one to another." Phillips (*The New World of English Words*, 1658, 1671) does not include entries for these two words. Kersey had published *Dictionarium Anglo-Britannicum; or, A General English Dictionary* (London, 1708), with the same definitions but without indicating that he was revising Phillips's work.

13. See Parker, *Biography*, esp. 689–93n10 and 735–37n41, as well as French, *Life Records* and *Milton in Chancery*, and Campbell, *A Milton Chronology*.

14. *Pro populo anglicano defensio secunda* (1654), 83; YP 4:1.614.

15. Compare my discussion in "Arms of the Family," 75–76 and passim.

16. Simpson, *History of Land Law*, 186.

17. Parker, *Biography*, 748–49n11.

18. British Library, Cottonian Charters 1/5/5.

19. The Committee for Compounding was formed to come to agreement for payment with those who had not paid their assessment. Obviously, the more property owned, the higher the assessment. Christopher's taxable lands were specifically questioned a couple of times; see my "Arms of the Family," 16–18.

20. See Parker, *Biography*, 737n42.

21. Ibid., 397, 996n165. The referral to Excise Bonds comes from "To the Reader," in *Mr John Miltons Character of the Long Parliament and Assembly of Divines* (1681), A_2–A_2v. See French, *Life Records*, 2:279, for the text; hereafter cited in the text.

22. Milton's comment is in Latin: "usuram peccare in naturam, et in artem ait *Dantes* in naturam quia facit ut nummi pariant nummos qui est partus non naturalis, in artem quia non laborat &c."

23. John T. Shawcross, *John Milton: The Self and the World* (Lexington: University Press of Kentucky, 1993), 76–78, 281–84.

24. The entry from John Speed's *Historie of Great Britaine* is from the 1623 edition, and its frequent appearances in the

Commonplace Book are dated 1639–1641(?). Milton is using André Rivet's *Prælectiones in Caput XX Exodi* in its 1637 edition from Leyden; the handwriting of the holograph entry places it in late 1639 or after. (He was abroad from May 1638 through August 1639.)

25. Hanford's work on the *Commonplace Book* was published as "The Chronology of Milton's Private Studies," *PMLA* 36 (1921): 251–314, and was reprinted in *John Milton, Poet and Humanist: Essays by James Holly Hanford*, ed. John S. Diekhoff (Cleveland: The Press of Western Reserve University, 1966), 75–125.

26. See *"Arms of the Family,"* 73–75 and 80–82; the lower date of 1650 for the Machiavelli scribes' entries is also questioned, for some of the amanuenses may have been students and did include Milton's nephew Edward Phillips and perhaps John Phillips.

27. Hanford, "The Chronology," 101.

28. Hoxby, *Mammon's Music,* discusses Milton, economics, and trade in a number of places. He sees the "Lady's denunciation of luxury and her call for distributive justice" in *A Mask* as never rescinded, but also a development in the 1640s of argument for the benefit of circulation and free commerce (233–34). Later, Milton realized "that if economic discourse could serve as an instrument of liberation and a source of intellectual inspiration, short-term material grievances could lead men to surrender civic and religious freedoms" (235); he "is conscious of how readily a work ethic can degenerate into a compulsion to labor" (238). The upshot becomes a reformist ideal of active citizenship and of trust and faith. It also has much to indicate for us of "conceptual development."

29. References to Rivet appear in the second edition of *Doctrine and Discipline of Divorce* (YP 2:246, 292, 296, 297, 298) and *Tetrachordon* (YP 2:659). Those on 296–98 are in chapter 4 of the second book, in disagreement with Rivet on the question of God's dispensation in the matter of divorce, referring to his *Theologicæ & Scholasticæ Exercitationes* (Leyden, 1633).

30. Other appearances of the word "usury" will be found in the second edition of *Doctrine and Discipline of Divorce* (1644; YP 2: 289); *The Judgement of Martin Bucer* (1644; YP 2:425); and *Tetrachordon* (YP 2:661, 714).

31. Kerry MacLennan, "Milton's Contract for *Paradise Lost:* A New Reading" (paper presented at the Eighth International Milton Symposium at Grenoble, France, June 2005).

32. Jonathan Richardson, *Explanatory Notes and Remarks on Milton's* Paradise Lost (London, 1734), cxv.

33. Facsimile printed in *John Milton's Complete Poetical Works Reproduced in Photographic Facsimile*, 4 vols., ed. Harris F. Fletcher (Urbana: University of Illinois Press, 1945), 2:112.

34. See my *Rethinking Milton Studies*, chap. 6, 103–21.

35. The Savonarola entry is in Italian in Milton's hand, from *Oracolo della Renovatione della chiesa* (YP 1:48–49), and is dated 1639–40(?). The Speed entry is in English in Milton's hand (*Historie*, 614–16), and is dated 1639–41(?). The third item is from Paolo Sarpi's *Historia* (1619), in Latin in Milton's hand, and is dated 1641–43(?).

36. CM 18:221–26, 509–10 prints what it calls an "Index Legalis" and assumes Milton's authorship since these commonplace book notes appear in a manuscript including "Proposalls of certaine expedients for the preventing of a civil war now feard, & the settling of a firme government" (an attributed and accepted tract), "A Letter to a Friend Occasioned by the Ruptures in the Commonwealth," and a number of state papers. The manuscript, known as the Columbia Manuscript, is owned by Columbia University Library, MS X823 M64/S52. In the hands of two scribes and dating after 1659 for at least one scribe's work, these items appear, in modern pagination, on pp. 19–21, 21–23, 23–79, respectively, from the front of the manuscript. Maurice Kelley in YP 1:954–60, discusses the manuscript, and the notes are given in a translation by Ruth Mohl. The "Legal Index," in the hand of a different scribe from the one recording the above-mentioned Miltonic work, begins from the back of the manuscript on pp. 7–1 (or 144–50 in modern, straightforward pagination). The date of these entries may be before or after those already cited, and there seems to be no connection between these two parts of this manuscript. Whoever wrote the notes down either made many errors or did not know Latin well, or both. The notes have not been accepted as Milton's despite the Columbia editor's belief that "Milton prepared an elaborate page with twenty capital letters for the Index" (509) and that it "is an interesting sidelight on his interest in law" (510). Kelley states, "the form of the notes and table of the *Index* differs markedly from that of Milton's authentic *Commonplace Book*" (956). The amazing and foundationless Columbia pronouncement is: "This unfinished collection of notes on legal matters, which exactly parallels the entries on other subjects in the *Commonplace Book*" (509). The approach to content is, on the contrary, very different.

37. See Jacob Philipp Tomasini's *Petrarcha Redividus* (1635), in Latin in Milton's hand, which is dated 1643–44(?); and William Schickhard's *Jus Regium Hebræorum* (1625), in Latin in Milton's hand. Hanford left the date indeterminate and Mohl gives 1639–50(?). Handwriting indicates that the entry was made much earlier than 1650; it appears on p. 186 of the *Commonplace Book* (the second page that concerns "The King of England"), which was begun by 1639–41, and this entry had to have been made before the third page on "The King of England" (195), which was begun in 1640–42(?). Other entries on p. 186 are dated 1639–41?), 1642–47(?), and 1644–47(?). Three entries are cited as 1644–47(?), but they clearly follow the entry of the Schickhard item. Thus, perhaps, this entry was made in 1640–42.

Notes to Chapter 3, "Milton the Republican"

1. Barbara K. Lewalski, "How Radical Was the Young Milton?" in *Milton and Heresy*, ed. Stephen B. Dobranski and John P. Rumrich, 49–72 (Cambridge: Cambridge University Press, 1998), 49, 64.
2. David Loewenstein, "The Radical Religious Politics of *Paradise Lost*," in *A Companion to Milton*, ed. Thomas N. Corns, 348–62 (Oxford: Basil Blackwell, 2001), 355.
3. Matthew Biberman, "'The Earth Is All Before Me': Wordsworth, Milton, and the Christian Hebraic Roots of English Republicanism," in *Romantic Generations: Essays in Honor of Robert F. Gleckner*, ed. Ghislaine McDayter, Guinn Batten, and Barry Milligan, 102–28 (Lewisburg, Pa.: Bucknell University Press, 2001), 103 and passim. Biberman finds roots in Hebraic thought and action; thus, note 18 to his chapter 1 provides further significant reference. He notes that ancient Israel stands at the top of a hierarchy of republican models and views the Eden of *Paradise Lost* "as a republic where the only contract binding individuals to other individuals is marriage, a law Milton places above all other" (110). Taking a different tack to the question, David Harris Sacks, "Adam's Curse and Adam's Freedom: Milton's Concept of Liberty," in *Milton, Rights, and Liberties*," ed. Christophe Tournu and Neil Forsyth, 69–98 (Bern, Switzerland: Peter Lang, 2007), concludes that Milton "fits the category" of "republican" later in his career (70), basing it on the concept of "liberty" as central to "the freedom granted on the voluntary rendering of godly service for the common good" and thus "loyal service to the republic, with Christian liberty" (that is, "absolute

obedience to God's commands" [95]). Compare both Lewalski, "Milton on Liberty," and Martin Dzelzainis, "Liberty and the Law," in Tournu and Forsyth, wherein he concludes that for Milton it is not only an abstract right but also "the space within which we are free from interference and coercion" (66).

4. On the entwining of religion and government at this time, see Charles W. A. Prior, *Defining the Jacobean Church: The Politics of Religious Controversy, 1603–1625* (Cambridge: Cambridge University Press, 2005), who examines clerical attention to governmental control over church governance, ritual, and liturgy instead of clerical concerns about theological matters. David Reid, "Milton's Royalism," *Milton Quarterly* 37 (2003), discusses "how Milton's poetry turns royalism in the sublime mode to libertarian ends," and concludes that Milton "exalts the Kingdom of God in order to set Christians free from subjection to earthly kingdom" (31). Likewise, see Bryson's argument in *Tyranny of Heaven* of God the Father's "tyranny" and true kingship being that of the Son, through love.

5. John F. Wilson, *Pulpit in Parliament: Puritanism during the English Civil Wars, 1640–1648* (Princeton: Princeton University Press, 1969).

6. *Table Talk of John Selden*, ed. Frederick Pollock (London: Quaritch, 1927), 89, and see Rosenblatt, *Renaissance England's Chief Rabbi*, 264.

7. N. H. Keeble, "Milton and Puritanism," in Corns, *A Companion to Milton*, 132, 133–34.

8. John Rogers, *The Matter of Revolution: Science, Poetry, and Politics in the Age of Milton* (Ithaca, N.Y.: Cornell University Press, 1996), 109; Dzelzainis, "Republicanism," in Corns, *A Companion to Milton*, 308. Also compare my comments in "Arms of the Family," 158.

9. See also the very important analysis of the tracts of this period by Barbara K. Lewalski in "Milton: Political Beliefs and Polemical Methods, 1659–60," *PMLA* 74 (1959): 191–202.

10. Diane Purkiss, *Literature, Gender, and Politics during the English Civil War* (Cambridge: Cambridge University Press, 2005), 192n26. She also epitomizes *Areopagitica* as being Milton's giving "birth" by appropriating the powers of a father, becoming both father and mother to himself (189).

11. See also Ann Hughes, *The Causes of the English Civil War* (New York: St. Martin's Press, 1991).

12. Andrew Milner, *John Milton and the English Revolution: A Study in the Sociology of Literature* (Totowa, N.J.: Barnes & Noble Books, 1981), 136. Generally Milner views pre-Restoration

times as one that triumphs, whereas the post-Restoration period sees Reason embattled; thus, Milton's major poems result from the quandary of why Reason failed (137).

13. Selden, *Table Talk,* 433; Rosenblatt, *Renaissance England's Chief Rabbi,* 263.

14. Mark Fortier, *The Culture of Equity in Early Modern England* (Burlington, Vt.: Ashgate, 2005), 89.

15. Milton's use of "citizen" seems to mean a person living in a city (the word's etymology): "For the Citizens of *London* rising to apprehend a riotous servant of the Bishop of *Salisbury*...were by the Bishop...so complained of, that the King therewith seized on their liberties, and set a Governour over the Citie" ("A Postscript," YP 1:971); or, a fellow Englishman: "I apply'd my selfe...to be an interpreter & relater of the best and sagest things among mine own Citizens throughout this Iland in the mother dialect" (*Reason of Church-Government,* YP 1:811–12); or, a resident of a specific country, whether noble or not: Poland "thenceforth turned her thoughts upon some one in her own Nation...neither did she seek long among her Citizens whom she should prefer above the rest...for although in the equality of our Nobles many might be elected, yet the vertue of a Hero appeared above his equals, therefore the eyes and minds of all men were willingly and by a certain divine instinct turned upon the High Marshal of the Kingdom, Captain of the Army *John Sobietski*" (*A Declaration, or Letters Patents,* YP 8:446–47). While he does not distinguish "citizen" in terms of class or gender, the electorate referred to in the last item (a "translation") was undoubtedly only "men," which word here may be precise. Milton's "people" are only "some people."

Hugh Jenkins, "*Quid nomine populi intelligi velimus:* Defining the 'People' in *The Second Defense,*" in *Milton Studies,* vol. 46, ed. Albert C. Labriola, 191–209 (Pittsburgh: University of Pittsburgh Press, 2007), asks, "who exactly are the English people Milton is defending?" (193), and his examination of "populace," "plebs" (which counters "class assumptions"), or "vulgi," and "cives" leads to the awareness of Milton's ambiguity in his argument against Salmasius (and More, that is, du Moulin). The "firmest" distinction is between Protestant citizenship and Catholic "superstition," and "contrasting the 'people' and the 'mob' enlarges the former category while further restricting the latter" (201), leading to "two forms of *cives.*" Jenkins recognizes Milton's "elitism" as a "moral and intellectual vanguard" (203).

16. Milton's reference to a "Gynæcocratiæ" may lampoon Salmasius's jab that the English government would overthrow all states, but it also most clearly pokes fun at the influence of women upon Salmasius's world and is dismissive of rule by women. Further, his turning of his opponent's words to mean "the dregs of the populace, but hardly of the middle class" likewise banishes those not "of the middle class, which produces the greatest number of men of good sense and knowledge of affairs" (in distinction from those of excessive wealth and luxury and those of want and poverty). See YP 7:470–71, as well as CM 7:391. Donald Roberts's note (YP 7:470–71n30) should be attended to by those arguing for meaningful accuracy in Milton's language: "Milton...frequently telescopes scattered quotations or gives as direct quotations his own paraphrases and probably his own notes on Salmasius' text. Many of these are fair to Salmasius' general sense, but quite a few are inaccurate and misleading—implications that Milton has made in terms of his own bias and not existent in either Salmasius' text or his mind."

17. Michael Wilding, "Milton's *Areopagitica:* Liberty for the Sects," *Prose Studies* 9, no. 2 (1986): 17. Usually it seems men thought of women as nonentities in these "serious" matters of religion and politics; they were represented by their male counterparts (father, husband) or otherwise not very often given any status. See Keith L. Springer's information on women in the seventeenth-century Reformed church, *Dutch Puritanism: A History of English and Scottish Churches of the Netherlands in the Sixteenth and Seventeenth Centuries* (Leiden: E. J. Brill, 1982).

18. Thomas N. Corns, "Milton and Class," in *Running Wild: Essays, Fictions, and Memoirs Presented to Michael Wilding,* ed. David Brooks and Brian Kiernan, 55–68 (Manohar: Sydney Association for Studies in Society and Culture, 2004), 64.

19. Ibid., 57, 59, 60.

20. See, for one instance, the one-sheet broadside *A Declaration of the Well Affected to the Good Old Cause in the Cities of London, Westminster, and Southwark: with the joynt consent and concurrence of all the well-affected in all other the cities, towns and boroughs of England and Wales, for the return and session of the Long Parliament, [interrupted by the late Protector April 20. 1653.] directed to the surviving Members of that Parliament,* dated May 2, 1659.

21. An earlier usage provides a similar general meaning: "Well may the Parliament and best-affected People not now be

troubl'd at his calumnies and reproaches, since he binds them in the same bundle with all other the reformed Churches" (*Eikonoklastes, YP* 3:512).

22. Peter Coleman, "The Good Old Cause: John Milton's *Areopagitica* Revisited," *Quadrant* 49 (October 2005): 64-70; available at http://www.quadrant.org.au/php/article_view.php?article_id .-1211.

23. Elizabeth Skerpan Wheeler, "Early Political Prose," in Corns, *A Companion to Milton*, 264. Distinguishing different positions concerning "republicanism" in Milton's diffuse epic and the prose, and bothered by a superficial application of "Machiavellianism," William Walker, "Towards Assessing 'Milton's Republicanism' in *Paradise Lost*," in Tournu and Forsyth, *Milton, Rights, and Liberties*, 241–62, argues that *Paradise Lost* stresses the virtue of the fallen individual (not the virtue of other individuals) through such qualities as "temperance,...patience, hope, faith, charity" (246). These are Pauline virtues, not Aristotelian, and even condemned by Machiavelli.

24. See, for example, my *Paradise Regain'd: "Worthy T'Have Not Remain'd So Long Unsung"* (Pittsburgh: Duquesne University Press, 1988): "*Paradise Regain'd* in its own way is a political document put in metaphysical terms. The way to fashion one's worthiness is to be so worthy within that all external action demonstrates that inner being. Worth is not shown by a mere following of command or maintenance of prohibition. It is by self-action" (82). See "The Higher Wisdom of *The Tenure of Kings and Magistrates*,"in *Achievements of the Left Hand: Essays on the Prose of John Milton*, ed. Michael Lieb and John T. Shawcross, 142–59 (Amherst: University of Massachusetts, 1974): "the answer to the world's political dilemma in a re-formation of the democratic citizen, not of institutions" (155); and in my "'Connivers and the Worst of Superstitions': Milton on Popery and Toleration," *Literature & History* 7 (August 1998): 51–69, remark his admonition in *Of True Religion:* "Let us therefore amend our lives with all speed" (63).

25. Michael Chappell, "De-fencing the Poet: The Political Dilemma of the Poet and the People in Milton's *Second Defense* and Shelley's *Defence of Poetry*," in *Milton, the Metaphysicals, and Romanticism*, ed. Lisa Low and Anthony John Harding, 136–50 (Cambridge: Cambridge University Press, 1994), 136, 137, 141, 138; Charles Geisst, *The Political Thought of John Milton* (London: Macmillan, 1984), 40; Sharon Achinstein, *Milton and the Revolutionary Reader* (Princeton: Princeton University Press, 1994), 224, 16, 14.

26. Rachel J. Trubowitz, "Body Politics in *Paradise Lost,*" *PMLA* 121 (2006): 391.

Notes to Chapter 4, "Milton, the Church, and Theology"

1. See Stephen R. Honeygosky, *Milton's House of God: The Invisible and Visible Church* (Columbia: University of Missouri Press, 1993), for a full discussion of this important and much misunderstood subject.

2. See Thomas Burgess, *Milton Not the Author of the Lately D iscovered Arian Work* De Doctrina Christiana (London: H. P., 1829), and William B. Hunter, *Visitation Unimplor'd: Milton and the Authorship of* De Doctrina Christiana (Pittsburgh: Duquesne University Press, 1998).

3. See my rebuttal of Hunter's position, especially those arguments he advanced as most indicative of Milton's nonauthorship, in *Rethinking Milton Studies,* chaps. 6 and 7, 103–51. Further, we must always remember that *Paradise Lost* is a literary work and *De doctrina Christiana* a treatise compiling theological information and positions. A recent comment on the Milton-L Web site, in trying to remind other contributors that *Paradise Lost* is a literary work, however, calls its "religion" "offensive" and its ethical stance for an individual "outrageous"—another example of one's personal beliefs entering a supposedly objective reading.

4. This seems to be generally true even today, but, regardless, Milton writes: "On the whole the moderns are of the opinion that everything was formed out of nothing (which is, I fancy, what their own theory is based on!)" (YP 6:305). For discussion of the significance of "All in All," see the first three essays in *"All in All": Unity, Diversity, and the Miltonic Perspective,* ed. Charles W. Durham and Kristin A. Pruitt (Selinsgrove, Pa.: Susquehanna University Press, 1999), by Diane Kelsey McColley (21–38), Albert C. Labriola (39–47), and Diana Treviño Benet (48–66).

5. The Hebrew verb *merachepath* and various commentators on it are discussed by David Daiches, "The Opening of *Paradise Lost,*" in *The Living Milton,* ed. Frank Kermode, 55–69 (London: Routledge & Kegan Paul, 1960), 65–67. In *De doctrina Christiana,* Milton discusses this verse as "the spirit of God brooded" (which "birth" symbolism is not pursued), relating it to the "divine breath which creates and nourishes everything" but then writing, "It seems more likely, however, that we

should here interpret the word as a reference to the Son, through whom, as we are constantly told, the Father created all things" (YP 6:282; see also 6:304–05).

6. He comments, citing Hebrews 11:3, "That the world was created, must be considered an article of faith" and that "CREATION IS THE ACT BY WHICH GOD THE FATHER PRODUCED EVERYTHING THAT EXISTS BY HIS WORD AND SPIRIT, that is, BY HIS WILL" (YP 6:300). He rejects the interpretation that the Hebrew, Greek, and Latin word for "create" means "to make out of nothing"; "each of them always means 'to make out of something'" (305–06). "It is clear, then, that the world was made out of some sort of matter.... That matter should have always existed independently of God is inconceivable.... There remains only this solution...that all things came from God" (307).

7. Aside from the significance for Milton that his comments on heresy, which follow here, point to, we should admit that "heretic" is loosely employed by people to apply to anyone who has any belief or opinion that does not coincide exactly with what purports to be every "orthodox" belief or opinion. Were that an accurate definition, it would mean that most (even "all"?) people are heretics.

8. Whether Milton used Arminius's writing or extensively employed the Remonstrants' summary of the synod in 1618–19 is uncertain. According to Maurice Kelley (YP 6:85–86), he may have used *Acta et Scripta Synodalia Dordracena Ministrorum Remonstrantium in Foederato Belgio* (1620) "in setting up his Remonstrant doctrines at the beginning of his treatise," but "conclusive verbal parallels between chapters iii–iv of the *Christian Doctrine* and the *Acta* are not readily apparent, and such is the case with Milton's chapters and the writings of Arminius and Episcopius."

9. James Holly Hanford, *A Milton Handbook*, 4th ed. (New York: F. S. Croft, 1946), 228–31; 5th ed., rev. James G. Taaffe (New York: Appleton-Century-Crofts, 1970), 191–94.

10. Milton cites Arminius, Arminianism, and Arminians in *A Postscript* (in the Smectymnuan 1641 *An Answer*, which is ascribed to him; YP 1:975); *Apology for Smectymnuus* (1642; 1:917); *The Doctrine and Discipline of Divorce* (1644, 2nd ed., 1:287, 293); and *Areopagitica* (1644; 1:519–20). These references seem negative or at best incidental. On the other hand, later comments are positive or at least accepting; see *The Ready and Easy Way* (1660, 1st ed.; 7:381–82), *Of True Religion* (1673; 8:423, 425–26, 437). (Of course, it should be remembered that in all of these works he is engaged in argumentation.) Hanford

tells us that "These radical ideas [of predestination, transubstantiation, and the like] deeply affected the currents of thought at Cambridge, and Milton could not have escaped being impressed by them. His own later Arminianism, maintained against the doctrines of the very group with which he was at first politically allied, may have its roots in the discussion which raged around Montagu's pronouncements" (*A Milton Handbook*, 362 in 4th ed.; omitted in 5th ed.). The reference is to the contention of Richard Montagu of King's College (*A Gagg for the new Gospell? NO: A New Gagg for An Old Goose* [London: Printed by Thomas Snodham for Matthew Lownes and W. Barrett, 1624]; *Apello Caesarem* [1625]) who sought to repudiate the alleged errors of Protestantism as practiced by the state church charged by Calvinists and Roman Catholics.

11. Hill, *John Milton*, 77. Lares, *Milton and the Preaching Arts*, 18–29, minimizes the significance of the events in Milton's life and in the ecclesiastical life of England during the 1630s and argues that it is the *Canons* of 1640, specifically its required "Et Cetera" oath (cited just below in my text), that was the decisive turning point for Milton. Milton refers to this oath in *Reason of Church-Goverment* (YP 1:822–23). But the substance of this oath of allegiance and supremacy to monarch and church had existed in prior documents as well as in the 1604 and 1612 *Canons*, though in briefer form. The specific sentence in the 1640 *Canons* that gave rise to the labeling of the oath (and this is stressed by Lares) is: "Nor will I ever give my consent to alter the Government of this Church, by Arch-bishops, Bishops, Deanes, and Arch-deacons, &c. as it stands now established" (YP 1:990–91). But this was standard expression. In *Constitutions and Canons* (1633) — the rest of the title is that of the 1640 version given here in note 12, except for "their synod begun at London, Anno dom. 1603" and "London, Printed by John Norton, for Joyce Norton, and Richard Whitabker, 1633" — canons 1 and 2 assert the king's supremacy, and canons 7 and 8 discuss, respectively, "Impugners of the Government of the Church of England by Archbishops, Bishops, &c. Censured" and "Impugners of the form of consecrating and ordering Archbishops, Bishops, &c. censured." In the required "Oath against Simony at institution into Benefice," the phrase "Arch-bishops, Bishops, or other person or persons" appears twice. And similarly Laud's "Metropolitical Articles for Lincoln Diocese, 1634" (Fincham, *Visitation Articles and Injunctions of the Early Stuart Church*, vol. 2 [Woodbridge, Suffolk: Boydell, 1998], 92–93; Article 5.19) includes the sentence: "Or against the governement of the

Church of England under the kings most excellent maiesty, by arch-bishops, bishops, deanes, arch-deacons, and other officers of the same: affirming, that the same is repugnant to the word of God, and that the said ecclesiasticall officers, are now lawfully ordained?" The "Et Cetera" and the whole idea of this 1640 *Canons* had existed for some years and had had its influence upon other bishops' visitations and orders. While a facing up to what the church and its discipline had become may have only gradually sunk in since his days at Christ's College, Milton's rejection of being a minister and thus a preacher had surely occurred prior to his trip to the Continent. But his ministerial background and its sermonizing remained a strong force as divine vocation and its emergence in authorship proceeded.

Barbara K. Lewalski, *The Life of John Milton: A Critical Biography* (Oxford: Blackwell, 2000), is less specific when she writes of the 1630s period and Milton's situation: "Milton rejoiced in his escape from business and the law, and the ministry seemed less and less viable to him as the Laudian takeover of the church accelerated. If he did not overtly reject a clerical role, neither did he imagine himself undertaking it" (53). However, the matter of business and the law, as we saw in chapter 2, continued to exist for Milton, albeit a different kind from what we normally think of, allowing him to engage in a divine vocation rather than a workaday one.

12. See *Constitutions and Canons Ecclesiasticall; Treated upon by the Archbishops of Canterbury and York, Presidents of the Convocations for the respective Provinces of Canterbury and York, and the rest of the Bishops and Clergie of those Provinces, And agreed upon with the Kings Majesties Licence in their severall Synods begun at London and York, 1640* (London: Printed by Robert Barker, and by the Assignes of John Bill. 1640); selections in YP 1:985–98.

13. The "University Subscription Books" (signed on March 26, 1629, and July 3, 1632) assert:

> (1.) That the King's Majesty, under God, is the only supreme governor of this realm, and of all other his Highness's dominions and countries, as well in all spiritual or ecclesiastical things or causes, as temporal.... (2.) That the Book of Common Prayer, and of ordering of bishops, priests, and deacons, containeth in it nothing contrary to the Word of God, and that it may lawfully so be used. (3.) That we allow the Books of Articles of Religion agreed upon by the

Archbishops and bishops of both provinces, and the whole Clergy in the Convocation holden in London in the year of our Lord 1562; and acknowledge all and every the Articles therin contained... to be agreeable to the Word of God. (French, *Life Records*, 1:190, 271)

One must wonder whether Milton realized what he was signing or whether expedience triumphed over hypocrisy.

14. See *The First and Large Petition of the Citie of London and of other Inhabitants thereabouts: For a Reformation in Church-government, as also for the abolishment of Episcopacy: With A Remonstrance thereto annexed, of the many Pressures and Grievances occasioned by the Bishops, and the sundry inconveniences incident to Episcopacie. The Tyrannie and Extortion practised in Ecclesiasticall Courts, together with the vnlawfulnesse of the Oath Ex Officio: preferred to the high and honourable Court of Parliament* (Printed Anno Dom. 1641), in YP 1:976–84.

15. Andrew Foster, "Church Policies of the 1630s," in *Conflict in Early Stuart England: Studies in Religion and Politics, 1603–1642*, ed. Richard Cust and Ann Hughes, 193–223 (London: Longman, 1989).

16. Shawcross, *Self and the World*, 61–70.

17. Hill, *John Milton*.

18. Montagu, *A Gagg for the new Gospell?*, A_2r, 140, 145.

19. See Fincham, *Visitations Articles*, 82. A copy of Archbishop of Canterbury William Juxon's "Articles" will be found in the Public Record Office, SP16/308/43, in the hand of Edward Nicholas, Clerk of the Privy Council. The diary of Walter Yonge (British Library, Additional MS 35331, f. 62v), dated April 1635, copies Juxon's "Articles" (omitting number 8 on bowing), and reports "that their author was Laud, who aimed 'to drawe all ministers to subscribe unto certayne newe positions, and as many as shall refuse to bee suspended, or dealt withall in the Highe Commission'" (Fincham, 126n1).

20. See also Emma Rhatigan, "Knees and Elephants: Donne Preaches on Ceremonial Conformity," *John Donne Journal* 23 (2004): 185–213. The concern with kneeling echoes in *Paradise Lost* quite tellingly. Satan rejects the concept ("To bow and sue for grace / With suppliant knee" [1.112–13]; "None left but by submission" [4.81]; "to receive from us / Knee-tribute yet unpaid, prostration vile" [5.781–82]; "Will ye submit your necks, and chuse to bend / The supple knee?" [5.787–88]), but, of course, the hypocritical Satan "Oft... bowd / His turret Crest, and sleek

enamel'd Neck, / Fawning, and lick'd the ground whereon she trod" (9.524–26). It all depends on circumstances and desires. Proper knee tribute is defined when the Father proclaims, of the Son, that "All knees to thee shall bow" (3.321) and "to him shall bow / All knees in Heav'n" (5.607–08). (A source of these lines is Philippians 2:10, "that at the name of Jesus every knee should bow, of *things* in heaven, and *things* in earth, and *things* under earth.") Abdiel repeats this in his challenge to Satan: "to his only Son.../ every Soul in Heav'n / Shall bend the knee" (5.815–17), and causes Satan to kneel with the "noble stroke" of "His massie Spear": "ten paces huge / He back recoild; the tenth on bended knee" (6.189–94). Adam and Eve, in the morning hymn, "Lowly...bow'd adoring, and began / Thir orisons, each Morning duly paid" (5.144–45). At the end of book 10, they pray to God and "prostrate fall / Before him reverent" (10.1087–88), repeated by the narrator and reprised in the first lines of book 11: "Thus they in lowliest plight repentant stood / Praying." While the words "kneel" or "knees" are not used here, the "prostration" contrasts Satan's "prostration vile," and the word "stood" creates ambiguity alongside "fall" and "lowliest." Not every act of kneeling or its equivalent is to be abjured seems to be the message and Milton's attitude.

At times there seems to be ambiguity, and again the circumstances and personal intention are the measuring stick of appropriateness. In 11.148–51, Adam remarks:

> For since I saught
> By Prayer th' offended Deitie to appease,
> Kneel'd and before him humbl'd all my heart,
> Methought I saw him placable and mild.

But does Eve's clasping of Adam's knees as his "suppliant" (10.917–18) raise the point of proper knee-tribute? Should it not be accorded only to God specifically, and to no other person and no other "thing?" And doesn't Michael really subtly rebuke Adam on this point in 11.249–52?

> *Adam* bow'd low, hee Kingly from his State
> Inclin'd not, but his coming thus declar'd.
> *Adam,* Heav'ns high behest no Preface needs:
> Sufficient that thy Prayers are heard.

The repeated kneeling and standing in the service at church even when the words from the litany are recited becomes blasphemous to Milton and to other Puritans. Psalm 81 rebukes bowing to "a forein God" (62–65), Psalm 86 praises bowing low before the Lord (29–32). The false act is ridiculed when Belial says to Satan, "Women...beguil'd the heart / Of wisest *Solomon*,...And made him bow to the Gods of his Wives" (*PR* 2.169–710; and see 1 Kings 11.1–8). The divine act of bowing culminates *A Mask:* "Or if Vertue feeble were, / Heav'n it self would stoop to her." (Instead of "would stoop," the Trinity Manuscript first had "would bow," which is changed to "stoope" and copied in the revised epilogue.)

21. See *Articles to be inquired of, in the first metropoliticall visitation, of the most reverend father, George, by Gods providence, Arch-bishop of Canterbury, and Primate of all England; in, and for the dioces of Glocester, in the yeare of our Lord God, 1612 and in the second yeare of his graces translation,"* Fincham, *Visitation Articles*, 100–14. Similar is Abbot's "Articles" for Coventry and Lichfield in 1631, published the next year. "Bishop John Williams's Order to Rail in the Communion Tables in Lincoln Diocese, 1635" (August 25, 1635, at St. Mary's Leicester and at other places and dates) is cited in Fincham (*Visitation Articles*, 127).

22. William Juxon, "Articles for the London Ministry, 1635," in Fincham, *Visitation Articles*, 126, 126n1; Bishop Richard Bancroft's articles are found at Fincham, 183.

23. *Constitutions and Canons Ecclesiastical Treated vpon by the Bishop of London, President of the Convocation for the Provinces of Canterbury, and the rest of the Bishops and Clergie of the sayd Prouinces And agreed vpon with the Kings Maiesties Licence in their Synode begun at London Anno dom. 1602. And in the yeare of the raigne of our Soueraigne Lord Iames by the grace of God King of England, France and Ireland the first, and of Scotland the 37* (Imprinted at London by Robert Barker, 1612). *Articles to be enquired of within the diocesse of London. In the third trienniall visitation of the right honourable, and right reverend father in God, William, Lord Bishop of London, Lord High Treasurer of England. Holden in the yeare of our Lord God, 1640* (Printed in London, 1640). We might note that a schoolmaster needed a license to teach and be "conformable to the religion now established," "bring his schollers to the church, to heare divine service and sermons," and "instruct his schollers in the grounds of the religion now established in this Church of England." ("The duty of Schoolmasters" is canon 79 in the 1633 *Constitutions and Canons.*) "Preaching for Conformity" demanded the ministers "submit themselves unto the authority and government of the Church as it is now established under

the Kings Majestie." And parishioners, among other things, are admonished about kneeling and standing and covering their heads during the time of divine service.

24. Fincham, *Visitation Articles*, 223, 233–34.

25. Citation here is from Laud's 1634 *Metropolitan Articles for Lincoln Diocese;* see ibid., 87.

26.. Laud, *A Speech Delivered in the Starr-Chamber, On Wednesday, the XIVth of Iune, MDCXXXVII. At the Censvre, of [Iohn Bastwick, Henry Burton, & William Prinn's Concerning pretended Innovations In the Church* (London: Printed by Richard Badger, 1637); page numbers hereafter cited in the text.

27. See John Jewell, *The Works of John Jewell; and a Briefe Discourse of his Life* (London: J. Norton, 1609).

28. See *The Works of the Most Reverend Father in God, William Laud, D. D. Sometimes Lord Archbishop of Canterbury*, vol. 4, *History of Troubles and Trial, &c.* (Oxford: John Henry Parker, 1854), 337, 392, 404. But see Reid Barbour, *Literature and Religious Culture in Seventeenth-Century England* (Cambridge: Cambridge University Press, 2002), concerning the difference between "circumstances" and "fundamentals" (4–6): for orthodox English Protestantism, "'circumstance' is not narrowly political, and not reducible to policies foisted on the public by a king's ideological obsessions and personal paranoia" (5).

29. "Ceremonialists" in the church were "those who embraced the English church's rituals and ceremonies," as Achsah Guibbory, *Ceremony and Community from Herbert to Milton: Literature, Religion, and Cultural Conflict in Seventeenth-Century England* (Cambridge: Cambridge University Press, 1998), 5–6, tells us; further, they remained loyal to *The Book of Common Prayer* and to episcopacy after 1642, thus distinguishing them from "Anglican" members.

30. David Cressy, *Birth, Marriage, and Death: Ritual, Religion, and the Life-Cycle in Tudor and Stuart England* (Oxford: Oxford University Press, 1997), 403, 108.

31. See Kenneth Fincham, ed., *The Early Stuart Church, 1603–1642* (Stanford: Stanford University Press, 1993), "Introduction," 3, 3–6, and following. This collection of essays engages the questions that continue to weigh down our understanding of religion and its intertwining with politics in the earlier seventeenth century, and indeed the essays disagree among themselves over the many assumptions and arguments that have lain behind the plethora of pertinent scholarly studies on the subject.

Notes to Chapter 5, "Theological Concerns, Especially the Trinity"

1. See Harris Francis Fletcher, *The Use of the Bible in Milton's Prose* (Urbana: University of Illinois Press, 1929), and Michael Bauman, *A Scripture Index to John Milton's* De doctrina christiana (Binghamton, N.Y.: Medieval & Renaissance Texts & Studies, 1989), for citations of the Bible in Milton's prose. From the Apocrypha Fletcher lists citations of Ecclesiasticus (three) and 1 Esdras (two) in the prose, and Wisdom, 1 Maccabees (two), and 2 Maccabees in *De doctrina Christiana;* Bauman indexes Wisdom, 1 Maccabees (two), and 2 Maccabees (two). Milton comments (YP 6:306): "I might also mention the apocryphal writers, as closest to the scripture in authority" (Wisdom 11:17 and 2 Macc. 7:28); "Or again, take a writer whom my opponents consider canonical: I Macc. i.59, 60" (YP 6:578). He does not, however, cite 2 Maccabees 12:42–45 (CM 15:348, and YP 6:455), which Bauman lists. That apocryphal text deals with Judas's taking up the bodies of those slain in pursuit of Gorgias, praying for the dead and their resurrection: "So he made a reconciliation for the dead that they might be deliuered from sinne"; the pages in the treatise cited, in the chapter on renovation and vocation, speak of "Christ's perfect sacrifice [which] is in every way sufficient even for those who have never heard of his name, but who only believe in God." For Milton, "The books usually added to these [the canonical ones], and known as the APOCRYPHAL books, having nothing like the same authority as the canonical, and are not admitted as evidence in deciding points of faith" (YP 6:574). Yet influence from both the Apocrypha and the Pseudepigrapha has been traced in the prose and the poetry; see Virginia R. Mollenkott, "Apocrypha and Pseudepigrapha," in *A Milton Encyclopedia*, vol. 1, gen. ed. William B. Hunter (Lewisburg, Pa.: Bucknell University Press, 1978), 61–62. In chapter 1, note 24, I refer to the New Testament apocryphal Book of James, with which Milton seems to have no connection, and in chapter 5 and chapter 6, to the Jewish-Christian Apocryphon of "The Martyrdom and Ascension of Isaiah," which offers a position concerning the Father, the Son, and the Holy Spirit that can be read as consonant in different ways with Milton's views. But there is no evidence of Milton's knowledge of this noncanonical narrative.

2. Rhu, "*Paradise Lost* and Traditional Exegesis," 487–88, citing James L. Kugel, *Traditions of the Bible* (Cambridge, Mass.: Harvard University Press, 1998).

3. The translation of Isaiah 7:14 iterates Matthew 1:23, but see my discussion of the problem of the text of Isaiah in *Rethinking Milton Studies*, 158–64.

4. The line is important as well in its compositional substance. Line 3, "Of wedded Maid, and Virgin Mother born"—three connoting the Trinity for those accepting numerological significances—not only implies the "Trinal Unity" of line 11, the number of which mystically was a symbol of regeneration and thus salvation, but it is a chiasmus, a chi, X, the sign of Christ (as in the popular but nonsacred Xmas). That is, "wedded" contrasts "Virgin," and "Maid" contrasts "Wife," yielding a kind of repetition of "wedded" and "Mother" and of "Maid" and "Virgin."

5. The poem, of course, is a telling of the temptation in the wilderness as presented in Luke 4:1–13 (as well as Matthew 4:1–11, with a reversal of the second and third temptations, and its brief mention in Mark 1:12–13). It is *not* a telling of his ministry; the Jesus of the temptation is *not* the Christ, and Milton, theologically correct, does not use the term for his character. Unfortunately, Herman, *Destabilizing Milton*, like so many Miltonists, has not paid attention to this or its theological importance and use. Although he quotes the angels' words, "Now enter, and begin to save mankind" (*PR* 4.635), Herman takes the last four lines of the poem to mean that Jesus does not do that: he only "unobserv'd / Home to his Mothers house private return'd." Does Herman's comment mean that Jesus was supposed to go off and wander around immediately after the period in the wilderness, acting as minister, citing his Father, and doing good deeds? That is *not* the subject or theme of this poem, but most significantly Jesus engages his ministry *only* from Luke 4:14 onward, the verse of the Bible *after* "the devil had ended all the temptation, [and] he departed from him *for a season*" (my emphasis). On the one hand, what the Bible then says is: "And Jesus *returned* in the power of the Spirit into Galilee; and there went out a fame of him through all the region round about" (verse 14; emphasis mine). Matthew, on the other hand, tells us, "Then the devil leaveth him, and, behold, angels came and ministered unto him" (as Milton also presents it), and "Now when Jesus had heard that John was cast into prison, he departed into Galilee" (verse 12). Mark (the earliest of the Gospels, of course) has: "And he was there in the wilderness forty days tempted of Satan; and was with the wild beasts; and the angels ministered unto him," followed by "Now after that John was put in prison,

Jesus came into Galilee, preaching the gospel of the kingdom of God" (verse 14). In all three accounts, but particularly the last two *earlier* gospels, time of some duration has expired between the departure of Satan and the beginning of the ministry of Jesus. Milton is *not* treating the ministry, the period when Jesus, anointed, performs miracles, such as healing the blind man at Bethsaida, and is now "the Christ" ("Christ" requires the anointing of Jesus). Not incidentally, the first appearance of "Christ" in Mark is the report after that time when Jesus and the disciples came to Caesarea Philippi: "And he saith unto them, But whom say ye that I am? And Peter answereth and saith unto him, Thou art the Christ" (8:29). For Matthew it is the same time (14:16). For Luke it is also Peter's statement (9:20), except for the foretelling of the advent of Christ in 2:11, 2:26, and in 4:41 after the healing of the sick (again well into Jesus' ministry). Luke 9:20 has the Greek "ὁ χριστος του θεου," which is literally "God's anointed one," but is translated as "the Messiah of God," which, according to the *New Oxford Annotated Bible*, 3rd ed., ed. Michael D. Coogan et al. (Oxford: Oxford University Press, 2001), is "a title that typically named a royal Davidic leader who would reconstitute the former political glory of Israel for the people and the nation" (114). See also the reading of Milton's poem by Ken Simpson, *Spiritual Architecture and* Paradise Regained: *Milton's Literary Ecclesiology* (Pittsburgh: Duquesne University Press, 2007).

The comment that "The emphasis on 'private' in the poem's final lines thus upends our expectations at the poem's end" (Herman, *Destabilizing Milton*, 162) indicates a gross misreading of the text and the biblical account on which it is based. Milton has supplied a necessary transition between the ending of the temptation and the beginning of the ministry. Jesus will, soon enough, "enter, and begin to save mankind." He has been "exercise[d]...in the Wilderness," where he has "first [laid] down the rudiments / Of his great warfare, *e're I* [the Father] *send him forth / To conquer Sin and Death*" (*PR* 1.156–59; emphasis mine). And refer to the very important essay by Marjorie O'Rourke Boyle, "Home to Mother: Regaining Milton's Paradise," *Modern Philology* 97 (2000): 499–527. The source for this closure, as she demonstrates, is the tradition of "the Catholic medieval *Meditationes vitae Christi*, with its derivatives" (502), that has Jesus returning to his mother's home. (Incidentally, previously published remarks in *"Arms of the Family"* and in this book are given weight by Boyle's significant observation:

"Milton was capable of distinguishing between institutional Catholicism, which he hated, and individual Catholics, many of whom he liked, especially their literature" [507]).

6. Isaiah 9:6–7 also alludes to what Christianity has interpreted as a prophecy of the birth of the Son of God: "For unto us a child is born, unto us a son is given: and the government shall be upon his shoulder: and his name shall be called Wonderful, Counselor, The mighty God, The everlasting Father, The Prince of Peace. / Of the increase of *his* government and peace *there shall be* no end, upon the throne of David, and upon his kingdom, to order it, and to establish it with judgment and with justice from henceforth even for ever." Milton cites these verses in *De doctrina Christiana* four times (YP 6:260, 432, 436, 624), emphasizing the names and their significance, and primarily the Son as counselor and prince of peace.

7. Again, see my discussion of Isaiah in *Rethinking Milton Studies*.

8. See YP 6:574–92; the basic statement was quoted before in chapter 4. He continues, "the scriptures are, both in themselves and through God's illumination[,] absolutely clear", "The scriptures, then, are plain and sufficient in themselves" (578, 580). Reference is made to canonicity, and in chapter 6 on the Holy Spirit, which is accepted as the "Spirit of God and the Holy Spirit of God" (YP 6:288), and in chapter 5 on the Son of God the question of the canonicity of 1 John 5:7 is raised (297–98, 221–22). "This verse, however, is not found in the Syriac or the other two Oriental versions, the Arabic and the Ethiopic, nor in the majority of the ancient Greek codices...(if John really wrote the verse)" (221); "the whole doctrine of the TRINITY seems to have been wrested primarily from this one sentence, which is almost the only foundation for it" (298). The text, 1 John 5:7, has been called the "Johannine comma" and has had a long history of discussion because its rejection has caused such authors to be called "Arians." Two excellent articles on the matter are Dayton Haskin, "Milton's Strange Pantheon: The Apparent Tritheism of *De Doctrina Christiana*," *Heythorpe Journal: Quarterly Review of Philosophy and Theology* 16 (April 1975): 129–48, and Joseph M. Levine, "Erasmus and the Problem of the Johannine Comma," *Journal of the History of Ideas* 58 (1997): 573–96.

9. I have previously explored the question of the Trinity for Milton at length in *Rethinking Milton Studies*, 103–08, 126–31, 133–35, 137, 139, 207–08n28, and throughout.

10. 1 Corinthians 12:3–6 has been noted (especially verse 3: "no man can say that Jesus is the Lord, but by the Holy Ghost").

Reference is given only in *De doctrina Christiana* (YP 6:286, 295, 471, 524). Milton comments on verse 3 in a related group of verses: "Thus the Spirit is called the Spirit of God, the Spirit of the Father, and even the Spirit of Christ" (noted elsewhere), and on verses 4–6, "Here the three are named again in inverse order, but, as we are continually taught, there is one God who works in all things, even in the Son and the Spirit." Verse 3 is cited with others to explicate "BY THE GIFT OF GOD" and to iterate that the Gospel is communicated "THROUGH THE HOLY SPIRIT." The word employed in verse 3 in Greek is: πνευιον, "a current of air, breath," which thence is interpreted as a spirit, that is, a rational soul, angel, dæmon, God, Christ's spirit, the Holy Spirit. The Latin translation of verse 3 is generally "spiritus sanctus."

11. References to the Spirit are frequent in the prose: for example, "by devout prayer to that eternall Spirit who can enrich with all utterance and knowledge" (*Reason of Church-Government*, YP 1:820–21), where the Spirit is clearly that of Isaiah 6:6–7, a text employed in line 28 of the Nativity ode, or "the Spirit of God who is purity it selfe" (*Apology*, YP 1:901). Even usage with the adjective does not indicate the third person of the Trinity: "according to the will of God & his Holy Spirit within us...no other within us but the Illumination of the Holy Spirit" (*Civil Power*, YP 7:242); "to interpret convincingly to his own conscience none is able but himself guided by the Holy Spirit" (ibid., 249); "by prayer for Illumination of the holy Spirit" (*Of True Religion*, YP 8:423).

Then there is the term "Holy Ghost." The four occurrences in the antiprelatical tracts of 1641 give the term without decisiveness as to Trinity but also not in opposition ("which is revel'd for the better by the holy Ghost," (YP 1:561); "I wish the like to all those that resist not the holy Ghost" (YP 1:729); "that durst dispose and guide the living arke of the holy Ghost" (754); "For which cause the holy Ghost by the Apostles joyn'd to the minister" (YP 1:838). It appears often in the "translation" (1644) of Martin Bucer and its biblical citations where the "Holy Ghost" seems assuredly a person and thus seems to represent an orthodox concept; for example, "the second mariage of *Fabiola* was permitted her by the holy Ghost himself for the necessity which she suffer'd" (YP 2:449–50); "Heer it is certain that the holy Ghost had no purpose to determine ought of mariage" (459); "and that most evidently, when as the holy Ghost, I *Cor.* 7. so frees the deserted party from bondage, as that he may not only send a just divorce in case of desertion" (474). This apparent acceptance, although it is translation of a mid sixteenth century author, may or may not continue in this attack on Charles I in *Eikonoklastes* (1649): "Who would have imagin'd so little feare in him of the true all-seeing Deitie, so little reverence of the Holy Ghost, whose office is to dictat and present our Christian Prayers" (YP 3:362). Is such expression including the Holy Ghost a result of continued belief in the third person of the Trinity? By 1653/1659, two instances in *Hirelings* (YP 7:279, 310), and one instance in *Civil Power* (YP 7:260), "and so, instead of forcing the Christian, they force the Holy Ghost; and, against that wise forewarning of *Gamaliel,* fight against God," are ultimately vague as to this issue.

12. Other citations of Matthew 27:19 in *De doctrina Christiana* are: 433, 457, 544, 563, 567, 569, 573, where the point is not pertinent to the present discussion (sometimes having to do only with teaching). "Spirit," "Holy Spirit," and "Holy Ghost" appear often in the poetry and prose, but they are not construed usually as a person of the Trinity (see note 10 for a possible exception). Aside from these theological examinations and the lines in *Of Reformation* already cited, the Trinity appears in the prose only in *Of True Religion* (YP 8:424–25), where Milton reviews "some Points of Doctrin" of various sects:

> The Arian and Socinian are charg'd to dispute against the Trinity: they affirm to believe the Father, Son, and Holy Ghost, according to Scripture, and the Apostolic Creed; as for terms of Trinity, Triunity, Coessentiality, Tripersonality, and the like, they reject them as Scholastic Notions, not to be found in Scripture, which by a general Protestant Maxim is plain and perspicuous abundantly to explain its own meaning in the properest words, belonging to so high a Matter and so necessary to be known; a mystery indeed in their Sophistic Subtilties, but in Scripture a plain Doctrin.

And in the translation of *Diploma Electionis S. R. M. Poloniæ* (*A Declaration; or, Letters Patents of the Election of this present King of Poland*), the epigraph "In the name of the most holy and Individual Trinity, the Father, Son, and Holy Spirit" is found in YP 8:445.

13. C. G. Jung, *Psychology and Religion: West and East,* trans. R. F. C. Hull (New York: Pantheon Books, 1958), makes an interesting cultural conclusion about any Father/Son concept and the "Spirit" (who is "not a human figure") that may exist between them: "The intellectual operation that lies concealed

in the higher father-son relationship consists in the extrapolation of an invisible figure, a 'spirit' that is the very essence of masculine life" (132–33). We are aware that the Holy Spirit is the one who metes out God's justice, unrelenting as such justice might be.

14. John Owen, *A Brief Declaration and Vindication of the Doctrine of the Trinity: As also of the Person and Satisfaction of Christ.... John 5.39. Search the Scriptures* (London: Printed by R. W. for Nath. Ponder, 1669), refers to such readers of the Bible as *"the Adversaries of the Truth": "But whilest they deny the Mysteries in these things them selves, which are such as every way because the glorious* Being *and* Wisdom *of God, they are forced to assign such ænigmatical sense unto the Words, Expressions and Propositions wherein they are revealed and declared in Scripture, as to turn almost the whole Gospel into an* Allegory, *wherein nothing is properly expressed, but in some kind of Allusion unto what is so elsewhere"* ("To the Reader," A4v, A6v–A7r).

15. It is usually the Holy Ghost who is cited in relation to the birth of Jesus; it would not illogically include the Son. Matthew 1:18, 20, reads "she was found with child of the Holy Ghost," "for that which is conceived in her is of the Holy Ghost"; Luke 1:35, "The Holy Ghost shall come upon thee, and the power of the Highest shall overshadow thee: therefore also that holy thing which shall be born of thee shall be called the Son of God." Milton, as we would expect, follows Scripture.

16. Albert C. Labriola, "The Son as an Angel in *Paradise Lost,"* in *Milton in the Age of Fish: Essays on Authorship, Text, and Terrorism,* ed. Michael Lieb and Albert C. Labriola, 105–18 (Pittsburgh: Duquesne University Press, 2006), 111. See also *The Old Testament Pseudepigrapha,* ed. James H. Charlesworth (Garden City, N.Y.: Doubleday, 1985).

17. Again the translation misleads: the Latin does not say "before the Son was made." The Latin is: "ut credible est, mundi fundamenta, post Filium, filioque longe inferiorem." The Columbia translation is: "after the foundations of the world were laid, but later than the Son, and far inferior to him" (14:402/403).

18. The question has really been resolved in two articles by Michael Lieb: Milton is certainly *not* an Arian and he did respond to Socinianism at various points in his career, inclining those of that persuasion "to draw upon certain elements in Milton's work to proclaim him as one of their own" (260). See "Milton and 'Arianism,'" *Religion and Literature* 32 (2000): 197–220, and "Milton and the Socinian Heresy," in *Milton and*

the *Grounds of Contention*, ed. Mark R. Kelley, Michael Lieb, and John T. Shawcross, 234–81 (Pittsburgh: Duquesne University Press, 2003). Both articles are reprinted in Lieb, *Theological Milton*, 261–78, as chapter 8, "Arianism and Godhead"; and 213–60, as chapter 7, "The Socinian Imperative."

19. *The Interpreter's Bible* (Nashville: Abington, 1957), vol. 12, 293–94.

20. See R. S. Franks, *The Doctrine of the Trinity* (London: Gerald Duckworth, 1953), 134, 138.

21. Geoffrey F. Nuttall, *The Holy Spirit in Puritan Faith and Experience* (Oxford: Basil Blackwell, 1947), 104.

22. Philip Dixon, *"Nice and Hot Disputes": The Doctrine of the Trinity in the Seventeenth Century* (London: T. & T. Clark, 2003), 24, 102, 208–09, 102. "Enthusiasm" refers to various sects who, through belief in direct divine inspiration, exhibited religious fervor involving wild bodily action and speaking in tongues. There are vague likenesses to other groups (such as Antinomians) believing in a more direct connection with God, thereby with emphasis upon the individual's moral law and rejection of churchly intervention. The manifestation of God in nature, thus, becomes increasingly the source of belief in God and God's ways, and develops into strong pantheism and transcendental thought. With the growing precedence of this kind of "concrete" manifestation (and the rise in scientific investigations contributes strongly to this) there is a sharp decline in belief in or necessity for revelation as a base for religious thought. See chapter 9 here.

23. Herbert Croft, *The Naked Truth; or, The True State of the Primitive Church* [London, 1674], 102. Edward Stillingfleet, *The Doctrine of the Trinity and Transubstantiation Compared, as to Scripture, Reason, and Tradition, In a New Dialogue between a Protestant and a Papist. The first Part* (London, Printed by J. D. for W. Rogers, 1687), 5, 6, 8.

24. Owen, *Brief Declaration*, 26–28.

25. Various clergymen ran afoul of the Church of England after the Restoration, through charges of refuting Arminian concepts (such as John Owen, 1616–83), emphasizing conscience (such as Anthony Horneck, 1641–97), or defending Catholic doctrine (such as George Bull, 1634–1710, who argued most erroneously in 1685 that there was no doctrinal difference between Ante-Nicene Fathers and the Council of Nicaea). Some attacked passive obedience and divided kingship (such as William Atwood, who died in 1712). William Sherlock, an advocate of passive obedience, proposed three "infinite minds" or "self-consciousnesses"

that were distinct from one another, "and yet entirely each one conscious of the thoughts of the others" and thus numerically one (*A Vindication of the Holy and Blessed Trinity and the Incarnation of the Son of God,* 1691), rebutted by Robert South in *Animadversions upon Dr. Sherlock's Book Entituled A Vindication of the Holy and Ever-Blessed Trinity* (1693). South proposed a doctrine of three persons (or subsistances) with one essence. Sherlock's earlier tract, *The Case of Resistance to the Supreme State and Resolved According to the Doctrine of the Holy Scriptures* (London: F. Gardiner, 1684), argues for the "absolute obedience or submission to the authority of ruler," despite his opposition to James II's Catholicism; such passive obedience was mandatory even under an execrable king, and derives primarily from the "doctrine" of the divine right of kings. See also his *The Case of the Allegiance Due to Sovereign Powers* (1691).

26. See *Encyclopedia of Early Christianity,* 2nd ed., ed. Everett Ferguson (New York: Garland, 1997), vol. 2, 804, for citations concerning the early history; hereafter cited in the text. Carl Jung's discussion in "Versuch zu einer psychologischen Deutung des Trinitätsdogmas," *Symbolik des Geistes* (Zurich: Rascher, 1948), is most pertinent. "Triads of gods appear very early, at a primitive level.... Arrangement in triads is an archetype in the history of religion, which in all probability formed the basis of the Christian Trinity. Often these triads do not consist of three different deities independent of one another; instead, there is a distinct tendency for certain family relationships to arise within the triads." He also comments that "Trinitarian speculation had long passed its peak when the Council of Nicaea, in 325, created a new creed, known as the 'Nicene.'" See Carl Jung, *Psychology and Religion: West and East,* trans. R. F. C. Hull (New York: Pantheon Books, 1958), 113, 143.

27. I am greatly indebted to Anne Barbeau Gardiner for alerting me to the significance of Cyril Lucaris in the theological discussions during the seventeenth century and the settlement within the Eastern church finally in 1672.

28. John Biddle, *A Confession of Faith Touching the Holy Trinity, According to the Scripture* (London, 1648). See also Lieb, "Milton and the Socinian Heresy."

29. Interestingly, Lucaris, through the agency of Sir Thomas Roe, English ambassador to the Dutch during the 1620s, gave the Codex Alexandrinus (an early fifth century Greek manuscript of the Bible) to James I; it did not arrive until after James's death in 1625 and was thus presented to Charles I in 1627. It will be found in the British Library as Royal MS 1 D. v–viii. It

was employed by Brian Walton in his *Biblia Sacra Polyglotta* in 1655–57, and we know that Milton aided Walton in publication of his compilation of various language versions of the Bible. See Parker, *Biography*, 419–20. (Prior to Lucaris's being at Constantinople, he was the patriarch of Alexandria.)

30. Dr. Edward Pocock, rector of Childrey and professor of Orientalism at Christ's Church, Oxford, informed Archbishop Laud of the circumstances of Lucaris's death in 1638 (Thomas Smith, *An Account of the Greek Church* [1680], 287).

31. The account of the Synod of Jerusalem is found in *The Acts and Decrees of the Synod of Jerusalem, sometimes called the Council of Bethlehem, Holden under Dositheus, Patriarch of Jerusalem in 1672, Translated from the Greek, with an Appendix containing the Confession, Published with the name of Cyril Lucar, Condemned by the Synod*, ed. J. N. W. B. Robertson (London, 1899; repr., New York: AMS Press, 1969). It is in Greek with an English translation of the *Confessio*. The translation is longer and verbally different from its first edition (1629), to be discussed below, since it derives from the augmented Greek version.

32. See George A. Hadjiantoniou, *Protestant Patriarch: The Life of Cyril Lucaris (1572–1638), Patriarch of Constantinople* (Richmond, Va.: John Knox Press, 1961), 102–06, for a discussion of authorship. Lucaris not only did not deny authorship, but he made references to "his" *Confession*. A most important instance of the latter will be cited shortly.

33. Leger was pastor of the Church of St. Martin's, Geneva. From February through 28 June 2, 1628, the Synod of the Reformed Church took action to send him to Constantinople as chaplain to the Dutch Embassy. A letter of March 24, signed by Diodati and others, urged his acceptance of the position. He arrived there in early autumn. He is the author of "Fragmentum Vitæ D. Cyrilli per D. Antonium Legerum," published in Thomas Smith's *Collectanea de Cyrillo Lucaris, Patriarcha Constantinopolitano* (London: Typis Gul. Bowyer, & Impensis Galfredi Wale, 1707), item 3, pp. 77–83.

34. *The Confession of Faith of...Cyrill, Patriarch of Constantinople...Written at Constantinople, 1629* (London, Printed for Nicholas Bourne, 1629). A copy is owned by the Bodleian Library and a copy of a different edition, also 1629, is owned by Emmanuel College, Cambridge.

35. Ibid., 1. Fletcher mentions Lucaris in talking of Sir Thomas Roe, who is not known to have been connected with Milton, and the presentation of the Codex Alexandrinus, cited above in

note 29. See Harris Francis Fletcher, *The Intellectual Development of John Milton*, vol. 1 (Urbana: University of Illinois Press, 1956), 62.

36. Lucaris, *Confession of Faith*, chap. 2, p. 10.

37. Thomas Smith, *An Account of the Greek Church, as to Its Doctrine and Rites of Worship...To which is added, An Account of the State of the Greek Church, under* Cyrillus Lucaris *Patriarch of* Constantinople, *with a Relation of his Sufferings and Death* (1680), a₄r, A₄v, 200–201.

38. Lucaris, *Confession of Faith*, 2. The version printed with *The Acts and Decrees of the Synod of Jerusalem*, from the Greek which reflects the addition in 1633 indicated above, has differences: "We believe the Sacred Scriptures to be God-taught; whose Author is the Holy Spirit, and none other. Which we ought to believe without doubting;...And so the witness of the Sacred Scriptures is of higher authority than that of the Church" (186). Smith, *An Account of the Greek Church*, also refers to Roe's gift of Lucaris's manuscript to Charles I at 252.

39. Lucaris, *Confession of Faith*, 4; *Confessio*, 2; Montagu, *A Gagg for the new Gospell?*, "To the Reader," 217n246. Compare the previous notice of Montagu in chapter 4.

40. Smith's account, 273, is that Lucaris said "That truly it was his Confession" when he was shown the version printed at Rome in 1632 by the French ambassador to Constantinople, Count de Marcheville, at dinner, citing a letter from Sir Cornelius Van Haghe, ambassador from the States of the Netherlands at Constantinople, dated January 17, 1632. Smith's *Collectanea de Cyrillo Lucaris, Patriarcha Constantinopolitano* (London: Gul. Bowyer, & Impensis Galfredi Wale, 1707), also includes, among other pertinent items, his own "Narratio de Vitâ" of Lucaris with an appendix concerning the connection with James I and Charles I, and Van Haghe's letter.

Notes to Chapter 6, "Theological Concerns, the Son, and the Divine Presence"

1. See, for example, C. A. Patrides, "Milton on the Trinity: The Use of Antecedents," in *Bright Essence: Studies in Milton's Theology*, ed. William B. Hunter, C. A. Patrides, and Jack Adamson, 3–13 (Salt Lake City: University of Utah Press, 1971), "The hard core of Milton's thesis remains, nevertheless, the 'subordinationism' espoused by the early Fathers whose views Tertullian

well summarized:... 'the Father is the entire substance but the Son is a derivation and portion of the whole'" (9 and n26).

2. It is interesting to compare Kersey's dictionary definitions as what would be standard in the late seventeenth and early eighteenth centuries: "Arianism, the Doctrine and Opinions of *Arius*, a noted Heretick in the Time of the Emperour *Constantine* the Great, who deny'd the Son of God to be of the same Substance with the Father, and began to broach that damnable Heresy about it *A.C.* 315" (which, of course, does *not* represent Milton's position, despite repeated charges by those Milton critics who do not comprehend Arianism beyond a separation of Father and Son), and "Trinitarians, or rather Anti-Trinitarians, a Sect of new *Arian* Hereticks that deny the Mystery of the Blessed Trinity, and all Distinctions of the Divine Persons. The Orthodox that believe the Trinity are also called *Trinitarians* by the *Socinians*," and "The Trinity, one only God in three Persons; the Godhead being one and the selfsame for Essence, and for Substance and Personality, three *viz. Father, Son and Holy Ghost*, and these three are one, 1 *Joh.* 5.7."

3. Referring to texts enumerated, Milton writes, "All these passages prove that the Son existed before the creation of the World, but not that his generation was from eternity" (YP 6:206). Compare the expression "eternally begotten" in the *Confession of Faith*.

4. The relationship of husband and wife is resultant from the biblical tradition of Adam's being first created and Eve's being created from him; the dominance of a masculinist attitude for both men and women in all things where gender appears is difficult (if not impossible) to shake because of humankind's belief in the Bible as the Word of God and its interpretations. In discussing the divorce tracts, although Milton may be masculinist and may accept Paul's word in regard to woman and the relationship of husband and wife, critics keep forgetting that he is arguing for a position that his *male* audience, "The Parlament of *England* with the Assembly" (title page to the second edition), would have to act on to effect the "Seasonable [action] to be now thought on in the Reformation intended" (title page to the first edition). We cannot overemphasize the strategy needed to get affirmative action when one, like Milton, is in argument about politics, religion, social/"œconomic" affairs. It is not really different in the divorce tracts from the reason for Bathsua Makin's masquerade as a masculine persona in an attempt at persuasion in *An Essay to Revive the Antient Education of Gentlewomen* (1673, though written earlier). A pertinent article that disputes

the use of the word and concept "misogynist" for Milton is David Boocker's "Milton and the Woman Controversy," in *A Search for Meaning: Critical Essays on Early Modern Literature*, ed. Paula Harms Payne, 125–43 (New York: Peter Lang, 2004).

    5. Looking backward, we recognize a different yet similar secular approach to "Father" (Ens) and "Son" or "Sons" in "At a Vacation Exercise" (1632?), a seeming conceptual development that emerges a decade later in 1641. It may have existed in embryo while Milton was still in college, and amid much religious controversy that would raise these issues. Here Milton enacts "Ens," who is *represented as Father of the Predicaments his ten Sons, whereof the eldest stood for Substance with his Canons* (fundamental principles or properties common to Substance). Is not his later thought on the Godhead observable in Milton's thinking, with Substance being addressed by the Father: "Good luck befriend thee Son...thou should'st still / From eyes of mortals walk invisible" (59, 65–66)?

> O're all his Brethren he shall Reign as King,
> Yet every one shall make him underling,
> And those that cannot live from him asunder
> Ungratefully shall strive to keep him under;
> In worth and excellence he shall out-go them,
> Yet being above them, he shall be below them. (75–80)

Indeed, a punning reference to Jesus' treatment on earth and to the Eucharist also appears: "Yet shall he live in strife, and at his dore / Devouring war shall never cease to roar" (85–86). The rejection of the Catholic doctrine of transubstantiation and the Real Presence we would expect from Milton, of course, as a Protestant.

    6. *The Confession of Faith, and the Larger & Shorter Catechism* (London, for the Company of Stationers, 1656), 8, 10.

    7. I have reviewed much of this before in "Milton and 'Of Christian Doctrine': **D**oubts, **D**efinitions, **C**onnotations," in *Explorations in Renaissance Culture* 27 (2001): 161–78; and in *Rethinking Milton Studies*, 133–38.

    8. The citation is John 14:28: "If ye loved me, ye would rejoice, because I said, I go unto the Father: for my Father is greater than I." The matter appears in the work of contemporary, supposedly orthodox ministers who take a similar position. For example, George Bull, *Defensio Fidei Nicænæ, Ex scriptis, quæ extant Catholicorum doctorum, qui intra tria prima Ecclesiæ christianæ secula floruerunt. In qua Obiter quoque*

Constantinopolitan a Confessio, de Spiritu Sancto, antiquiorum testimoniis adstruitur. Authore Georgio Bullo Presbytero Anglicano (Oxonii: e Theatro Sheldoniano, 1685), where section 4 is "De Subordinatione Filii ad Patrem," and chapter 4 in this section discusses "usus Doctrinæ de subordinatione Filii explicator."

9. On *genuit* and its forms, see, for example, CM 14:188/189, and YP 6:209; or *genuisse*, CM 14:188/189, and YP 6:210.

10. Lucaris, *Confessio*, 198–99, 201.

11. As I have pointed out in *Rethinking Milton Studies*, 103–08.

12. The Hebrew *mashiah*, meaning "anointed," was always used when referring to an actual ruler rather than a future king; see the *New Oxford Annotated Bible*, 177.

13. Labriola, "The Son as an Angel," 105, 106.

14. Examining the epistemological significance of Milton's proof-texts, Lieb, *Theological Milton*, concludes, "What emerges is a God who is defined by...his Son....He assumed the form of a servant [in] order to provide a means for humankind to experience God in all his glory. The proof-texts cited leave no doubt that it is only through the Son that a true knowledge of the Father is possible" (84). We should also heed Gerardus van der Leeuw, *Religion in Essence and Manifestation: A Study in Phenomenology*, 2 vols., trans. J. E. Turner (New York: Harper & Row, 1963), who writes that "the typology of Christianity needs only *one* word: *Love*. This is because in Christianity, God's activity and the reciprocal activity of man are essentially the same: the movement of Power towards the world is love, while that of the world towards God is reciprocal love" (646). (I have previously argued that the theme of *Paradise Lost* is love; see Shawcross, *With Mortal Voice: The Creation of* Paradise Lost [Lexington: University Press of Kentucky, 1982], 27–29.)

My argument in the book on *Paradise Regain'd* disclaims the idea that the Son should be imitated, but rather that the qualities of the Son should be so inculcated that one acts automatically with love and obedience and faith. As R. A. Shoaf, *Milton, Poet of Duality: A Study of Semiosis in the Poetry and the Prose* (New Haven: Yale University Press, 1985), presents "Christ: Son of God, Lord of Difference," we have another way of saying this: "Why would Christ want to make someone else such as he? Such a desire would argue at least a deficiency, if not also a perversion, of self-love. Rather, Christ wants every man and woman to be only or—more daringly, but also more truthfully—singularly such as he or she is" (155–56). The observation also underlies the concept of the paradise regained: it is the "paradise within," which will prepare one for the heavenly ascent at the end of time. Indeed, it seems to me that Milton's poem and title have almost consistently been misread about this point.

15. See chapter 4 in this volume and the studies there cited.

16. 133 (2), 148 (3), 194, 150 (2), 151. The reference on p. 148 reads, "it [the New Testament] asserts that this one God is the Father of Our Lord Jesus Christ." But as in this reference, "God the Father" is not otherwise named except in reference to the Son. These are: John 6:46 (2); 1 Corinthians 8:6; Ephesians 4:6; John 5:26; Luke 6:36; 2 Corinthians 1:3; Matthew 5:48; and the reference above.

17. The text is also given in Mark 14:22–24, Luke 22:19–20, and 1 Corinthians 11:20, 23–29 (compare Revelation 19:9, 17–18.) Corinthians is specifically important, for Paul calls this "the Lord's supper" and says of it, "this do in remembrance of me," "this do ye, as oft as ye drink it, in remembrance of me," "for as often as ye eat of this bread, and drink of this cup, ye do show the Lord's death till he come." See Lee Palmer Wandel, *The Eucharist in the Reformation: Incarnation and Liturgy* (Cambridge: Cambridge University Press, 2006), for a full discussion of these matters. Wandel thoroughly examines the meanings of "This Is," "My Body," "This Do," and "In Remembrance of Me" in the various religious positions developed in the sixteenth century. She also details the structure of the Protestant service (no longer a Mass), which is "radically simplified" on p. 74.

18. The denial of efficacy of the Lord's Supper for the unworthy who partake of it, as given in 1 Corinthians 11:27–28, is alluded to in *Of Reformation* (YP 1:561) and *A Treatise of Civil Power* (YP 7:268). In *The Judgement of Martin Bucer* (YP 2:443) Milton relates the rejection of Jewish use of circumcision, sacrifice, and bodily washings to how the faithful "may rightly learn, with what purity and devotion both Baptism and the Lords Supper should be administerd and receav'd."

19. Milton's ridicule occurs often: in *Of True Religion* (YP 8:431–32), for example, "But first we must remove their [popery's] Idolatry, and all the furniture thereof, whether Idols, or the Mass wherein they adore their God under Bread and Wine: for the Commandment forbids to adore." (The charge of Catholic idolatry in the interpretation of the Real Presence in this action in the Catholic Mass—that is, in the worship of the host as the true body of Christ—will appear in many discussions that I note.) See also note 31 to chapter 9 here. In *Of Reformation* (YP 1:548), objecting to the Laudian alteration of the altar and

its Catholic similarities, he remarks, "while the obscene, and surfeted Priest scruples not to paw, and mammock the sacramentall bread, as familiarly as his Tavern Bisket." Reading the interpretation of Mosaic law to forbid all but adultery as a reason for divorce, Milton parallels it with the corporal interpretation of the Lord's Supper: "as much against plain equity, and the mercy of religion, as those words of *Take, eat, this is my body,* elementally understood, are against nature and sense"; that is, they should not be taken literally (*Doctrine and Discipline of Divorce,* YP 2:325).

Examinations of *Paradise Lost* 5.433–43, the description of the meal set out for Raphael and its satiric use of the verb "to transubstantiate," are explored by Anne Barbeau Gardiner, "Milton's Parody of Catholic Hymns in Eve's Temptation and Fall: Original Sin as a Paradigm of 'Secret Idolatries,'" *Studies in Philology* 91 (1994): 216–31, and "'Division in Communion: Symbols of Transubstantiation in Donne, Milton, and Dryden," *Symbolism: An International Annual of Critical Aesthetics* 4 (2005): 15–39; John N. King, *Milton and Religious Controversy: Satire and Polemic in Paradise Lost* (Cambridge: Cambridge University Press, 2000); and Regina M. Schwartz, "Real Hunger: Milton's Version of the Eucharist," *Religion and Literature* 31 (1999): 1–17. The scene takes on the appearance of a communion but with a table rather than an altar (we have already discussed the rejection of some alterations in and attitudes toward a church altar by archbishops, including Laud, in chapter 4). "The Table of Communion now become a Table of separation stands like an exalted platforme upon the brow of the quire, fortifi'd with bulwark, and barricado, to keep off the profane touch of the Laicks" (*Of Reformation,* YP 1:547–48). Reformers rejected the concept of an altar because no sacrifice occurred with the observance of the Lord's Supper; the partaking of the host makes its location a "table." I have already noted the importance of "table" in chapter 4, for in *Paradise Lost,*

> various fruits the Trees of God
> Have heap'd this Table. Rais'd of grassie terf
> Thir Table was, and mossie seats had round,
> And on her ample Square from side to side
> All *Autumn* pil'd. (5.390–94)

The description achieves a squaring of the circle, creating in a kind of parallel the square of heaven and the unending circle that is God (compare Rev. 21:10–18, and the "glory of God" and "the tree of life, which bare twelve manner of fruits, and yielded her fruit every month."} Squaring of the circle (that is, quadrature of the circle) is impossible to achieve by limited geometric methods; it attempts to find the side of a square exactly equal in area to a given circular area. Milton ridicules Satan by having Sin pronounce that, with the disobedience of Eve and Adam, "henceforth Monarchie with thee divide / Of all things, parted by th' Empyreal bounds, / His Quadrature, from thy Orbicular World. (*PL* 10.379–81). The passage in book 5 implies that this impossibility has been achieved and thus that Divine Presence is there as nourisher and as "Celestial Father [who] gives to all." As Schwartz elucidates the results of the repast, "this whole process is really about...man turning into God"; the body is assimilated "perpetually and naturally turns matter into spirit" (referring to *PL* 5.404–26; see 8–9).

20. In his most important study, Thomas N. Corns, *The Development of Milton's Prose Style* (Oxford: Clarendon Press, 1982), understandably, does not include Latin texts and therefore not *De doctrina Christiana*. His attention is largely on language and expositional form, dealing with imagery more structurally than tonally, although he does cite Milton's "comic strain." Since we are concerned in this book with "conceptual development," we should absorb the significance of Corns's statement, "The comparison of Milton's first [1641–42, and 1643–1645, 1649, which are akin] and final [1659–73] groups of tracts disclosed a radical shift in his prose style" (101). "Style" and "concept" are not equivalents, but has there been a realization finally—the kind of stylistic realization that *Paradise Regain'd*, produced after *Paradise Lost*, exhibits—that a different style needed to be sought to clarify concepts for Milton's reader—and perhaps even for himself? "Step by step Milton dismantled what was possibly the most exhilarating and inventive prose style of the seventeenth century," Corns tells us, "and replaced it with a spare functionalism" (101–02). Does *De doctrina Christiana*, indeed, exhibit early, middle, and later style?

On the question of compositional dates (plural), I suggest that the answer to Lieb's concern about "a very curious reference to the Jews, who, for not learning the lesson of true faith in God and the principles of Christian doctrine, must suffer the fate of having been dispersed throughout all parts of the world up to and including the present day (YP 6:132)....[I]t is entirely out of keeping with the discussion that has gone before and the discussion that follows it" (*Theological Milton*, 290n34), may be that it is another example of earlier composition and of a lack of attention for publication. The statement ends the first section on "De Deo," just preceding a second section investigating the need to study "the word or message of God" in order to derive "correct ideas about God."

21. Saint Hilary, *Sancti Hilarii de trinitate contra arianos* (1489).

22. William Forbes, *Considerationes Modestæ et Pacificæ Controversiarum de...Eucharista. Editio quarta. Tom. II* (Oxonii: Apud J. H. Parker, 1856), 381, 389, 411, 413.

23. This information comes from Richard Hakluyt, *Principal Navigations, Voyages, Traffiques, and Discoveries of the English Nation*, vol. 1 (London: G. Bishop, R. Newberie and R. Barker, 1598–1600), 253.

24. See Forbes, *Considerationes Modestæ et Pacificæ*, book 2, chap. 1, "Wherein the questions of Communion under one or both kinds...are briefly treated of" (509–31); he quotes numerous commentators on the subject, such as Bellarmine, Lorichius, J. Barnes, Bucer, and Andrewes.

25. Montagu, "The Preface," *A Gagg for the new Gospell?*, ¶¶2v. Joseph Mede, *The Apostasy of the Latter Times; or, The Gentiles Theology of Dæmons* (1641), reprinted in *The Works of the Pious and Profoundly Learned Joseph Mede. B. D. Sometime Fellow of Christ's College in Cambridge. Corrected and Enlarged according to the Author's own Manuscripts* (London: Printed by Roger Norton for Richard Royston, 1672), 688.

Timothy O'Keeffe, *Milton and the Pauline Tradition: A Study of Theme and Symbolism* (Washington, D. C.: University Press of America, 1982), points out John Colet's earlier statement regarding Christ's Real Presence in the Eucharist and acknowledging Christ as the body of the church, "then He 'feeds on HIMSELF' as the body of the church" (215, quoting John Colet, *An Exposition of St. Paul's First Epistle to the Corinthians*, trans. J. H. Lupton [Ridgewood, N.J.: 1965], 116). O'Keeffe remarks that "Richard Hooker is concerned with both the real presence in the sacrament and also the spiritual condition of the believer, but he insists that there is a reality to the concept.... 'The real presence' is better sought in the person who receives the sacrament rather than in the sacrament itself" (215–16). See Hooker, *Of the Laws of Ecclesiastical Polity* (London, 1963), 1:324–25, 2:322.

26. Laud, *Works*, 404, 337–38, 336.

27. *Confession of Faith* (1649), 59–62; my emphasis.

28. The word is the term generally used by Protestant writers, for example, Thomas Chubb in *The Comparative Excellence and Obligation of Moral and Positive Duties, Fully Stated and*

Considered (1730): "the Benefits of the Lord's Supper, described in the Catechism by the strengthening and refreshing of our Souls by the Body and Blood of Christ, as our Bodies are by the Bread and Wine" (6). *The New Schaff-Herzog Encyclopedia of Religious Knowledge*, vol. 7 (New York: Funk & Wagnalls, 1908), tells us that from Zwingli onward "The body and blood of Christ" were not the "sign of the Sacrament" but "the benefit" which only the faithful, "spiritually eating," received (35).

29. *Confession of Faith*, 62; my emphasis.

30. Lucaris, *Confessio*, 6. It is interesting to note a further remark by Lucaris in comparison with the imagery and analogy, discussed before, of *Paradise Lost* 6.779: "When therefore we haue been partakers of the body and blood of Christ worthily, and haue communicated entirely, we acknowledge our selues to be reconciled, *vnited to our Head of the same body*, with certaine hope to be coheires in the Kingdome to come" (5; my emphasis). Note as well Lucaris's image of the "teeth," which also appears in Saint Augustine and those, like Forbes, who quote him. Milton's language in both *De doctrina Christiana* and *Paradise Lost* repeats that of many writers on these subjects who preceded him.

31. Smith, *An Account of the Greek Church*, 142, 144–45.

32. Robertson, *Acts and Decrees of the Synod of Jerusalem*, 203, 205.

33. William Atwood, *A Seasonable Vindication of the Truly Catholick Doctrine of the Church of England: In Reply to Dr. Sherlock's Answer to Anonymous his three Letters concerning Church-Communion* (London: Printed for Jonathan Robinson, 1683), 23; William Payne, *A Discourse Concerning the Adoration of the Host, As it is Taught and Practiced in the Church of Rome* (London: Printed for Brabazon Aylmer, 1685), 2.

34. Stillingfleet, *Doctrine of the Trinity*, 8, 46.

35. Anthony Horneck, *The Crucified Jesus; or, A full Account of the Nature, End, Design and Benefits of the Sacrament of the Lords Supper.... The Third Edition, Corrected and Amended* (In the Savoy, Printed for Samuel Lowndes, 1695), declares that transubstantiation was a word created by Stephen, Bishop of Autun, in 1112, and confirmed by Pope Innocent III in 1215 (126–27). Quotations in text from page 4.

36. Historical summaries, definitions, and incisive discussions appear in numerous religious studies, of course. See, for examples and much information, Rudolf Otto, *Religious Essays: A Supplement to "The Idea of the Holy,"* trans. Brian Lunn (London: Oxford University Press, 1931), chap. 6, "The Lord's

Supper as a Numinous Fact," 45–52; van der Leeuw, *Religion in Essence and Manifestation*, particularly book 2, chap. 52, "The Sacrament," 365–72; John C. Ulreich Jr., "Milton on the Eucharist: Some Second Thoughts about Sacramentalism," in *Milton and the Middle Ages*, ed. John Mulryan (Lewisburg, Pa.: Bucknell University Press, 1982), 33–56; and Schwartz, "Real Hunger," 1–17.

37. Van der Leeuw, *Religion in Essence and Manifestation*, 2:368–69. The term "epiclesis" signifies the invocation of the Holy Spirit for the purpose of consecrating the Eucharist; at the moment that the word is said in the ceremony the transubstantiation has occurred. The term *maran atha* is a formula from the Aramaic/Syrian, meaning "our Lord has come." It is associated with the Lord's Supper and it is used without explanation by Paul in the First Epistle to the Corinthians 16:22: "If any man love not the Lord Jesus Christ, let him be Anath'ema, Maranath'a."

38. Jung, *Psychology and Religion*, 255. Dionysus Zagreus was "torn to pieces by the Titans, from whose mangled remains the neos dionysos arises" (255).

39. See the *Encyclopedia of Religion and Ethics*, ed. James Hastings (New York: Charles Scribner's Sons, 1914), 548, 561.

40. Otto, *Religious Essays*, 50.

41. See Laud, *Works*, 7:619.

42. Anthony Milton, *Catholic and Reformed: The Roman and Protestant Churches in English Protestant Thought, 1600–1640* (Cambridge: Cambridge University Press, 1995), 385.

43. Lieb, *Poetics of the Holy*, 212, 215, with quotations coming from *PL* 11.315–33, 11.340–41.

44. Forbes, *Considerationes Modestæ et Pacificæ*, 423, 425, 403.

45. Lieb, *Theological Milton*, 117–20. The word *kabod* was translated in the Septuagint by the Greek *doxa*, creating a narrowing of meaning with an emphasis on praise for the object of worship. See Rumrich, *Matter of Glory*, 14–15, 39, and following.

46. See also the quotations from *De doctrina Christiana* to which note 3 above refer.

47. Rumrich, *Matter of Glory*, 81.

48. Guibbory, *Ceremony*, 227, 226, 215.

Notes to Chapter 7, "Conceptual Reflections in Milton's Poetry and Prose"

1. See John Hollander, *The Figure of Echo: A Mode of Allusion in Milton and After* (Berkeley and Los Angeles: University of California Press, 1981), for a full discussion of allusion and its forms in echo, metalepsis, and transumption. See also Leonard, "'Thus They Relate Erring.'"

2. Stanley E. Fish, *Surprised by Sin: The Reader in* Paradise Lost (London: Macmillan, 1967), argues the ways in which the reader's understanding of *Paradise Lost* alters as the reader proceeds through the poem. The further reading of the text aids in correcting what the reader first concluded, and thus, referring to an allusion to the last line of Virgil's *Aeneid* in *Paradise Lost* 4.1015, Fish remarks, "Whatever the allusion adds to the richness of the poem's texture or to Milton's case for superiority in the epic genre, it is also one more assault on the confidence of a reader who is met at every turn with demands his intellect cannot even consider" (37). The reader must grapple with the ambiguities of Milton's text, the destabilization of its language, and the successive reading that equates for the reader a conceptual development as he or she proceeds through this textured writing, and most significantly upon rereading it.

3. Shawcross, *With Mortal Voice*, 183–84n1. A demonstration of "Sources as Meaning and Structure" is found in this study as chapter 7, 68–83. These citations may be meaningful sources, and I suggest as an "excellent study of indebtedness and meaningfulness" for Milton's texts Davis P. Harding, *The Club of Hercules* (Urbana: University of Illinois Press, 1961).

4. Hollander, *The Figure of Echo*; Leonard, "'Thus They Relate Erring.'"

5. George Sandys, *Ovid's Metamorphosis. Englished by G. S.* (London: W. Stansby, 1626).

6. David N. Dickey reviews various gendered readings in *A Study of the Place of Women in the Poetry and Prose Works of John Milton* (Lewiston, Maine: Edwin Mellen Press, 2000).

7. The contrast of the prelapsarian Adam and Eve in book 4 and the now postlapsarian couple, each seducing the other and engaging in erotic sex, *nothing loath*, in book 9 is the subject of a multitude of e-mails as I write, many correspondents concerned over nudity and who might enact these characters in a literal cinematic transcription of the poem.

8. His description ("enclos'd / In Serpent") when he first addresses Eve is:

> not with indented wave,
> Prone on the ground, as since, but on his rear,
> Circular base of rising foulds, that tour'd
> Fould above fould a surging Maze. (PL 4.494–99)

9. The other two "horsemen" of the Apocalypse (Rev. 6:1–8), famine and death, are Satan's son, Death.

10. > Hee boulder now, uncall'd before her stood;
> But as in gaze admiring: Oft he bowd
> His turret Crest, and sleek enamel'd Neck,
> Fawning, and lick'd the ground whereon she trod.
> His gentle dumb expression turnd at length
> The Eye of *Eve* to mark his play. (PL 9.523–28)

11. Harold Fisch, "Hebraic Style and Motifs in *Paradise Lost*," *Language and Style in Milton: A Symposium in Honor of the Tercentenary of* Paradise Lost, ed. Ronald David Emma and John T. Shawcross (New York: Frederick Ungar, 1967), 50, 49. For one instance of the phallic reference, see Wolfgang Rudat, "Godhead and Milton's Satan. Classical Myth and Augustinian Theology in *Paradise Lost*," *Milton Quarterly* 14 (1980): 17–21.

12. > I nearer drew to gaze;
> When from the boughs a savorie odour blown
> Grateful to appetite, more pleas'd my sense
> Then smell of sweetest Fenel, or the Teats
> Of Ewe or Goat dropping with Milk at Eevn,
> Unsuckt of Lamb or Kid, that tend thir play. (PL 9.578–83)

Note the four senses involved in just this passage alone: sight, smell, touch, taste, as well as the animals' "play." Milton repeatedly implies Satan's libidinousness.

13. See my "Allegory, Typology, and Didacticism: *Paradise Lost* in the Eighteenth Century," in *Enlightening Allegory: Theory, Practice, and Contexts of Allegory in the Late Seventeenth and Eighteenth Centuries*, ed. Kevin L. Cope, 41–74 (New York: AMS Press, 1993), specifically 61–62 and 73nn35–36. In reference to Julia Kristeva's article, "Stendhal and the Politics of the Gaze: An Egotist's Love," *Tales of Love* (New York: Columbia University Press, 1987), 341–64, we can observe that "The gaze in Kristeva's Lacanian interpretation indicates both the fascination with what one is not sexually and with one's own sexuality."

I also wish to remark upon a point that seems to have been generally ignored concerning Adam. The poem reads that Adam "scrupl'd not to eat / Against his better knowledge, not deceav'd" (9.997–98); it is the narrative voice that records this, but Milton's acceptance of this culpability on Adam's part is assured when we remember that 1 Timothy 2:14 explicitly pronounced—and Milton repeatedly asserts his belief in Scripture—"And Adam was not deceived, but the woman being deceived was in the transgression." We can thus appreciate that, although "Milton" did not say this in the poem, he believed it. He employed the previous scriptual text twice in *De doctrina Christiana:* on marriage and a husband's authority (YP 6:355) and on the Fall (6:382). A. W. Verity in 1910 first cited this verse as a gloss on Milton's poetic line.

Notes to Chapter 8, "The Three Major Poems"

1. Thomas Ellwood, *The History of the Life of Thomas Ellwood* (London: J. Sowle, 1714), 233–34.
2. Milton, *John Milton's Complete Poetical Works*, ed. Fletcher, 3:10.
3. See my discussion of this important issue in *The Uncertain World of* Samson Agonistes (Cambridge: D. S. Brewer, 2001), 28–29. Significantly the prosodic evidence of the translations of Psalms 80–88 in April 1648 and those of Psalms 1–8 in August 1653, as well as sonnets dated prior to 1649 and those from 1652 and after bears out the alteration in Milton's prosodic work in terms of run-on lines.
4. Michael Wilding, *Dragons Teeth: Literature in the English Revolution* (Oxford: Clarendon, 1987), 243, 258. The conclusion to which Bryson, in *Tyranny of Heaven,* proceeds iterates the significance of the "paradise within" as the means of "regaining" paradise.
5. Cited are *PL* 2.406 and 12.188, describing hell and the plague of darkness visited upon Pharaoh's land.
6. Jackie Di Salvo, "'The Lord's Battells': *Samson Agonistes* and the Puritan Revolution," in *Milton Studies,* vol. 4, ed. James D. Simmonds (Pittsburgh: University of Pittsburgh Press, 1972), 39–62.
7. Joseph Wittreich, *Interpreting* Samson Agonistes (Princeton: Princeton University Press, 1986), 187.
8. Jean-Baptiste Mosneron-De Launay, ed., *Le Paradis perdu, traduction nouvelle* (Paris: Chez Royez, 1786), 3 vols.; see "Préface," 1:iii–iv, and its new edition in 1804.
9. Bryson, *Tyranny of Heaven,* 115, 146, 170.

10. James D. Driscoll, *The Unfolding God of Jung and Milton* (Lexington: University Press of Kentucky, 1993), 30.
11. Joseph Addison, *The Spectator*, no. 297 (February 9, 1712).
12. Shawcross, *Uncertain World*, 144.
13. Ibid., 144. See 60–64 for an examination of "renovation" instead of "regeneration," which has often—erroneously, I believe—been employed to describe Samson's final actions.

Notes to Chapter 9, "Unchanging Belief and the Changed Mind"

1. See Shawcross, *Self and the World*, 269–71.
2. Gordon Teskey, *Delirious Milton: The Fate of the Poet in Modernity* (Cambridge, Mass.: Harvard University Press, 2006), 3, 5–6.
3. Rumrich, *Matter of Glory*, 72, 73, 74, 72.
4. Lieb, *Theological Milton*, 66–67.
5. Ibid., 117–18. Milton writes (translated on CM 14:61): "Some description of this divine glory has been revealed, as far as it falls within the scope of human comprehension," and various texts such as the following are cited: "they saw the God of Israel, and there was under his feet as it were a paved work of a sapphire stone, and as it were the body of heaven in his clearness" (Exodus 24:10, etc.); "I saw Jehovah sitting on his throne" (1 Kings 22:19).
6. Ibid., 184. Radzinowicz, *Toward* Samson Agonistes, proposes "progressive revelation" as underlying various poems from *Lycidas* onward. She remarks, "The arrangement of Samson's despair, conveyed in the language of Scripture and predicting progressive revelations in time, is a form of consolation apt for tragedy but not annihilative of it. It is an assuagement that enables ethical action" (265). This concept arises from her view that "The meaning of Scripture cannot simply be distilled once and for all from the text and kept fixed in its original purity. Scripture also contains truth which will be progressively discerned.... The progressive discernment of the truth does not imply that human beings may add to the meaning of Scripture but simply that they may progressively discover the truth always latent in the text. Milton read Scripture in the way one should read Milton, attentive to progressive relevancies" (279). In one way she is talking about "build" or "climax" as Kenneth Burke employed the term, a literary/compositional development and unfolding through the movement and placement of text.

There has been disagreement (mistakenly, I believe) among Miltonists about "progressive revelation," yet it is basic to the definition in the *New Catholic Encyclopedia* (Washington, D.C.: Catholic University of America Press, 2003), 2nd ed., vol. 12: "Primarily, revelation is the act of God, seen in the progressive unfolding of His eternal plan of Salvation in Christ, by which He manifests and communicates Himself to people, calls the Church into being, and invites the loving response of assent and obedience; secondarily, it is the body of truth that is made known through God's unfolding plan" (187).

7. Thomas Chubb, *The Posthumous Works of Mr. Thomas Chubb*, vol. 1 (London: Printed for R. Baldwin, jun., and sold by E. Easton, 1748), 3, 5. His middle position as to the question at hand can be seen in *A Discourse Concerning Reason, with Regard to Religion and Divine Revelation. Wherein is shewn, That Reason either is, or else that it ought to be, a sufficient guide in Matters of Religion* (London: Printed for T. Cox, 1731). Chubb writes, "Let me then intreat my *fellow Protestants*, especially the *laity*, to contend for, and hold fast their *reason*, and to follow its guidance in matters of religion, and divine revelation: this being their best security against *popery*, which some think gains ground among us" (31).

8. Lieb, *Theological Milton*, 70–71, 209.

9. Shawcross, *Rethinking Milton Studies*, 155, and see Richard Elliott Friedman, *The Disappearance of God* (Boston: Little Brown, 1995).

10. Shawcross, "Arms of the Family," 143–44. See Joseph Glanvil, "The Agreement of Reason, and Religion," *Essays on Severall Important Subjects in Philosophy and Religion* (London: J. D. for John Baker and Henry Mortlock, 1676), 7–10.

11. John Rogers, *The Matter of Revolution: Science, Poetry, and Politics in the Age of Milton* (Ithaca, N.Y.: Cornell University Press, 1996), 49–51, 150.

12. Glanvil, "The Agreement of Reason," 25. We can realize this in between philosophic world for Restoration and Augustan times by looking at one like Richard Cumberland, Lord Bishop of Peterborough, who, though antagonistic to deism and deistic principles, yet writes: "GOD, the Author of Nature, has imprinted characters of His independent Power, Wisdom, Goodness, Providence, &c. upon his Works; he has given us Reason, by which we cannot but discover, if we attend, these his Attributes, and the Relation we have to him"; see "Concerning the City, or Kingdom, of GOD in the Rational World, and the Defects of HEATHEN DEISM," *A Treatise of the Laws of Nature*, trans. John Maxwell (London: R. Phillips, 1727), vi.

13. *Sir Isaac Newton's Mathematical Principles of Natural Philosophy and His System of the World*, 2 vols., trans. Andrew Motte (in 1729), ed. Florian Cajori (Berkeley and Los Angeles: University of California Press, 1973), 2:543–44. Roger Cotes in a preface to the second edition (1713) pertinently remarks "the most beautiful frame of the System of the World" that Newton has set before humankind's eyes:

> Therefore we may now more nearly behold the beauties of Nature, and entertain ourselves with the delightful contemplation; and, which is the best and most valuable fruit of philosophy, be thence incited the more profoundly to reverence and adore the great Maker and Lord of all. He must be blind who from the most wise and excellent contrivances of things cannot see the infinite Wisdom and goodness of their Almighty Creator, and he must be mad and senseless who refuses to acknowledge them.
>
> *Newton's* distinguished work will be the safest protectation against the attacks of atheists. (xxxii–xxxiii)

I cite Newton (and Cotes) at such length because his words are reflective of the kinds of arguments presented even today to prove the existence of God.

14. See, for example, Diane McColley, *A Gust for Paradise: Milton's Eden and the Visual Arts* (Urbana: University of Illinois Press, 1993) and "Milton and Ecology," 157–73, in Corns, *A Companion to Milton*; Karen L. Edwards, *Milton and the Natural World: Science and Poetry in* Paradise Lost (Cambridge: Cambridge University Press, 1999); G. Stanley Koehler, "Milton and the Art of Landscape," in *Milton Studies*, vol. 8, ed. James D. Simmonds (Pittsburgh: University of Pittsburgh Press, 1975), 3–49; John Dixon Hunt's "Milton and the Making of the English Landscape Garden," in *Milton Studies*, vol. 15, ed. James D. Simmonds (Pittsburgh: University of Pittsburgh Press, 1981), 81–105; Ken Hiltner, *Milton and Ecology* (Cambridge: Cambridge University Press, 2003); and Hiltner, *Renaissance Ecology: Imagining Eden in Milton's England* (Pittsburgh: Duquesne University Press, 2008). One should also consider John R. Knott's argument that *Paradise Lost* is an epic with a pastoral center; see *Milton's Pastoral Vision: An Approach to* Paradise Lost (Chicago: University of Chicago Press, 1971).

15. George Mason, *An Essay on Design in Gardening, First Published in MDCCLXVIII. Now Greatly Augmented* (London,

1795); Thomas Tyers, *An Historical Rhapsody on Mr. Pope*, 2nd ed. (London, 1782); Horace Walpole, *The Works of Horatio Walpole, Earl of Orford*, vol. 1 (London, 1798), [517]–45; Daniel Malthus, trans., preface to René Louis, Marquis de Girardin's *An Essay on Landscape; or, On the Means of Improving and Embellishing the Country Round Our Habitation* (London, 1783).

16. See Scott Robinson, "The Eighteenth-Century Novel," in *The Oxford Handbook of English Literature and Theology*, ed. Andrew Haas, David Jasper, and Elisabeth Jay, 431–47 (Oxford: Oxford University Press, 2007), 433, 435.

17. John Reichardt, *Milton's Wisdom: Nature and Scripture in* Paradise Lost (Ann Arbor: University of Michigan Press, 1992), 21. See also Herman Rapaport's limited reading of the issue in *Milton and the Postmodern* (Lincoln: University of Nebraska Press, 1983), 210–12, and Georgia B. Christopher's lack of understanding (to my way of reading it) of Adam's and Michael's speeches that I cite below in the text; see Christopher, *Milton and the Science of the Saints* (Princeton: Princeton University Press, 1982), 176. Reichardt discusses such statements on 39–41. Note also his questioning of Kathleen Swaim's assignment of Raphael's instruction only from the book of Nature and Michael's only from Scripture (272n9). Reference is to Kathleen Swaim, *Before and After the Fall: Contrasting Modes in* Paradise Lost (Amherst: University of Massachusetts Press, 1986).

18. One might compare Adam's commemoration and "monument" with the memorial Manoa speaks of for Samson (*SA* 1733–44), which is not only misplaced remembrance and externality for public show, but a great irony in using flowers, nature, living things to celebrate the past and death "In yonder nether World."

19. Edwards, *Milton and the Natural World*, discusses "the book of knowledge" and the debate over it: "in its representation of the creatures of the natural world, *Paradise Lost* precisely registers the complex historical moment of the making," and thereby joins the debate over classical and biblical interpretations and the new philosophy (6). She reminds us that Raphael's interpretation of the world is incomplete, and is thus demanding of a disengagement from interpretations of the Bible to allow ongoing and continual rethinking as experimental science expands (42).

20. Zera Fink, *The Classical Republicans* (1945; repr., Evanston, Ill.: Northwestern University Press, 1962), 91–122; cited is my translation of Milton's poem, lines 33–37.

21. Marjorie Hope Nicolson, *Mountain Gloom and Mountain Glory: The Development of the Aesthetics of the Infinite* (Ithaca, N.Y.: Cornell University Press, 1959).

22. See, as examples, Leibniz's letters to Burnet dated February 18, 1699, and February 2/13, 1700, in *Die Philosophischen Schriften von Gottfried Wilhelm Leibniz. Herausgegeben von C. J. Gerhardt. Dritter Band* (Berlin: Unveränderter Nachdruck der Ausgabe, 1887), 262–63, 270. Much attention is given to John Toland and his use of Milton in offering his own Socinian views in *The Life of John Milton* (London: John Darby, 1798).

23. John Knott, "Milton and the Spirit of Truth," *The Sword of the Spirit: Puritan Responses to the Bible* (Chicago: University of Chicago Press, 1980), 108–17.

24. Ken Simpson, "'That Sovran Book': The Discipline of the Word in Milton's Anti-Episcopal Tracts," in *Of Poetry and Politics: New Essays on Milton and His World*, ed. P. G. Stanwood, 313–25 (Tempe, Ariz.: Medieval & Renaissance Texts & Studies, 1997). The term *sola scriptura* was employed by Martin Luther and then by William Tyndale in England to indicate the "primacy of the Bible in spiritual affairs without clerical mediation, and heeded the humanistic call to return *ad fontes* by working directly from Hebrew texts and Erasmus's Greek New Testament (1516)," as John King explains. It is a major doctrine in the attitude and divisive acts of the Protestant movement in the sixteenth and seventeenth centuries, and therewith a major influence upon Milton's thinking, it would seem from early years without change. See King's entry on "English Bible" in *The Oxford Encyclopedia of the Reformation*, ed. Hans J. Hillerbrand (New York: Oxford University Press, 1996), 2:48–49.

25. See Cressy, *Birth, Marriage, and Death*, on this matter. Disagreement continued over the *Book of Common Prayer* in the ejection of many ministers on Black Bartholomew Day, August 24, 1662, after the royalist control of the government reinstated it as mandate. The "Black Rubric" reinstated kneeling, for example, since "no Adoration is intended, or ought to be done."

26. Simpson, "'That Sovran Book,'" 320, 316; King, *Milton and Religious Controversy*.

27. A. B. Chambers, "Christmas: The Liturgy of the Church and English Verse of the Renaissance," *Literary Monographs*, vol. 6, *Medieval and Renaissance Literature*, ed. Eric Rothstein and Joseph Anthony Wittreich Jr. (Madison: University of Wisconsin Press, 1975), 142–44. William B. Hunter Jr., *Milton's* Comus:

Family Piece (Troy, N.Y.: Whitston, 1983), chap. 2, "The Creation of *Arcades*," 17–18.

28. Lieb, *Poetics of the Holy*, 338n96.

29. Hannibal Hamlin, *Psalm Culture and Early Modern English Literature* (Cambridge: Cambridge University Press, 2004), 213–14, 215. See also 237–240 for discussion of Psalm 137 and the "Te Deum laudamus."

30. Diane McColley, "The Copious Matter of My Song," in *Literary Milton: Text, Pretext, Context*, ed. Diana Treviño Benet and Michael Lieb (Pittsburgh: Duquesne University Press, 1994), 69–78. McColley explicitly writes, "Milton's distrust of high-church ritual does not apply in heaven, where 'the beauty of holiness' is innocent of snobbery or manipulation and the angels raise their hymns in impromptu jubilation" (71).

31. Reichardt, *Milton's Wisdom*, offers a number of examples in *Paradise Lost* of "unmediated" orisons (42–50) that "are at least closely related to established liturgical forms" (43). Curiously, however, he quotes *Eikonoklastes* (1649) to indicate Milton's "great contempt for the Book of Common Prayer" "*In his earlier years*" (my italics). Milton, of course, was nearly 41 when he wrote that tract, and the beginnings of what became the poem date from 1640. The date of rejection of the prayer book's liturgy may, however, predate his travel on the Continent.

32. See especially Gardiner, "Milton's Parody" and "'Division in Communion.'" (King, *Milton and Religious Controversy*, also has some extensive comments on transubstantiation.) Gardiner points out that "Milton puts in the mouth of Eve words and phrases from the hymns of Fortunatus invoking the Cross as a 'tree' and from the hymns of Thomas Aquinas invoking the Sacrament as heavenly food. He also puts in the mouth of the Serpent phrases found in the hymns to Mary" (231). In the other article cited, she proposes that Milton suggests that "matter is constantly transmuted into spirit.... When Milton teaches that matter moves up by feeding what is more spirit-like, he leaves little room for the Eucharist, where the purer (Christ) comes to nourish the grosser (the communicant)" (26–27). The "diabolical illusion of transubstantiation" lies in book 9 as well when "Satan persuades Eve that a nectar powerful enough to give her divine life has been infused into the Fruit of the forbidden Tree" (28). Here Satan himself is transubstantiated to "Man / Internal Man," 9.710–11, parodying the Anglican Lord's Supper, which afforded an "interior transubstantiation or deification of the receiver after communion" (29). Milton's rejection of much in

the state church that we have glanced at here is over and over again an equating of Roman Catholicism with certain practices and ideas in that church, all of which point, for him and his fellow Puritans, to incomplete reformation. The "false" religion, Roman Catholicism, can be lampooned; therefore, its remnants in Protestant forms can also be lampooned with impunity.

33. See Ramie Targoff, *Common Prayer: The Language of Public Devotion in Early Modern England* (Chicago: University of Chicago Press, 2001) for a full exposition of this topic and for relationships with the Puritan attitude toward prayer concerning spontaneity and conformity. Adam and Eve's prayer is discussed on 89–90; see also the important view of prayer and Satan and the concept of hope examined by Mary C. Fenton, *Milton's Places of Hope: Spiritual and Political Connections of Hope with Land* (Burlington, Vt.: Ashgate, 2006), 97–126, and passim.

34. "Milton's differences with the Presbyterians over church discipline and social policy expose more fundamental differences of theological and anthropological opinion," Rumrich writes ("Radical Heterodoxy and Heresy," in Corns, *A Companion to Milton*, 147). "The prose works Milton published in the 1640s...track his increasing divergences from the Presbyterian orthodoxy with which he had allied himself early in the decade" (152), which offers us another example of Milton's changed mind.

35. In disagreement with the uncertain author of *A Modest Confutation,* Milton writes: "Nor is unity lesse broken, especially by our Liturgy, though this author would almost bring the Communion of Saints to a Communion of Liturgicall words. For what other reformed Church holds communion with us by our liturgy, and does not rather dislike it? and among our selves who knowes it not to have bin a perpetuall cause of disunion" (*Apology*, YP 2:937).

36. The Hebrew meaning of Michael is "one who is like unto God," and he was the equivalent of the mythic Hermes as conductor of the dead to the afterlife.

37. Debora K. Shuger, "Subversive Fathers and Suffering Subjects: Shakespeare and Christianity," in *Religion, Literature, and Politics in Post-Reformation England, 1540–1688*, ed. Donna B. Hamilton and Richard Strier, 46–69 (Cambridge: Cambridge University Press, 1996), 60.

38. Fenton, *Milton's Places of Hope*, 33.

39. A reinterpretation of Adam's observation to the Almighty that Man, in "unitie defective," without "Collateral love, and

deerest amitie," "by number is to manifest / His single imperfection" (*PL* 8.422–26) leads Thomas Luxon, *Single Imperfection: Milton, Marriage and Friendship* (Pittsburgh: Duquesne University Press, 2005), to a reading that "solitude, far from being a problem is actually what made Paradise before Eve a happy state" (104), and "It is not entirely good for man to need company, especially when the partner may fall short of being what classical friendship defined as fundamental—an equal, other self" (156).

40. See Shawcross, "Higher Wisdom," 155–56. Milton's emphasis upon the individual and the individual's "education" and "growth" ultimately is interrelated with the hope for *Paradise Lost*'s effectiveness: that it will reach a "fit audience though few." Achievement comes only step by step, person by person, not by mandate, not by blanket, rote conformity, not even by imitation. His talent that is death to hide has not always been successful—"to argue against ignorance, to educate his readers, to inculcate virtue and advance right reason"—well, there have been a few.

WORKS CITED

Abbot, George. "Articles to be inquired of, in the first metropolitan visitation, of the most reverend father, George, by Gods providence, Arch-Bishop of Canterbury, and Primate of England...1612." In Fincham, *Visitation Articles*.

Achinstein, Sharon. *Milton and the Revolutionary Reader*. Princeton: Princeton University Press, 1994.

Addison, Joseph. *The Spectator*. No. 297, February 9, 1712.

Articles whereupon it was agreed by the Archbishoppes and Bishoppes of both prouinces and the whole cleargie in the Convocation holden in London in the yere of our Lorde GOD, *1562 according to the composition of the Churche of Englande,...Put foorth by the Queenes autoritie*. London: Deputies of Christopher Barker, 1590.

Atwood, William. *A Seasonable Vindication of the Truly Catholick Doctrine of the Church of England: In Reply to Dr. Sherlock's Answer to Anonymous his Three Letters concerning Church-Communion*. London: Printed for Jonathan Robinson, 1683.

Barbour, Reid. *Literature and Religious Culture in Seventeenth-Century England*. Cambridge: Cambridge University Press, 2002.

Bauman, Michael. *A Scripture Index to John Milton's* De doctrina christiana. Binghamton, N.Y.: Medieval & Renaissance Texts & Studies, 1989.

Benet, Diana Treviño. "'All in All': The Threat of Bliss." In Durham and Pruitt, *"All in All,"* 49–66.

Biberman, Matthew. "'The Earth Is All Before Me': Wordsworth, Milton, and the Christian Hebraic Roots of English Republicanism."

In *Romantic Generations: Essays in Honor of Robert F. Gleckner*, edited by Ghislaine McDayter, Guinn Batten, and Barry Milligan, 102–28. Lewisburg, Pa.: Bucknell University Press, 2001.

———. *Masculinity, Anti-Semitism, and Early Modern English Literature: From the Satanic to the Effeminate Jew.* Burlington, Vt.: Ashgate, 2004.

Biddle, John. *A Confession of Faith Touching the Holy Trinity, According to the Scripture.* London, 1648.

Boocker, David. "Milton and the Woman Controversy." In *A Search for Meaning: Critical Essays on Early Modern Literature*, edited by Paula Harms Payne, 125–48. New York: Peter Lang, 2004.

Book of Common Prayer, The. London: Bonham Norton and John Bill, 1621.

Boyle, Marjorie O'Rourke. "Home to Mother: Regaining Milton's Paradise." *Modern Philology* 97 (2000): 499–527.

Brooks, Cleanth, and John Edward Hardy. *Poems of Mr. John Milton: The 1645 Edition with Essays in Analysis.* New York: Harcourt, Brace, 1951.

Bryson, Michael. *The Tyranny of Heaven: Milton's Rejection of God as King.* Newark: University of Delaware Press, 2004.

Bull, George. *Defensio Fidei Nicænæ, Ex scriptis, quæ intra tria prima Ecclesiæ Christianæ secula floruerunt. In qua Ob iter quoque Constantinopolitana Confessio, de Spiritu Sancto, Antiquiorum testimoniis adstruitur. Authore Georgio Bullo Presbytero Anglicano.* Oxonii e Theatro Sheldoniano, 1685.

Burgess, Thomas. *Milton Not the Author of the Lately Discovered Arian Work De Doctrina Christiana.* London, 1829.

Burnet, Thomas. *Telluria Theoria Sacra.* London: Typis R. N.; Impensis Gualt. Kettilby, 1681. Translated as *The Theory of the Earth* (London: R. Norton, for Walter Kettilby, 1684) and *The Sacred Theory of the Earth* (1691), 4th ed. augmented (London: John Hoole, 1719).

Campbell, Gordon. *A Milton Chronology.* London: Macmillan Press, 1997.

Chambers, A. B. "Christmas: The Liturgy of the Church and English Verse of the Renaissance." In *Literary Monographs*, vol. 6, *Medieval and Renaissance Literature*, edited by Eric Rothstein and Joseph Anthony Wittreich Jr., 111–53. Madison: University of Wisconsin Press, 1975.

Chappell, Michael. "De-fencing the Poet: The Political Dilemma of the Poet and the People in Milton's *Second Defense* and Shelley's *Defence of Poetry*." In *Milton, the Metaphysicals, and Romanticism,* edited by Lisa Low and Anthony John Harding, 136–50. Cambridge: Cambridge University Press, 1994.

Charlesworth, James H., ed. *The Old Testament Pseudepigrapha*. Garden City, N.Y.: Doubleday, 1985.

Christopher, Georgia B. *Milton and the Science of the Saints*. Princeton: Princeton University Press, 1982.

Chubb, Thomas. *The Comparative Excellence and Obligation of Moral and Positive Duties, Fully Stated and Considered*. London: Printed for J. Roberts, 1730.

———. *A Discourse Concerning Reason, with Regard to Religion and Divine Revelation, wherein is shewn, That Reason either is, or else that it ought to be, a sufficient guide on Matters of Religion*. London: Printed for T. Cox, 1731.

———. *The Posthumous Works of Mr. Thomas Chubb*. 2 vols. London: Printed for R. Baldwin, jun, and sold by E. Easton, 1748.

Cleland, John. *Memoirs of a Woman of Pleasure*. 2 vols. London: For G. Fenton, 1749.

Coleman, Peter. "The Good Old Cause: John Milton's *Areopagitica* Revisited." *Quadrant* 49 (October 2005): 64–70; available at http://www.quadrant.org.au/php/article_view.php?article_id.-1211.

Colet, John. *An Exposition of St. Paul's First Epistle to the Corinthians*. Translated by J. H. Lupton. Ridgewood, N.J.: N.p., 1965.

Constitutions and Canons Ecclesiastical. Imprinted at London by Robert Barker, 1612. [Another edition], London: Printed by John Norton, for Joyce Norton and R. Whitaker, 1633. For 1640 edition, see Laud.

Corns, Thomas N. *The Development of Milton's Prose Style*. Oxford: Clarendon Press, 1982.

———. "Milton and Class." In *Running Wild: Essays, Fictions, and Memoirs Presented to Michael Wilding*, edited by David Brooks and Brian Kiernan, 55–68. Manohar: Sydney Association for Studies in Society and Culture, 2004.

Corns, Thomas N., ed. *A Companion to Milton*. Oxford: Basil Blackwell, 2001.

Creaser, John. "'Fear of Change': Closed Minds and Open Forms in Milton." *Milton Quarterly* (forthcoming).

Cressy, David. *Birth, Marriage, and Death: Ritual, Religion, and the Life-Cycle in Tudor and Stuart England*. Oxford: Oxford University Press, 1997.

Croft, Herbert. *The Naked Truth; or, The True State of the Primitive Church.* [London], 1675.

Cumberland, Richard. *A Treatise of the Laws of Nature.* Translated by John Maxwell. London: R. Phillips, 1727.

Daiches, David. "The Opening of *Paradise Lost.*" In *The Living Milton,* edited by Frank Kermode, 55–69. London: Routledge & Kegan Paul, 1960).

Darbishire, Helen, ed. *The Early Lives of Milton.* London: Constable, 1932.

Declaration of the Well Affected to the Good Old Cause in the Cities of London, Westminster, and Southwark, A. London: Printed by J. C., 1659.

Dickey, David N. *A Study of the Place of Women in the Poetry and Prose Works of John Milton.* Lewiston, Maine: Edwin Mellen Press, 2000.

Di Salvo, Jackie. "'The Lord's Battells': *Samson Agonistes* and the Puritan Revolution." In *Milton Studies,* vol. 4, edited by James D. Simmonds, 39–62. Pittsburgh: University of Pittsburgh Press, 1972.

Dixon, Philip. *"Nice and Hot Disputes": The Doctrine of the Trinity in the Seventeenth Century.* London: T. & T. Clark, 2003.

Driscoll, James P. *The Unfolding God of Jung and Milton.* Lexington: University Press of Kentucky, 1993.

Durham, Charles W., and Kristin A. Pruitt, eds. *"All in All": Unity, Diversity, and the Miltonic Perspective.* Selinsgrove, Pa.: Susquehanna University Press, 1999.

Dzelzainis, Martin. "Liberty and the Law." In Tournu and Forsyth, *Milton, Rights, and Liberties,* 57–67.

———. "Republicanism." In Corns, *A Companion to Milton,* 294–308.

Edwards, Karen L. *Milton and the Natural World.* Cambridge: Cambridge University Press, 1999.

Eliot, T. S. "A Note on the Verse of John Milton." *Essays and Studies by Members of the English Association* 21 (1936): 156–64.

Ellrodt, Robert. "Milton's Unchanging Mind and the Early Poems." *Milton Quarterly* 22 (1988): 59–62.

Ellwood, Thomas. *The History of the Life of Thomas Ellwood.* London: J. Sowle, 1714.

Fallon, Stephen. "'Elect above the rest': Theology as Self-representation in Milton." In *Milton and Heresy,* edited by Stephen B. Dobranski and John P. Rumrich, 93–116. Cambridge: Cambridge University Press, 1998.

Fenton, Mary C. *Milton's Places of Hope: Spiritual and Political Connections of Hope with Land.* Burlington, Vt.: Ashgate, 2006.

———. "Milton's View of Ireland: Reform, Reduction, and National Polity." In *Milton Studies*, vol. 44, edited by Albert C. Labriola, 203–29. Pittsburgh: University of Pittsburgh Press, 2005.

Ferguson, Everett, ed. *Encyclopedia of Early Christianity.* Vol. 2. 2nd ed. New York: Garland, 1997.

Fincham, Kenneth, ed. *The Early Stuart Church, 1603–1642.* Stanford, Calif.: Stanford University Press, 1993.

———. *Visitation Articles and Injunctions of the Early Stuart Church.* Vol. 2. Woodbridge, Suffolk: Boydell, 1998.

Fink, Zera. *The Classical Republicans: An Essay in the Recovery of a Pattern of Thought in Seventeenth Century England.* Evanston, Ill.: Northwestern University Press, 1945.

First and Large Petition of the City of London and of other Inhabitants thereabouts, The. Printed Anno Dom. 1641. Known as the "London Petition."

Fisch, Harold. "Hebraic Style and Motifs in *Paradise Lost.*" In *Language and Style in Milton: A Symposium in Honor of the Tercentenary of Paradise Lost,* edited by Ronald David Emma and John T. Shawcross, 30–64. New York: Frederick Ungar, 1967.

Fish, Stanley E. *Surprised by Sin: The Reader in* Paradise Lost. London: Macmillan, 1967.

Fletcher, Harris Francis. *The Intellectual Development of John Milton.* Vol. 1. Urbana: University of Illinois Press, 1956.

———. *The Use of the Bible in Milton's Prose.* Urbana: University of Illinois Press, 1929.

Forbes, William. *Considerationes Modestæ et Pacificæ Controversiarum de...Eucharista. Editio quarta. Tom. II.* Oxonii: Apud J. H. Parker, 1856. "Consideratio Æqua et Pacifica Controversiæ Hodiernæ Gravissimæ de Sacramento Eucharistiæ" ("A Moderate and Peaceful Consideration of the Present Very Serious Controversy Concerning the Sacrament of the Eucharist," 378–613 (Latin and English on alternate pages).

Fortier, Mark. *The Culture of Equity in Early Modern England.* Burlington, Vt.: Ashgate, 2005.

Foster, Andrew. "Church Policies of the 1630s." In *Conflict in Early Stuart England: Studies in Religion and Politics, 1603–1642,* edited by Richard Cust and Ann Hughes, 193–223. London: Longman, 1989.

Franks, R. S. *The Doctrine of the Trinity*. London: Gerald Duckworth, 1953.

French, J. Milton, ed. *The Life Records of John Milton*. 5 vols. New Brunswick: Rutgers University Press, 1949–58.

———. *Milton in Chancery: New Chapters in the Lives of the Poet and His Father*. New York: Modern Language Association, 1939.

Friedman, Richard Elliott. *The Disappearance of God: A Divine Mystery*. Boston: Little, Brown, 1995.

Gardiner, Anne Barbeau. "Division in Communion: Symbols of Transubstantiation in Donne, Milton, and Dryden." *Symbolism: An International Annual of Critical Aesthetics* 4 (2005): 15–39.

———. "Milton's Parody of Catholic Hymns in Eve's Temptation and Fall: Original Sin as a Paradigm of 'Secret Idolatries.'" *Studies in Philology* 91 (1994): 216–31.

Geisst, Charles. *The Political Thought of John Milton*. London: Macmillan, 1984.

Glanvil, Joseph. *Essays on Several Important Subjects in Philosophy and Religion*. London: J. D., 1676.

Goldberg, Jonathan. "Dating Milton." In *Soliciting Interpretation: Literary Theory and Seventeenth-Century English Poetry*, edited by Elizabeth D. Harvey and Katharine Eisaman Maus, 199–220. Chicago: University of Chicago Press, 1990.

Goodman, Godfrey. *The Fall of Man; or, The Corruption of Nature, proved by the Light of Our National Reason*. London: F. Kyngston, and Sold by R. Lee, 1616.

Guibbory, Achsah. *Ceremony and Community from Herbert to Milton: Literature, Religion, and Cultural Conflict in Seventeenth-Century England*. Cambridge: Cambridge University Press, 1998.

Hadjiantoniou, George A. *Protestant Patriarch: The Life of Cyril Lucaris (1572–1638), Patriarch of Constantinople*. Richmond, Va.: John Knox Press, 1961.

Hair, Christopher R. "Seventeenth Century Discord and the Paradise Within: Genesis in the Works of Winstanley, Milton, Hutchinson, and Cavendish." Unpublished Ph.D. dissertation, University of Kentucky, 2005.

Hakewill, George. *An Apologie or Declaration of the Power and Providence of God on the Government of the World*. Oxford: J. Lichfield and W. Turner, 1627.

Hakluyt, Richard. *Principal Navigations, Voyages, Traffiques, and Discoveries of the English Nation*. London: G. Bishop, R. Newberie, and R. Barker, 1598–1600.

Haller, William. *The Rise of Puritanism; or, The Way to the New Jerusalem as Set Forth in Pulpit and Press from Thomas Cartwright to John Lilburne and John Milton, 1570–1643*. New York: Columbia University Press, 1938.

Hamlin, Hannibal. *Psalm Culture and Early Modern English Literature*. Cambridge: Cambridge University Press, 2004.

Hanford, James Holly. "The Chronology of Milton's Private Studies." *PMLA* 36 (1921): 251–314. Reprinted in *John Milton, Poet and Humanist: Essays by James Holly Hanford*, edited by John S. Diekhoff. Cleveland: The Press of Western Reserve University, 1966.

———. *A Milton Handbook*. 4th ed. New York: F. S. Croft, 1946; 5th ed. rev. James G. Taaffe (New York: Appleton-Century-Crofts, 1970).

Harding, Davis P. *The Club of Hercules*. Urbana: University of Illinois Press, 1961.

Haskin, Dayton. "Milton's Strange Pantheon: The Apparent Tritheism of *De Doctrina Christiana*." *Heythorpe Journal: Quarterly Review of Philosophy and Theology* 16 (April 1975): 129–48.

Hastings, James, ed. *Encyclopedia of Religion and Ethics*. New York: Charles Scribner's Sons, 1914.

Hawkes, David. "The Concept of the 'Hireling' in Milton's Theology." In *Milton Studies*, vol. 43, edited by Albert C. Labriola, 64–85. Pittsburgh: University of Pittsburgh Press, 2004.

Hawkes, David, ed. *Paradise Lost: John Milton*. New York: Barnes and Noble Classics, 2004.

Herman, Peter C. *Destabilizing Milton:* Paradise Lost *and the Poetics of Incertitude*. New York: Palgrave Macmillan, 2005.

———. *Squitters-wits and Muse-haters: Sidney, Spenser, Milton, and Renaissance Antipoetic Sentiment*. Detroit: Wayne State University Press, 1996.

Hill, Christopher. *Milton and the English Revolution*. New York: Viking, 1978.

Hill, John Spencer. *John Milton: Poet, Priest, and Prophet. A Study of Divine Vocation in Milton's Poetry and Prose*. Totowa, N.J.: Rowman and Littlefield, 1979.

Hiltner, Ken. *Milton and Ecology*. Cambridge: Cambridge University Press, 2003.

Hiltner, Ken, ed. *Renaissance Ecology: Imagining Eden in Milton's England*. Pittsburgh: Duquesne University Press, 2008.

Hollander, John. *The Figure of Echo: A Mode of Allusion in Milton and After*. Berkeley and Los Angeles: University of California Press, 1981.

Honeygosky, Stephen R. *Milton's House of God: The Invisible and Visible Church*. Columbia: University of Missouri Press, 1993.

Hooker, Richard. *Of the Laws of Ecclesiastical Polity*. Introduction by Christopher Morris. London: N.p., 1963.

Horneck, Anthony. *The Crucified Jesus; or, A full Account of the Nature, End, Design and Benefits of the Sacrament of the Lords Supper. ... The Third Edition, Corrected and Amended*. In the Savoy, Printed for Samuel Lowndes, 1695.

———. *The Great Law of Consideration; or, A Discourse, wherein the Nature, Usefulness, and Absolute Necessity of Consideration, in Order to a Truly Serious and Religious Life, is laid open*. London: Printed by T. N., for Sam. Lowndes, 1677.

Hoxby, Blair. *Mammon's Music: Literature and Economics in the Age of Milton*. New Haven: Yale University Press, 2002.

Hughes, Ann. *The Causes of the English Civil War*. New York: St. Martin's Press, 1991.

Hunt, John Dixon. "Milton and the Making of the English Landscape Garden." In *Milton Studies*, vol. 15, edited by James D. Simmonds, 81–105. Pittsburgh: University of Pittsburgh Press, 1981.

Hunter, William B. *Milton's* Comus: *Family Piece*. Troy, N.Y.: Whitston, 1983.

———. *Visitation Unimplor'd: Milton and the Authorship of* De Doctrina Christiana. Pittsburgh: Duquesne University Press, 1998.

Hunter, William B., gen. ed. *A Milton Encyclopedia*. 9 vols. Lewisburg, Pa.: Bucknell University Press, 1978–83.

Interpreter's Bible, The. Nashville: Abington, 1957.

Jenkins, Hugh. "*Quid nomine populi intelligi velimus:* Defining the 'People' in *The Second Defense*." In *Milton Studies*, vol. 46, edited by Albert C. Labriola, 191–209. Pittsburgh: University of Pittsburgh Press, 2007.

Jewell, John. *The Works of John Jewell; and a Briefe Discourse of His Life*. London: Printed by J. Norton, 1609.

Johnson, Samuel. "The Life of John Milton." *Prefaces, Biographical and Critical to the Works of the English Poets*. London: J. Nichols, 1779.

Jung, C. G. *Psychology and Religion: West and East*. Translated by R. F. C. Hull. New York: Pantheon Books, 1958.

———. *Symbolik des Geistes*. Zurich: Rascher, 1948.

Juxon, William. "Articles for the London Ministry, 1635." In Fincham, *Visitation Articles*.

———. "Bishop William Juxon's Injunctions for Barstable Deanery, London Diocese, 1637." In Fincham, *Visitation Articles*.

Keeble, N. H. "Milton and Puritanism." In Corns, *A Companion to Milton*, 124–40.

Kersey, J. *Dictionarium Anglo-Britannicum; or, A General English Dictionary*. London: 1708.

———. *The New World of English Words; or, A General Dictionary*. Revised, corrected, and improved. London, 1710.

King, John N. "English Bible." In *The Oxford Encyclopedia of the Reformation*, vol. 2, edited by Hans J. Hillerbrand, 48–49. New York: Oxford, 1996.

———. *Milton and Religious Controversy: Satire and Polemic in* Paradise Lost. Cambridge: Cambridge University Press, 2000.

———. "Milton and the Bishops: Ecclesiastical Controversy and the Early Poems." In *Centered on the World: Literature, Scripture, and the Tudor-Stuart Middle Way*, edited by Daniel W. Doerksen and Christopher Hodgkins, 277–97. Cranbury, N.J.: Associated University Presses, 2004.

Knott, John R. Jr. "Milton and the Spirit of Truth." *The Sword of the Spirit: Puritan Responses to the Bible*, 106–30. Chicago: University of Chicago Press, 1980.

———. *Milton's Pastoral Vision: An Approach to* Paradise Lost. Chicago: University of Chicago Press, 1971.

Koehler, G. Stanley. "Milton and the Art of Landscape." In *Milton Studies*, vol. 8, edited by James D. Simmonds, 3–40. Pittsburgh: University of Pittsburgh Press, 1975.

Kristeva, Julia. "Stendhal and the Politics of the Gaze: An Egotist's Love." In *Tales of Love*, 341–64. New York: Columbia University Press, 1987.

Kugel, James L. *Traditions of the Bible*. Cambridge, Mass.: Harvard University Press, 1998.

Labriola, Albert C. "'All in All' and 'All in One': Obedience and Disobedience in *Paradise Lost*." In Durham and Pruitt, *"All in All,"* 39–47.

———. "The Son as an Angel in *Paradise Lost*." In *Milton in the Age of Fish: Essays on Authorship, Text, and Terrorism*, edited by Michael

Lieb and Albert C. Labriola, 105–18. Pittsburgh: Duquesne University Press, 2006.

Lares, Jameela. *Milton and the Preaching Arts*. Pittsburgh: Duquesne University Press, 2001.

Laud, William. *Articles to be enquired of within the diocesse of London...Holden in the yeare of our Lord God, 1640*. Printed in London, 1640.

——. *Constitutions and Canons Ecclesiasticall. Treated upon by the Archbishops of Canterbury and York, Presidents of the Convocations for the respective Provinces of Canterbury and York, and the rest of the Bishops and Clergie of those Provinces, And agreed upon with the Kings Majesties Licence in their severall Synods begun at London and York, 1640*. London: Printed by Robert Barker, and by the Assignes of John Bill, 1640.

——. *Metropolitan Articles for Lincoln Diocese, 1634*. In Fincham, *Visitation Articles*.

——. *A Speech Delivered in the Starr-Chamber, On Wednesday, The XIVth of Iune, MDCXXXVII. At the Censure, Of [Iohn Bastwick, Henry Burton, & William Prinn; Concerning pretended Innovations In the Church*. London: Printed by Richard Badger, 1637.

——. *The Works of the Most Reverend Father in God, William Laud, D. D. Sometimes Lord Archbishop of Canterbury*. Vol. 4, *History of Troubles and Trial, &c*. Oxford: John Henry Parker, 1854.

Leavis, F. R. "Milton's Verse." *Sewanee Review* 2 (1933): 123–36.

Le Comte, Edward. "*Areopagitica* as a Scenario for *Paradise Lost*." In *Achievements of the Left Hand: Essays on the Prose of John Milton*, edited by Michael Lieb and John T. Shawcross, 121–41. Amherst: University of Massachusetts Press, 1974.

——. "Milton as Satirist and Wit." In *Th' Upright Heart and Pure*, edited by Amadeus P. Fiore, 45–59. Pittsburgh: Duquesne University Press, 1967.

——. *Milton's Unchanging Mind*. Port Washington, N.Y.: Kennikat Press, 1973.

——. *Yet Once More: Verbal and Psychological Pattern in Milton*. New York: Liberal Arts Press, 1954.

Leger, Antoine. "Framentum Vitæ D. Cyrilli." In Smith, *Collectanea de Cyrillo Lucaris*, 77–83.

Leibniz, Gottfried Wilhelm. *Die Philosophischen Schriften von Gottfried Wilhelm Leibnitz. Herausgegeben von C. J. Gerhardt. Dritter Band*. Berlin: Unveränderter Nachdruck der Ausgabe, 1887.

Leonard, John. "'Thus They Relate Erring': Milton's Inaccurate Allusions." In *Milton Studies*, vol. 38, *The Writer in His Works*, edited by Albert C. Labriola and Michael Lieb, 96–121. Pittsburgh: University of Pittsburgh Press, 2000.

Leslie, Charles. *The History of Sin and Heresy Attempted*. London: H. Hindmarsh, 1698.

Levine, Joseph M. "Erasmus and the Problem of the Johannine Comma." *Journal of the History of Ideas* 58 (1997): 573–96.

Lewalski, Barbara K. "How Radical Was the Young Milton?" In *Milton and Heresy*, edited by Stephen B. Dobranski and John P. Rumrich, 49–72. Cambridge: Cambridge University Press, 1998.

———. *The Life of John Milton: A Critical Biography*. Oxford: Blackwell, 2000.

———. "Milton: Political Beliefs and Polemical Methods, 1659–60." *PMLA* 74 (1959): 191–202.

———. "Milton on Liberty, Servility, and the Paradise Within." In Tournu and Forsyth, *Milton, Rights, and Liberties*, 31–53.

Lieb, Michael. "Milton and 'Arianism.'" *Religion and Literature* 32 (2000): 197–220.

———. "Milton and the Socinian Heresy." In *Milton and the Grounds of Contention*, edited by Mark R. Kelley, Michael Lieb, and John T. Shawcross, 234–81. Pittsburgh: Duquesne University Press, 2003.

———. *Poetics of the Holy: A Reading of* Paradise Lost. Chapel Hill: University of North Carolina Press, 1981.

———. *Theological Milton: Deity, Discourse, and Heresy in the Miltonic Canon*. Pittsburgh: Duquesne University Press, 2006.

Lilburne, John. *An Outcry of the Youngmen and Apprentices of London*. [London, 1649].

Liljegren, S. B. *Studies in Milton*. Lund: Gleerup, 1918.

Loewenstein, David. "The Radical Religious Politics of *Paradise Lost*." In Corns, *A Companion to Milton*, 348–62.

Lucaris, Cyril. *The Confession of Faith of...Cyrill, Patriarch of Constantinople...Written at Constantinople, 1629*. London: Printed for Nicolas Bourne, 1629.

Luxon, Thomas. *Single Imperfection: Milton, Marriage, and Friendship*. Pittsburgh: Duquesne University Press, 2005.

MacLennan, Kerry. "Milton's Contract for *Paradise Lost:* A New Reading." Paper presented at the Eighth International Milton Symposium at Grenoble, France, June 2005.

Makin, Bathsua. *An Essay to Revive the Antient Education of Gentlewomen*. London: Printed by J. D., and to be sold by Tho. Parkhurst, 1673.

Malthus, Daniel. *An Essay on Landscape; or, On the Means of Improving and Embellishing the Country Round Our Habitation*. London: J. Dodsley, 1783.

Mason, George. *An Essay on Design in Gardening, First Published in MDCCLXVIII. Now Greatly Augmented*. London: Printed by C. Roworth, for Benjamin and John White, 1795.

McColley, Diane Kelsey. "'All in All': The Individuality of Creatures in *Paradise Lost*." In Durham and Pruitt, *"All in All,"* 21–38.

———. "'The Copious Matter of My Song.'" In *Literary Milton: Text, Pretext, Content*, edited by Diana Treviño Benet and Michael Lieb, 69–78. Pittsburgh: Duquesne University Press, 1994.

———. *A Gust for Paradise: Milton's Eden and the Visual Arts*. Urbana: University of Illinois Press, 1993.

———. "Milton and Ecology." In Corns, *A Companion to Milton*, 157–73.

Mede, Joseph. *The Works of the Pious and Profoundly Learned Joseph Mede, B. D. Sometime Fellow of Christ's College in Cambridge. Corrected and Enlarged according to the Author's own Manuscripts*. London: Printed by Roger Norton, for Richard Royston, 1672. 3rd ed. edited by John Worthington.

Milner, Andrew. *John Milton and the English Revolution: A Study in the Sociology of Literature*. Totowa, N.J.: Barnes & Noble Books, 1981.

Milton, Anthony. *Catholic and Reformed: The Roman and Protestant Churches in English Protestant Thought 1600–1640*. Cambridge: Cambridge University Press, 1995.

Milton, John. *The Complete Poetry of John Milton*. Edited by John T. Shawcross. Garden City, N.Y.: Doubleday Anchor, 1971.

———. *Complete Prose Works of John Milton*. 8 vols. in 10. Edited by Don M. Wolfe et al. New Haven: Yale University Press, 1953–82.

———. *Comus, A Mask: (Now Adapted to the Stage)*. London: J. Hughs for R. Dodsley, 1738. Adaptation by John Dalton with music by Thomas Arne.

———. *John Milton Poems Reproduced in Facsimile from the Manuscript in Trinity College, Cambridge*. Menston: Scolar Press, 1970.

———. *John Milton's Complete Poetical Works Reproduced in Photographic Facsimile*. 4 vols. Edited by Harris F. Fletcher. Urbana: University of Illinois Press, 1945.

———. *The Prose of John Milton.* Edited by J. Max Patrick et al. Garden City, N.Y.: Doubleday Anchor, 1967.

———. *A Variorum Commentary on The Poems of John Milton.* 5 vols. Edited by Douglas Bush et al. New York: Columbia University Press, 1970–.

———. *The Works of John Milton.* 18 vols. in 21. Edited by Frank Allen Patterson et al. New York: Columbia University Press, 1931–38.

Mohl, Ruth, ed. "Commonplace Book." In YP 1:344–513.

Mollenkott, Virginia R. "Apocrypha and Pseudepigrapha." In *A Milton Encyclopedia*, vol. 1, edited by William B. Hunter et al., 61–63. Lewisburg, Pa.: Bucknell University Press, 1978.

Montagu, Richard. *A Gagg for the new Gospell? NO: A New Gagg for An Old Goose.* London: Printed by Thomas Snodham for Matthew Lownes and W. Barrett, 1624.

Mosneron-De Launay, Jean-Baptiste, ed. *Le Paradis perdu, traduction nouvelle.* 3 vols. Paris: Chez Royez, 1786.

Mutschmann, Heinrich. *Der andere Milton.* Bonn: K. Schrœder, 1920.

New Catholic Encyclopedia. Vol. 12. 2nd ed. Washington, D.C.: Catholic University of America Press, 2003.

New Oxford Annotated Bible. Third Edition, with the Apocryphal/Deuterocanonical Books, New Revised Standard Version. Edited by Michael D. Coogan; Marc Z. Brettler, Carol A. Newsom, Pheme Perkins, Associate Editors. Oxford: Oxford University Press, 2001.

New Schaff-Herzog Encyclopedia of Religious Knowledge, The. New York: Funk & Wagnalls, 1908.

Newton, Isaac. *Sir Isaac Newton's Mathematical Principles of Natural Philosophy and His System of the World.* Edited by Florian Cajori. Berkeley and Los Angeles: University of California Press, 1973.

Nicolson, Marjorie Hope. *Mountain Gloom and Mountain Glory.* Ithaca, N.Y.: Cornell University Press, 1959.

Nuttall, Geoffrey F. *The Holy Spirit in Puritan Faith and Experience.* Oxford: Basil Blackwell, 1947.

O'Keeffe, Timothy J. *Milton and the Pauline Tradition: A Study of Theme and Symbolism.* Washington, D.C.: University Press of America, 1982.

"Orders Agreed on by the General Vestry of St. Bartholomew Exchange, The." (1633). In Fincham, *Visitation Articles.*

Otto, Rudolf. *Religious Essays: A Supplement to "The Idea of the Holy."* Translated by Brian Lunn. London: Oxford University Press, 1931.

Owen, John. *A Brief Declaration and Vindication of the Doctrine of the Trinity: As also of the Person and Satisfaction of Christ.... John 5.39. Search the Scriptures.* London: Printed by R. W. for Nath. Ponder, 1669.

Parker, William Riley. *Milton: A Biography.* 2nd ed. Edited by Gordon Campbell. Oxford: Clarendon Press, 2nd ed. 1996.

———. *Milton's Contemporary Reputation.* Columbus: Ohio State University Press, 1940.

Patrides, C. A. "Milton on the Trinity: The Use of Antecedents." In *Bright Essence: Studies in Milton's Theology,* edited by William B. Hunter, C. A. Patrides, and Jack Adamson, 3–13. Salt Lake City: University of Utah Press, 1971.

Payne, William. *A Discourse Concerning the Adoration of the Host, As It Is Taught and Practiced in the Church of Rome.* London: Printed for Brabazon Aylmer, 1685.

Phillips, Edward. *The New World of English Words.* London: E. Tyler, for Nath. Brooke, 1658. Reprinted 1662, 1663, 1671, 1678.

Prior, Charles W. A. *Defining the Jacobean Church: The Politics of Religious Controversy, 1603–1625.* Cambridge: Cambridge University Press, 2005.

Purkiss, Diane. *Literature, Gender, and Politics during the English Civil War.* Cambridge: Cambridge University Press, 2005.

Radzinowicz, Mary Ann. *Toward* Samson Agonistes: *The Growth of Milton's Mind.* Princeton: Princeton University Press, 1978.

Raitt, William. *Vindication of the Reformed Religion, from the Reflection of a Romanist: Written for Information of All, Who will receive the truth in love.* Aberdene: Printed by Iohn Forbes the Younger, 1711.

Rapaport, Herman. *Milton and the Postmodern.* Lincoln: University of Nebraska Press, 1983.

Reichardt, John. *Milton's Wisdom: Nature and Scripture in* Paradise Lost. Ann Arbor: University of Michigan Press, 1992.

Reid, David. "Milton's Royalism." *Milton Quarterly* 37 (2003): 31–40.

Rhatigan, Emma. "Knees and Elephants: Donne Preaches on Ceremonial Conformity." *John Donne Journal* 23 (2004): 185–213.

Rhu, Lawrence F. "*Paradise Lost* and Traditional Exegesis." In *The Idea of Biblical Interpretation: Essays in Honor of James L. Kugel*, edited by Hindy Najman and Judith H. Newman, 485–512. Leiden: Brill, 2004.

Richardson, Jonathan. *Explanatory Notes and Remarks on Milton's Paradise Lost*. London: 1734.

Robertson, J. N. W. B., ed. *The Acts and Decrees of the Synod of Jerusalem*. 1899. New York: AMS Press, 1969.

Robinson, Scott. "The Eighteenth-Century Novel." In *The Oxford Handbook of English Literature and Theology*, edited by Andrew Haas, David Jasper, and Elisabeth Jay, 431–47. Oxford: Oxford University Press, 2007.

Rogers, John. *The Matter of Revolution: Science, Poetry, and Politics in the Age of Milton*. Ithaca, N.Y.: Cornell University Press, 1996.

Rosenblatt, Jason P. *Renaissance England's Chief Rabbi: John Selden*. Oxford: Oxford University Press, 2006.

———. *Torah and Law in Paradise Lost*. Princeton: Princeton University Press, 1994.

Ross, Charles. *Elizabethan Literature and the Law of Fraudulent Conveyance: Sidney, Spenser, and Shakespeare*. Burlington, Vt.: Ashgate, 2003.

Rudat, Wolfgang E. H. "Godhead and Milton's Satan: Classical Myth and Augustinian Theology in *Paradise Lost*." *Milton Quarterly* 14 (1980): 17–21.

Rumrich, John P. *Matter of Glory: A New Preface to Paradise Lost*. Pittsburgh: University of Pittsburgh Press, 1987.

———. *Milton Unbound: Controversy and Reinterpretation*. Cambridge: Cambridge University Press, 1996.

———. "Radical Heterodoxy and Heresy." In Corns, *A Companion to Milton*, 141–56.

Sacks, David Harris. "Adam's Curse and Adam's Freedom: Milton's Concept of Liberty." In Tournu and Forsyth, *Milton, Rights, and Liberties*, 69–98.

Sandys, George. *Ovid's Metamorphosis. Englished by G. S*. London: W. Stansby, 1626.

Sauer, Elizabeth. "Toleration, the Irish Crisis, and Milton's *On the Late Massacre in Piemont*." In *Milton Studies*, vol. 44, edited by Albert C. Labriola, 40–61. Pittsburgh: University of Pittsburgh Press, 2005.

Schwartz, Louis. *Conscious Terrors: Milton and Maternal Mortality.* Forthcoming.

Schwartz, Regina M. "Real Hunger: Milton's Version of the Eucharist." *Religion and Literature* 31 (1999): 1–17.

Selden, John. *Table Talk of John Selden.* Edited by Frederick Pollock. London: Quaritch, 1927.

Shawcross, John T. "Allegory, Typology, and Didacticism: *Paradise Lost* in the Eighteenth Century." In *Enlightening Allegory: Theory, Practice, and Contexts of Allegory in the Late Seventeenth and Eighteenth Centuries,* edited by Kevin L. Cope, 41–74. New York: AMS Press, 1993.

———. *"The Arms of the Family": The Significance of John Milton's Relatives and Associates.* Lexington: University Press of Kentucky, 2004.

———. "'Connivers and the Worst of Superstitions': Milton on Popery and Toleration." *Literature & History* 7 (August 1998): 51–69.

———. "The Higher Wisdom of *The Tenure of Kings and Magistrates.*" In *Achievements of the Left Hand: Essays on the Prose of John Milton,* edited by Michael Lieb and John T. Shawcross, 142–59. Amherst: University of Massachusetts Press, 1974.

———. *John Milton: The Self and the World.* Lexington: University Press of Kentucky, 1993.

———. "Milton and 'Of Christian Doctrine': Doubts, Definitions, Connotations." *Explorations in Renaissance Culture* 27 (2001): 161–78.

———. *Paradise Regain'd: "Worthy T'Have Not Remain'd So Long Unsung."* Pittsburgh: Duquesne University Press, 1988.

———. *Rethinking Milton Studies: Time Present and Time Past.* Newark: University of Delaware Press, 2005.

———. *The Uncertain World of* Samson Agonistes. Cambridge: D. S. Brewer, 2001.

———. *With Mortal Voice: The Creation of* Paradise Lost. Lexington: University Press of Kentucky, 1982.

Shawcross, John T., ed. *Milton 1732–1801: The Critical Heritage.* London: Routledge & Kean Paul, 1972.

Sherlock, William. *The Case of Resistance to the Supreme State and Resolved According to the Doctrine of the Holy Scriptures.* London: F. Gardiner, 1684.

———. *The Case of the Allegiance due to Sovereign Powers.* London: Printed for W. Rogers, 1691.

———. *A Vindication of the Holy and Blessed Trinity and the Incarnation of the Son of God*. London: Printed for W. Rogers, 1691.

Shoaf, R. A. *Milton, Poet of Duality: A Study of Semiosis in the Poetry and the Prose*. New Haven: Yale University Press, 1985.

Shoulson, Jeffrey S. *Milton and the Rabbis: Hebraism, Hellenism, and Christianity*. New York: Columbia University Press, 2001.

Shuger, Debora K. "Subversive Fathers and Suffering Subjects: Shakespeare and Christianity." In *Religion, Literature, and Politics in Post-Reformation England, 1540–1688*, edited by Donna B. Hamilton and Richard Strier, 46–69. Cambridge: Cambridge University Press, 1996.

Simpson, A. B. *An Introduction to the History of Land Law*. 2nd ed. Oxford: Clarendon Press, 1986.

Simpson, Ken. *Spiritual Architecture and* Paradise Regained: *Milton's Literary Eccesiology*. Pittsburgh: Duquesne University Press, 2007.

———. "'That Sovran Book': The Discipline of the Word in Milton's Anti-Episcopal Tracts." In *Of Poetry and Politics: New Essays on Milton and His World*, edited by P. G. Stanwood, 313–25. Tempe, Ariz.: Medieval & Renaissance Texts & Studies, 1997.

Sirluck, Ernest. See YP 2.

Smith, Thomas. *An Account of the Greek Church, as to Its Doctrine and Rites of Worship... To which is added, An Account of the State of the Greek Church, under* Cyrillus Lucaris *Patriarch of* Constantinople, *with a Relation of his Sufferings and Death*. London: Printed by Miles Fletcher for Richard Davis, 1680.

Smith, Thomas, ed. *Collectanea de Cyrillo Lucaris, Patriarcha Constantinopolitano*. Londini: Gul. Bowyer, & Impensis Galfredi Wale, 1707.

South, Robert. *Animadversions upon Dr. Sherlock's Book Entituled A Vindication of the Holy and Ever-Blessed Trinity*. London: Printed for Randal Taylor, 1693.

Spenser, Edmund. *The Faerie Queene*. Edited by Thomas P. Roche Jr. Harmondsworth: Penguin Books, 1978.

Springer, Keith L. *Dutch Puritanism: A History of English and Scottish Churches of the Netherlands in the Sixteenth and Seventeenth Centuries*. Leiden: E. J. Brill, 1982.

Stillingfleet, Edward. *The Doctrine of the Trinity and Transubstantiation Compared, as to Scripture, Reason, and Tradition, in a New Dialogue between a Protestant and a Papist. The first Part*. London: Printed by J. D. for W. Rogers, 1687.

Swaim, Kathleen M. *Before and After the Fall: Contrasting Modes in Paradise Lost*. Amherst: University of Massachusetts Press, 1986.

Targoff, Ramie. *Common Prayer: The Language of Public Devotion in Early Modern England*. Chicago: University of Chicago Press, 2001.

Teskey, Gordon. *Delirious Milton: The Fate of the Poet in Modernity*. Cambridge, Mass.: Harvard University Press, 2006.

Toland, John. *The Life of John Milton*. London: John Darby, 1699.

Tournu, Christophe, and Neil Forsyth, eds. *Milton, Rights, and Liberties*. Bern, Switzerland: Peter Lang, 2007.

Trubowitz, Rachel J. "Body Politics in *Paradise Lost*." *PMLA* 121 (2006): 388–404.

Tyers, Thomas. *An Historical Rhapsody on Mr. Pope. The Second Edition, Corrected and Enlarged*. London: Printed for T. Cadell, 1782.

Ulreich, John C. Jr. "Milton on the Eucharist: Some Second Thoughts about Sacramentalism." In *Milton and the Middle Ages*, edited by John Mulryan, 33–56. Lewisburg, Pa.: Bucknell University Press, 1982.

"University Subscription Books." See French, *Life Records*, 1:190 (1629); 1:271 (1632).

van der Leeuw, Gerardus. *Religion in Essence and Manifestation: A Study in Phenomenology*. 2 vols. Translated by J. E. Turner. New York: Harper & Row, 1963.

Verity, A. W., ed. *Milton: Paradise Lost*. Cambridge: Cambridge University Press, 1910.

von Maltzahn, Nicholas. "Making Use of the Jews: Milton and Philosemitism." Forthcoming.

———. "Naming the Author: Some Seventeenth-Century Milton Allusions." *Milton Quarterly* 27 (1993): 1–19.

Walker, William. "Towards Assessing 'Milton's Republicanism' in *Paradise Lost*." In Tournu and Forsyth, *Milton, Rights, and Liberties*, 241–62.

Walpole, Horace. *The Works of Horatio Walpole, Earl of Orford*. London: Printed for G. G. J. and J. Robinson, and J. Edwards, 1798.

Walton, Brian, ed. *Biblia Sacra Polyglotta*. 6 vols. London: Imprimebat Thomas Roycroft, 1655–57.

Wandel, Lee Palmer. *The Eucharist in the Reformation: Incarnation and Liturgy*. Cambridge: Cambridge University Press, 2006.

Westminster Assembly. *The Confession of Faith, and the Longer and Shorter Catechisme.* Edinburgh: Printed by Gedeon Lithgovv, 1649. First published as *The Humble Advice of the Assembly of Divines, now by Authority of Parliament sitting in Westminster, Concerning a Confession of Faith.* London: Printed for the Company of Stationers [1646].

Wheeler, Elizabeth Skerpan. "Early Political Prose." In Corns, *A Companion to Milton*, 263–78.

Whitby, Daniel. *A Dissuasive from Enquiring into the Doctrine of the Trinity; or, The Difficulties and Discouragement Which Attend the Study of the Doctrine.* London: J. Baker, 1714.

Wilding, Michael. *Dragons Teeth: Literature in the English Revolution.* Oxford: Clarendon Press, 1987.

———. "Milton's *Areopagitica*: Liberty for the Sects." *Prose Studies* 9, no. 2 (1986): 7–38.

Williams, John. "Bishop John Williams's Order to Rail to the Communion Tables in Lincoln Diocese, 1635." In Fincham, *Visitation Articles*.

Wilson, John F. *Pulpit in Parliament: Puritanism during the English Civil Wars, 1640–1648.* Princeton: Princeton University Press, 1969.

Wittreich, Joseph. *Interpreting* Samson Agonistes. Princeton: Princeton University Press, 1986.

———. *Why Milton Matters: A New Preface to His Writings.* New York: Palgrave Macmillan, 2006.

INDEX

Abbot, Archbishop George, 75, 80
Abdiel, 50, 170
Abraham, 193
accommodation, 173
Accedence Commenc't Grammar, 105
Achinstein, Sharon, 61
Adam, 138–39, 143, 146, 153–54, 156, 163, 182–83, 191; and Eve, 2, 14–15, 69–70, 117, 137–40, 146–48, 152, 170, 182, 188, 192, 245n7, 246–47n13
Addison, Joseph, 166
"Admonition to the Parliament," 79
Ad Patrem, 47
"All in All," 66–67, 120, 191–92
allusion, 135–37, 140–43, 146, 148–50
Ambrose, Saint, 128
Animadversions upon Smectymnuus, 73, 101, 157, 186
Anne (mother of the Virgin Mary), 86
ante-Nicene Fathers, 102–04

anti-Catholicism. *See* Catholicism
Antitrinitarian, 93
Apocrypha and Pseudepigrapha, 83, 225n1
Apology for Smectymnuus, 73, 87, 157, 191
Arcades, 154, 187
Areopagitica, 59, 70, 92, 140, 163
Arianism, 99, 101–02, 111, 113, 118, 178, 236n2
Aristotle, 60
Arminianism (Arminians), 67–70, 73–74, 118, 232–33n25
Arminius, Jacobus, 68–70, 218n8, 218–19n10
Articles of Faith (Thirty-Nine Articles), 107
Art of Logic, The, 105
At a Solemn Music, 92, 140
At a Vacation Exercise, 237n5
Atwood, William, 128
Augustine, Saint, 104, 187

Bancroft, Richard, 75, 80
baptism, 100

276 Index

Barbour, Reid, 223n28
Barrett, William, 31
Bastwick, John, 74, 76–77
Bauman, Michael, 225n1
"begot" ("begotten"), 107, 113–14, 119
Belial, 166–67
Berkeley, George, 178
Biberman, Matthew, 50, 212n3
Bible (Holy Scripture), ix, 36, 38–40, 45, 47, 67–68, 82–86, 89, 92–96, 98–99, 100, 103, 106, 108–09, 112, 115, 119–20, 122–25, 128–29, 131, 133, 137–41, 143, 169, 173, 176–77, 179, 181–86, 191, 193, 225n1, 226–28n5, 228nn6, 8, 236n4, 239n17. *See also* Apocrypha and Pseudepigrapha
Biddle, John, 105
Blake, William, 164
Boocker, David, 236–37n4
Book of Common Prayer, The, 76, 79, 162, 186–90, 252n25
Book of James, 203–04n24
Book of Nature, 251nn17, 19
Book of Sports, 73
Boyle, Marjorie O'Rourke, 227–28n5
bridge to hell, 150
Brief History of Moscovia, A, 105, 127
Brief Notes upon a Late Sermon, 58
Brooks, Cleanth, 6–7
Bryson, Michael, 117, 165–66
Bull, George, 237–38n8
Burgess, Thomas, 65
burial, 118, 120
Burnet, Thomas, 185
Burton, Dr. Samuel, 33
Burton, Henry, 74, 76–77
Bush, Douglas, 3

Calvin, John, 36, 38, 44, 68–70
Calvinism, 69–70, 105–06, 108, 118, 127
career, 6–7, 18–23, 63–64, 70–71, 77–78, 80, 93–94, 104
Catholicism, 72–73, 77–79, 100, 102–03, 105, 110, 122–23, 125–26, 128, 131, 150–51, 157, 190–91, 226–28n5, 253–54n32
Cerdogni, Count Camillo, 3, 110
ceremonialism, 134, 189, 224n29
Chambers, A. B., 187
Chappell, Michael, 60–61
Chappell, William, 78
Charles I, 50–52, 73, 87–88, 92
chiasmus, 139–40, 226n4
Christ, 81, 102, 105–06, 116–17, 120–22, 124–26, 130–32, 134, 140, 142, 155, 191–92, 226–27n5; benefits of death of, 123; and hope, 193. *See also* Godhead
Chrysostom, Saint John, 125
Chubb, Thomas, 176, 249n7
church, the, 23; and invisible church, 64; and visible church, 64
church-outed, 23, 64, 72
citizens. *See* people, the
Cleland, John, 146–47
Coleman, Peter, 59–60
Colet, John, 242n25
comet, 149
Committee for Compounding, 33
Commonplace Book, 34–38, 46–47; dating of, 36–37, 104–05
Comus, 17–18, 151, 159, 167, 170, 204–05n26; dating of, 159–62
Confessio Fidei. See Lucaris, Cyril

Confession of Faith
 (Westminster Assembly),
 97, 99, 107, 113–14,
 126–27
*Considerations Touching the
 Likeliest Means to Remove
 Hirelings*, 27–28, 57, 132,
 157–58
Constitutions and Canons,
 71–72, 75–76, 219–20n11,
 223–24n23. *See also* "Et
 Cetera" oath
consubstantiation, 121
convey (conveyance), 26–27,
 29–34, 41–46, 155–58
Cope, Sir John, 30, 34
Corns, Thomas N., 56,
 241–42n20
Cotes, Roger, 250n13
Cotton, Sir Thomas, 31–32
creatio de deo, 66–68, 112
creation, 113, 141
Cressy, David, 79
Croft, Herbert, 102
Cromwell, Oliver, 50–52, 60–61,
 78
Cross Keys, the, 31–33
Cumberland, Richard, 249n12

Daniello, Bernardino, 35
Dante, 35, 37–38
daughters, Milton's, 198n5
death, 137–39
De doctrina Christiana, 17,
 36, 42–44, 64–65, 67–68, 70,
 82–87, 93–95, 97–98, 102, 105,
 109, 111, 113–16, 118–20,
 122–23, 131, 133, 176, 181,
 188, 217n3, 217–18n5;
 dating of, 44–45, 83, 123–24,
 241–42n20
Deists, 185
development, 10–11, 17

Diggers, the, 177
Diodati, Giovanni (Jean, John),
 106, 109–10
Dioynsus Zagreus, 129
Di Salvo, Jackie, 163
discipline, church, 73–77
Divine Liturgy of James, 187
divorce (and divorce tracts),
 13–15, 39–40, 147
Dixon, Philip, 101–02, 112
*Doctrine and Discipline of
 Divorce*, 35, 38, 40, 70, 125,
 157
Donne, John, 138
Downer, Rose, 30
Driscoll, James, 165–66
Dryden, John, 166
Dzelzainis, Martin, 52

Eden. *See* nature
Eikonoklastes, 52, 87–88, 92,
 108
Elegia quarta, 120
Ellrodt, Robert, 6–7
Ellwood, Thomas, 160
Emerson, Ralph Waldo, 185
Enlightenment, the, 175
Enthusiasm, 178, 232n22
epiclesis, 129
episcopacy, 72, 78, 80, 101
equity, 54. *See also* usury
Erasmus, 93
"Et Cetera" oath, 219–20n11
Eucharist (and transformation),
 133–34. *See also* Holy
 Communion; Lord's
 Supper; Real Presence;
 transubstantiation
Eusebius, 104
Eve, 66, 139, 151, 153–54,
 190–91. *See also* Adam, and
 Eve
Evelyn, John, 177

fallen angels, 141–45
Fallon, Stephen, 27
Fenton, Mary C., 56, 193
Ferguson, Everett, 104
Fielding, Henry, 182
financial matters (status), 27–34, 42–45, 208–09n10
Fincham, Kenneth, 80
Fink, Zera, 184
Fisch, Harold, 153
Fish, Stanley, 245n2
Fletcher, Harris Francis, 161, 168, 225n1
Forbes, William, 124–25, 132
Fortier, Mark, 54
Foster, Andrew, 73
Franks, R. S., 100
fraud (fraudulent). *See* convey (conveyance)
French, J. Milton, 30
French Revolution, 164
Friedman, Richard Elliott, 177

"gaze," 152–54
Geisst, Charles, 61
gender, 13–16, 62, 147, 201–02n21, 236–37n4. *See also* woman/women
generation, 113–15, 118–19
Giants of the Earth, 141–44
Glanvill, Joseph, 178, 180
Godhead, 21–22, 65, 67–68, 73, 80, 82–83, 87, 94, 97–99, 102, 107, 109, 112–16, 118–20, 130, 132–34, 142–45, 150, 152, 163–64, 168–70, 172, 174–85, 193–94, 205–06n32, 218n6, 238–39n14, 239n16; and God the Father, viii, 66, 83, 89, 96–98, 103–05, 107–08, 111–20, 165, 184, 189; and God the Son, 83, 89, 91–92, 96–99, 107–08, 111–21, 139–43, 145, 154–55, 165–67,
189, 191–94, 228n6, 231n15, 236n3, 238–39n14. *See also* Trinity, the
Goldberg, Jonathan, 8–9, 18
Goodman, Godrey, 180
Guibbory, Achsah, 134

Hadjiantoniou, George, 234n32
Hair, Christopher R., 22–24
Hakewell, George, 184
Hamey, Baldwin, 42
Hamey, Jeremy, 42
Hamlin, Hannibal, 188–89
Hanford, James Holly, 36–37, 70
Hardy, John Edward, 6–7
Hawkes, David, 27–28
Hayley (Haley), Richard, 208n9
heresy, 67–68, 118–19, 121
Herman, Peter, 11–12, 14–15, 20, 62, 117, 226–27n5
hero, 163–66
Hesiod, 142
Hilary, Saint, 124
Hill, John Spencer, 19, 71
History of Britain, 105
Hobson, William, 32–33
Hollander, John, 140
Holy Communion, 122, 125; benefits of, 123; "both kinds" of, 125, 127–28
Holy Ghost. *See* Holy Spirit
Holy Spirit, 85–87, 94–101, 103–04, 107–16, 129–30, 172, 181, 191, 201n19, 228n8, 228–29n10, 229–30n11, 230n12, 231n15; as a dove, 96, 98
Hooker, Richard, 242n25
hope, 193
Horneck, Anthony, 128
Hoxby, Blair, 28–29, 210n28
Hunter, William B., 65, 181, 187
husband and wife. *See* gender

Index

idolatry, 76–77, 79, 126, 155
Immaculate Conception, 203–04n24
Incarnation, the, 115–17, 120–21
"Index Legalis," 211n36
individuation, 175, 184
In Quintum Novembris, 22, 151
Interpreter's Bible, The, 99
Irenaeus, 129

Jacob's Stairs, 151
James I, 80
Jenkins, Hugh, 214n15
Jesus, 89, 98, 167–69, 176, 193. See also Christ
Jewel, John, 77
Johannine comma (1, 2, 3 John), 83–84, 93, 99–100, 228n8, 236n2
Joshua, 193
Jung, Carl G., 129, 230–31n13, 233n26
justification, 106, 108
Justin Martyr, 129
Juxon, William, 75, 221n19

kabod (glory), 133, 244n45
Keeble, N. H., 51
Kelley, Maurice, 70, 118–19, 131–32
Kersey, John, 113, 236n2
King, John N., 22–23, 186, 189–90
kneeling, 77, 221–22n20, 223–24n23
Knott, John, 186
Kristeva, Julia, 246n13
Kugel, James L., 84

Labriola, Albert C., 117
landscape, 180–81
Lares, Jameela, 19, 219–20n11
Laud, William, 23, 71, 73–80, 110, 125, 130, 189
Le Comte, Edward, 3, 6–7

Leger, Antoine, 109, 234n33
Leibniz, Gottfried, 178, 185
Letter to a Friend, A, 57
Levellers, 56
Lewalski, Barbara K., 49–50, 220n11
Lieb, Michael, 131, 133, 175–77, 187, 231–32n18, 238n14, 241–42n20
Lilburne, John, 29
liturgy, 73, 87, 157, 186–91, 254n35
Loewenstein, David, 50
Lord's Supper, 78–79, 100, 121, 122–28, 130–33, 239n17, 239–41n18; benefits of, 126, 242–43n28. See also Eucharist; Holy Communion
love (*agape*), vii, 4, 117
Lucaris, Cyril, 105–10, 115, 123, 127, 233n29, 234nn30–34, 235nn38, 40, 243n30; and *Confessio Fidei*, 105–10, 114–15, 234nn31, 32, 34, 235n38, 243n30
Lucifer, 83, 89–92
Ludlow mask. See *Comus*
Luther, Martin, 130
Lutheranism, 130–31
Luxon, Thomas, 254–55n39
Lycidas, 12, 22–23

Machiavelli, Niccolò, 36
MacKennan, Kerry, 41
Makin, Bathsua, 236n4
Malthus, Daniel, 180
Maltzahn, Nicholas von, 27, 29, 208n10
manifestation, 174–86
maran atha, 129
Marshall, William, 88
Martyrdom and Ascension of Isaiah, The, 98, 116–17
Marvell, Andrew, 177

Mary, 89, 98. *See also* virgin birth
Mask Performed at Ludlow Castle, A. See Comus
Mason, George, 180
Maundy, Thomas, 32, 42
McColley, Diane, 189, 253n30
Mede, Joseph, 125
Michael (archangel), 99, 131, 148, 168, 182–83, 192
Milner, Andrew, 53–54
Milton, Christopher, 31–33
Milton, John (father), 27–33
Milton, Mary Powell, 28
Modest Confutation, A, 87
Mohl, Ruth, 35–37
monarchy, 6, 51
moneylending, 27–28, 30–35, 37–38. *See also* equity; usury
Montagu, Richard, 74, 109, 125, 218–19n10
Mosneron-De Launay, Jean-Baptiste, 164
mystery, 96–98, 100, 102–03, 112, 127, 151–52, 167
myth, 129, 141–46

Nativity ode, 12, 17, 68, 88, 90–91, 94, 187, 226n4
Naturam non pati senium, 183
nature, 102, 180–86
Neoplatonism, 104
Newton, Sir Isaac, 178–80, 250n13
Nicolson, Marjorie Hope, 185
Nimrod, 156, 193
Numenius, 104
numerology, 103–04
Nuttall, Geoffrey, 100–101

Observations on the Articles of Peace, 56
Ode on the Morning of Christ's Nativity. See Nativity ode
Ode to Rouse, 56

Of Education, 105, 157
Of Prelatical Episcopacy, 73, 113, 190
Of Reformation, 37, 73, 94
Of True Religion, 59, 121, 181
O'Keeffe, Timothy, 242n25
omnipresence. *See* presence
On the Forcers of Conscience, 190
"Orders Agreed on by the General Vestry," 74
Ovid, 142, 155
Owen, John, 103, 231n14

Paradise Lost, 2, 11–12, 14–15, 36, 41, 45, 47, 50, 62, 65–69, 74, 88–91, 95–97, 99, 101, 115–17, 120, 131–32, 137–57, 159–63, 170, 173, 175, 177–78, 182–86, 188–90, 192; dating of, 159–62, 241–42n20; Eve's dream in, 154; Sin and Death in, 150, 156; use of "dubious" in, 152; use of "play" in, 153; use of "pontifical" in, 150–51
Paradise Regain'd, 45, 47–48, 60, 81, 88–89, 91, 98, 101, 120, 160–62, 165–69, 180–81, 192–93, 226–27n5, 238–39n14; dating of, 159–62, 241–42n20
"paradise within," 23–24, 162, 165–66
Parker, William Riley, 6, 31, 34, 208–09n10
Parliament, 50–55, 57, 78
Passover, 122
Patrides, C. A., 235–36n1
Paul, Saint, 13–14, 16, 24, 122, 127, 194
Payne, William, 128
Pell, John, 208n9
people, the, 6, 29, 38, 53–61, 214n15, 215nn16–17
Phillips, Edward, 104–05

phoenix, 154–55
Picard, Jeremy, 36–37
Plotinus, 104
Postscript, A, 73
prayer, 188, 253n31, 254n33
predestination, 106, 108, 119
Presbyterianism, 190, 254n34
presence, 130–32
"proceeding," 107, 113–14
progressive revelation, 248–49n6
Pro Populo Anglicano Defensio, 54–55
Pro Populo Anglicano Defensio Secunda, 186
Proposals of Certaine Expedients, 57–58
protevangelium, 66, 191
providence, 108, 122, 148, 170, 182
Prynne, William, 74, 76–77
Psalm 1, 48, 247n3
Psalm 2, 115, 117, 173, 247n3
Psalm 51, 189
Psalm 114, 22, 124, 132–33, 168
Psalm 136, 133
Psalms 1–8, 247n3
Psalms 80–85, 161, 247n3
puns, 150
Puritans, 79–80, 101, 126, 189–90
Purkiss, Diana, 53
Pythagoras, 104

quadrature of the circle, 239–41n19

radicalism, 49–50, 61, 195
Radzinowicz, Mary Ann, 248–49n6
Raitt, William, 106
Raphael, 154–56, 194
Ready and Easy Way, The, 52, 58, 158
Real Presence, 122, 124–30, 242n25. *See also* Eucharist; Holy Communion; Lord's Supper; transubstantiation
reason, 102, 175, 178–80, 184
Reason of Church-Government, 73, 92, 152, 181, 191
Reformed belief, 131
Reichardt, John, 182–83, 251n17, 253n31
religion: and government, 50–53, 55, 59, 71–73, 213n4; Milton's, ix–x, 80–81, 185
remembrance, 122, 126–28, 130, 133
renovation, 169, 193
reprobation, 68–70
republicanism, 49, 52, 54–59, 165, 212–13n3, 216n23
revelation, 174–86
Rhu, Lawrence, 84
Richardson, Jonathan, 41
ritual, 253n30
Rivet, André, 35–38, 44
Roberts, Donald, 186
Rogers, John, 52, 177
"Root and Branch" petition, 72
Ross, Charles, 26
royalism, 50–51
Rumrich, John, 11, 133, 175, 254n34

Sacks, David Harris, 212–13n3
sacrifice, 124, 126, 128–29, 133
Salmasius, 54–55
Samson, 154, 162–63, 169–70, 193. *See also Samson Agonistes*
Samson Agonistes, 132, 160–63, 168–69; dating of, 159–62, 247n3; disillusionment in, 162
Sandys, George, 142
Satan, iii, 1–2, 45, 47, 89–91, 115, 117, 138, 142, 144–45, 148–50, 152–53, 155, 163–68, 173, 192
Sauer, Elizabeth, 56

Savonarola, 46
Schwartz, Louis, 200n5
science, 175, 178–80, 184–85
scriptura sola, 120, 186, 252n24
Selden, John, 51, 54
sexuality, 18, 152
Shawcross, John T., 177
Sherlock, William, 232–33n25
Shuger, Debra, 192
Simpson, A. B., 26
Simpson, Ken, 186
Sirluck, Ernest, 140
Smith, Thomas, 107–08, 235n40
Socinians, 67, 99, 105, 118, 178
"Song: On May Morning," 90
Sonnet XV (Fairfax), 45
Sonnet XVI (Cromwell), 27
Sonnet XIX ("When I consider"), 8–10, 18
South, Robert, 232–33n25
Speed, John, 37, 46
Spenser, Edmund, 140
Spirit (of God). *See* Holy Spirit
Stillingfleet, Edward, 102, 128
style, 241–42n20
subordinationism, 111–12, 116–18
Suckling, Sir John, 31
Synod of Jerusalem, 105–06, 108, 127, 234n31

Targoff, Ramie, 254n33
"Te Deum laudamus," 189
Tenure of Kings and Magistrates, 52, 60
Tertullian, 104, 113
Teskey, Gordon, 175
Tetrachordon, 13–16, 39–40
Thirty-Nine Articles. *See* Articles of Faith
Tindal, Matthew, 185
toleration, 6, 56, 59–60, 172
tradition, 103

transubstantiation, 106, 109, 121–29, 133, 237n5, 239n17, 239–41n19, 242n25, 243n30, 244n37, 253–54n32. *See also* Eucharist; Real Presence
Treatise of Civil Power, The, 132, 181
Trinity, the, 12, 17–18, 64, 83, 86, 92–104, 106–08, 110–11, 121, 185, 201n20, 228n8, 230n12, 233n26, 236n2
Trinity Manuscript, 70, 140–41, 161
Trubowitz, Rachel, 62
Tyers, Thomas, 180
typology, 85, 115, 173

ubiquity. *See* presence
"University Subscription Books," 220–21n13
usury, 29–34, 35–46, 208n8; and equity, 41. *See also* moneylending

van der Leeuw, Gerardus, 129, 238n14
virgin birth, 84–88, 93, 106, 108, 203–04n24
virginity, 151
Virgin Mary. *See* Mary
vocation. *See* career

Walker, William, 216n23
Walpole, Horace, 180
Warcupp, Robert, 34
well-affected, 56–58
Westminster Assembly, 190
Wheeler, Elizabeth Skerpan, 59–60, 216n23
Whitby, Daniel, 103
Wilding, Michael, 56, 162, 192
Williams, John, 92
Wilson, John F., 51

Wittreich, Joseph, 163
Wolfe, Don M., 71
Wollebius, Johannis, 43
woman/women, 54–56, 62, 117, 138, 147, 194. *See also* gender

Young, Thomas, 72, 78, 120

Zwingli, Huldrych, 122, 124